W9-AOH-646

MAJOR BLACK
AMERICAN WRITERS
THROUGH THE HARLEM RENAISSANCE

Writers of English: Lives and Works

Major Black American Writers

THROUGH THE HARLEM RENAISSANCE

Edited and with an Introduction by

Harold Bloom

CHELSEA HOUSE PUBLISHERS
New York   Philadelphia

Jacket Illustration: Horace Pippin, *Harmonizing* (1944) (courtesy of the Allen Memorial Art Museum, Oberlin College, Ohio; Gift of Joseph and Enid Bissett).

CHELSEA HOUSE PUBLISHERS

Editorial Director Richard Rennert
Executive Managing Editor Karyn Gullen Browne
Picture Editor Adrian G. Allen
Copy Chief Robin James
Creative Director Robert Mitchell
Art Director Joan Ferrigno
Production Manager Sallye Scott

Writers of English: Lives and Works

Senior Editor S. T. Joshi
Series Design Rae Grant

Staff for MAJOR BLACK AMERICAN WRITERS THROUGH THE HARLEM RENAISSANCE

Assistant Editor Mary Sisson
Picture Researcher Ellen Dudley

© 1995 by Chelsea House Publishers, a division of Main Line Book Co.

Introduction © 1995 by Harold Bloom

3 5 7 9 8 6 4

Library of Congress Cataloging-in-Publication Data

Major black American writers through the Harlem Renaissance / edited and with an introduction by Harold Bloom.
    p.   cm.—(Writers of English)
  Includes bibliographical references and index.
  ISBN 0-7910-2218-8.—ISBN 0-7910-2243-9 (pbk.)
  1. American literature—Afro-American authors—History and criticism. 2. American literature—Afro-American authors—Bio-bibliography. 3. Afro-Americans in literature. 4. Harlem Renaissance. I. Bloom, Harold. II. Series.
PS153.N5M243 1994
810.9'896073—dc20   94-5886
[B]   CIP

Contents

◈ User's Guide

THIS VOLUME PROVIDES biographical, critical, and bibliographical information on the eleven most significant black American writers through the Harlem Renaissance. Each chapter consists of three parts: a biography of the author; a selection of brief critical extracts about the author; and a bibliography of the author's published books.

The biography supplies a detailed outline of the important events in the author's life, including his or her major writings. The critical extracts are taken from a wide array of books and periodicals, from the author's lifetime to the present, and range in content from biographical to critical to historical. The extracts are arranged in chronological order by date of writing or publication, and a full bibliographical citation is provided at the end of each extract. Editorial additions or deletions are indicated within carets.

The author bibliographies list every separate publication—including books, pamphlets, broadsides, collaborations, and works edited or translated by the author—for works published in the author's lifetime; selected important posthumous publications are also listed. Titles are those of the first edition; variant titles are supplied within carets. In selected instances dates of revised editions are given where these are significant. Pseudonymous works are listed but not the pseudonyms under which these works were published. Periodicals edited by the author are listed only when the author has written most or all of the contents. Titles enclosed in square brackets are of doubtful authenticity. All works by the author, whether in English or in other languages, have been listed; English translations of foreign-language works are not listed unless the author has done the translation.

The Life of the Author
Harold Bloom

NIETZSCHE, WITH EXULTANT ANGUISH, famously proclaimed that God was dead. Whatever the consequences of this for the ethical life, its ultimate literary effect certainly would have surprised the author Nietzsche. His French disciples, Foucault most prominent among them, developed the Nietzschean proclamation into the dogma that all authors, God included, were dead. The death of the author, which is no more than a Parisian trope, another metaphor for fashion's setting of skirt-lengths, is now accepted as literal truth by most of our current apostles of what should be called French Nietzsche, to distinguish it from the merely original Nietzsche. We also have French Freud or Lacan, which has little to do with the actual thought of Sigmund Freud, and even French Joyce, which interprets *Finnegans Wake* as the major work of Jacques Derrida. But all this is as nothing compared to the final triumph of the doctrine of the death of the author: French Shakespeare. That delicious absurdity is given us by the New Historicism, which blends Foucault and California fruit juice to give us the Word that Renaissance "social energies," and not William Shakespeare, composed *Hamlet* and *King Lear*. It seems a proper moment to murmur "enough" and to return to a study of the life of the author.

Sometimes it troubles me that there are so few masterpieces in the vast ocean of literary biography that stretches between James Boswell's great *Life* of Dr. Samuel Johnson and the late Richard Ellmann's wonderful *Oscar Wilde*. Literary biography is a crucial genre, and clearly a difficult one in which to excel. The actual nature of the lives of the poets seems to have little effect upon the quality of their biographies. Everything happened to Lord Byron and nothing at all to Wallace Stevens, and yet their biographers seem equally daunted by them. But even inadequate biographies of strong writers, or of weak ones, are of immense use. I have never read a literary biography from which I have not profited, a statement I cannot make about any other genre whatsoever. And when it comes to figures who are central to us—Dante, Shakespeare, Cervantes, Montaigne, Goethe, Whitman, Tolstoi, Freud, Joyce, Kafka among them—we reach out eagerly for every scrap that the biographers have gleaned. Concerning Dante and Shakespeare we know much too little, yet when we come to Goethe and Freud, where we seem to know more than everything, we still want to know more. The death of the author, despite our current resentniks, clearly was only a momentary fad. Something vital in every authentic lover of literature responds to Emerson's battle-cry sentence: "There is no history, only biography." Beyond that there is a deeper truth, difficult to come at and requiring a lifetime to understand, which is that there is no literature, only autobiography, however mediated, however veiled, however transformed. The events of Shakespeare's life included the composition of *Hamlet,* and that act of writing was itself a crucial act of living, though we do not yet know altogether how to read so doubled an act. When an author takes up a more overtly autobiographical stance, as so many do in their youth, again we still do not know precisely how to accommodate the vexed relation between life and work. T. S. Eliot, meditating upon James Joyce, made a classic statement as to such accommodation:

> We want to know who are the originals of his characters, and what were the origins of his episodes, so that we may unravel the web of memory and invention and discover how far and in what ways the crude material has been transformed.

When a writer is not even covertly autobiographical, the web of memory and invention is still there, but so subtly woven that we may never unravel it. And yet we want deeply never to stop trying, and not merely because we are curious, but because each of us is caught in her own network of memory and invention. We do not always recall our inventions, and long before we age we cease to be certain of the extent to which we have invented our memories. Perhaps one motive for reading is our need to unravel our own webs. If our masters could make, from their lives, what we read, then we can be moved by them to ask: What have we made or lived in relation to what we have read? The answers may be sad, or confused, but the question is likely, implicitly, to go on being asked as long as we read. In Freudian terms, we are asking: What is it that we have repressed? What have we forgotten, unconsciously but purposively: What is it that we flee? Art, literature necessarily included, is regression in the service of the ego, according to a famous Freudian formula. I doubt the Freudian wisdom here, but indubitably it is profoundly suggestive. When we read, something in us keeps asking the equivalent of the Freudian questions: From what or whom is the author in flight, and to what earlier stages in her life is she returning, and why?

Reading, whether as an art or a pastime, has been damaged by the visual media, television in particular, and might be in some danger of extinction in the age of the computer, except that the psychic need for it continues to endure, presumably because it alone can assuage a central loneliness in elitist society. Despite all sophisticated or resentful denials, the reading of imaginative literature remains a quest to overcome the isolation of the individual consciousness. We can read for information, or entertainment, or for love of the language, but in the end we seek, in the author, the person whom we have not found, whether in ourselves or in others. In that quest, there always are elements at once aggressive and defensive, so that reading, even in childhood, is rarely free of hidden anxieties. And yet it remains one of the few activities not contaminated by an entropy of spirit. We read in hope, because we lack companionship, and the author can become the object of the most idealistic elements in our search for the wit and inventiveness we so desperately require. We read biography, not as a supplement to reading the author, but as a second, fresh attempt to understand what always seems to evade us in the work, our drive towards a kind of identity with the author.

This will-to-identity, though recently much deprecated, is a prime basis for the experience of sublimity in reading. *Hamlet* retains its unique position in the Western canon not because most readers and playgoers identify themselves with the prince, who clearly is beyond them, but rather because they find themselves again in the power of the language that represents him with such immediacy and force. Yet we know that neither language nor social energy created Hamlet. Our curiosity about Shakespeare is endless, and never will be appeased. That curiosity itself is a value, and cannot be separated from the value of *Hamlet* the tragedy, or Hamlet the literary character. It provokes us that Shakespeare the man seems so unknowable, at once everyone and no one as Borges shrewdly observes. Critics keep telling us otherwise, yet something valid in us keeps believing that we would know Hamlet better if Shakespeare's life were as fully known as the lives of Goethe and Freud, Byron and Oscar Wilde, or best of all, Dr. Samuel Johnson. Shakespeare never will have his Boswell, and Dante never will have his Richard Ellmann. How much one would give for a detailed and candid *Life of Dante* by Petrarch, or an outspoken memoir of Shakespeare by Ben Jonson! Or, in the age just past, how superb would be rival studies of one another by Hemingway and Scott Fitzgerald! But the list is endless: think of *Oscar Wilde* by Lord Alfred Douglas, or a joint biography of Shelley by Mary Godwin, Emilia Viviani, and Jane Williams. More than our insatiable desire for scandal would be satisfied. The literary rivals and the lovers of the great writers possessed perspectives we will never enjoy, and without those perspectives we dwell in some poverty in regard to the writers with whom we ourselves never can be done.

There is a sense in which imaginative literature *is* perspectivism, so that the reader is likely to be overwhelmed by the work's difficulty unless its multiple perspectives are mastered. Literary biography matters most because it is a storehouse of perspectives, frequently far surpassing any that are grasped by the particular biographer. There are relations between authors' lives and their works of kinds we have yet to discover, because our analytical instruments are not yet advanced enough to perform the necessary labor. Perhaps a novel, poem, or play is not so much a regression in the service of the ego, as it is an amalgam of *all* the Freudian mechanisms of defense, all working together for the apotheosis of the ego. Freud valued art highly, but thought that the aesthetic enterprise was no rival for psychoanalysis, unlike religion and philosophy. Clearly Freud was mistaken; his own anxieties about his indebtedness to Shakespeare helped produce the weirdness of his joining in the lunacy that argued for the Earl of Oxford as the author of Shakespeare's plays. It was Shakespeare, and not "the poets," who was there before Freud arrived at his depth psychology, and it is Shakespeare who is there still, well out ahead of psychoanalysis. We see what Freud would not see, that psychoanalysis is Shakespeare prosified and systematized. Freud is part of literature, not of "science," and the biography of Freud has the same relations to psychoanalysis as the biography of Shakespeare has to *Hamlet* and *King Lear,* if only we knew more of the life of Shakespeare.

Western literature, particularly since Shakespeare, is marked by the representation of internalized change in its characters. A literature of the ever-growing inner self is in itself a large form of biography, even though this is the biography of imaginary beings, from Hamlet to the sometimes nameless protagonists of Kafka and Beckett. Skeptics might want to argue that all literary biography concerns imaginary beings, since authors make themselves up, and every biographer gives us a creation curiously different from the same author as seen by the writer of a rival *Life.* Boswell's Johnson is not quite anyone else's Johnson, though it is now very difficult for us to disentangle the great Doctor from his gifted Scottish friend and follower. The life of the author is not merely a metaphor or a fiction, as is "the Death of the Author," but it always does contain metaphorical or fictive elements. Those elements are a part of the value of literary biography, but not the largest or the crucial part, which is the separation of the mask from the man or woman who hid behind it. James Joyce and Samuel Beckett, master and sometime disciple, were both of them enigmatic personalities, and their biographers have not, as yet, fully expounded the mystery of these contrasting natures. Beckett seems very nearly to have been a secular saint: personally disinterested, heroic in the French Resistance, as humane a person ever to have composed major fictions and dramas. Joyce, self-obsessed even as Beckett was preternaturally selfless, was the Milton of the twentieth century. Beckett was perhaps the least egoistic post-Joycean, post-Proustian, post-Kafkan of writers. Does that illuminate the problematical nature of his work, or does it simply constitute another problem? Whatever the cause, the question matters. The only death of the author that is other than literal, and that matters, is the fate only of weak writers. The strong, who become canonical, never die, which is what the canon truly is about. To be read forever is the Life of the Author.

▨ Introduction

AS A NARRATIVE FICTION, Zora Neale Hurston's *Their Eyes Were Watching God* (1937) evidently was an attempt at exorcism, written in seven weeks or so after the end of an intense love affair. It seems now to owe at least part of its fame to a more general exorcism, one that the fiercely individualistic Hurston might have scorned, since she was no ideologue, whether of race or of gender. Here vitalism allies her art to D. H. Lawrence's; like him she yields only to a visionary politics, and like him also she celebrates a rare sexual fulfillment as an image of finality. The madness of the later Lawrence of *The Plumed Serpent* might have amused her, yet I think of early Lawrence at times when I reread *Their Eyes Were Watching God* or "Sweat," the most memorable of her short stories. Delia Jones the washwoman, the protagonist of "Sweat," suffers the brutality of her husband, Sykes, who after fifteen years of marriage sees her only as an obstacle to his happiness. The story begins with Sykes maliciously frightening her by letting his bullwhip fall upon her from behind, so that she believes a snake is attacking her. At the story's conclusion, an actual rattlesnake, introduced into the house by Sykes, rids Delia of her oppressor forever.

> She saw him on his hands and knees as soon as she reached the door. He crept an inch or two toward her—all that he was able, and she saw his horribly swollen neck and his one open eye shining with hope. A surge of pity too strong to support bore her away from that eye that must, could not, fail to see the tubs. He would see the lamp. Orlando with its doctors was too far. She could scarcely reach the Chinaberry Tree, where she waited in the growing heat while inside she knew the cold river was creeping up and up to extinguish that eye which must know by now that she knew.

The dispassionate vitality of this terror is free of animus; we are nowhere in the neighborhood of any of our contemporary versions of the spirit of revenge in the defensive war of some African-American women writers against African-American men. What marks the passage, and so much else of Hurston's work, is its power, in the sense of Delia's thwarted potential for more life. The thwarting, in the broadest sense, brings death to Sykes, but brings no trite reflections or morality or of sexual politics, whether to Hurston or to her reader. What is given instead is vision of an eye shining with the desperate hope of survival until it approaches the extinction of a knowledge that destroys. Terror dominates Delia, but she experiences also a realization almost too subtle to convey, a mingling of compassion and of freedom. The triple repetition of that "one open eye" culminates a litany of destructions that have guaranteed Sykes's doom. Earlier in the story, when Delia begs Sykes to have mercy and remove the rattlesnake from the house, his reply is prophetic: "Ah aint gut tuh do nuthin'uh de kin'—fact is ah aint got tuh do nuthin' but die." In Hurston, freedom is always an image of pathos, and never a political metaphor. But Hurston, in literature as in life, was High Romantic, and for her the pathos of freedom always bordered upon death. Sykes dies so that Delia can live and be free; passion in Hurston, as in Lawrence, feeds upon life. It hardly matters that Delia, who once loved Sykes, now hates him, while Janie Crawford still loves Tea Cake when she is compelled to kill him. In Hurston the drive is always that of the heroic vitalist, a drive that seeks the freedom of more life, of the blessing. It was appropriate, even inevitable, that Hurston's hero should have an African Moses, who as man of the mountain ascended to bring back the only power that mattered, the blessings of more life for his people.

—H. B.

Charles W. Chesnutt
1858–1932

CHARLES WADDELL CHESNUTT was born in Cleveland, Ohio, on June 20, 1858. His parents were free blacks who moved to Fayetteville, North Carolina, after the Civil War. Chesnutt began teaching at age fourteen and from 1877 to 1880 was assistant principal of State Normal School in Fayetteville; he became principal in 1880. In 1878 he married Susan Perry, with whom he had four children. Chesnutt went to New York City in 1883 to work as a journalist; he soon relocated to Cleveland, where he studied law.

In 1887, the year he passed his bar examination, Chesnutt sold his first stories. He was "discovered" by the critic and editor Walter Hines Page, who promoted Chesnutt's work enthusiastically over the next decade. Chesnutt spent these years working as a Cleveland court reporter and writing stories. These were published in two volumes in 1899. *The Conjure Woman* contained the Uncle Julius stories, which retold tales from Ovid and Vergil in black dialect, while *The Wife of His Youth* collected a series of stories with mulatto protagonists. Encouraged by the success of these books and of his biography, *Frederick Douglass*, published the same year, Chesnutt left his job to write full-time and made a southern lecture tour. His most controversial prose works, essays concerning his hope of miscegenation in America, were published in the *Boston Transcript* in 1900. Also at this time he began exchanging letters with Booker T. Washington and was instrumental in having Macmillan withdraw from publication the antiblack volume *The American Negro*. His most popular novel was his first, *The House Behind the Cedars* (1900), which poignantly, if somewhat melodramatically, etches the difficulties of mixed-race offspring in the South.

The Marrow of Tradition (1901) was a sweeping condemnation of racial prejudice and greed, less sentimental than its predecessor and correspondingly less popular. Chesnutt was disappointed by the book's failure, and in 1902 he returned to his court reporting position. He wrote another novel, *The Colonel's Dream* (1905), as well as at least five more that remain unpublished. An outspoken advocate for black rights, he successfully shut down the showing of *The Birth of a Nation* in Ohio, often protested the treatment of black soldiers, and was honored with the NAACP's Spingarn Medal in 1928. After years of strokes and ill health Charles Chesnutt died at his home in Cleveland on November 15, 1932. His daughter Helen published a memoir of him in 1952.

Critical Extracts

WILLIAM DEAN HOWELLS   The critical reader of the story called "The Wife of His Youth," which appeared in these pages two years ago, must have noticed uncommmon traits in what was altogether a remarkable piece of work. The first was the novelty of the material, for the writer dealt not only with people who were not white, but with people who were not black enough to contrast with white people—who were in fact of that near approach to the ordinary American in race and color which leaves, at the last degree, every one but the connoisseur in doubt whether they are Anglo-Saxon or Anglo-African. Quite as striking as this novelty of the material was the author's thorough mastery of it, and his unerring knowledge of the life he had chosen in its peculiar racial characteristics. But above all, the story was notable for the passionless handling of a phase of our common life which is tense with potential tragedy; for the attitude, almost ironical, in which the artist observes the play of contesting emotions in the drama under his eyes; and for his apparently reluctant, apparently helpless consent to let the spectator know his real feeling in the matter. Anyone accustomed to study methods in fiction, to distinguish between good and bad art, to feel the joy which the delicate skill possible only from a love of truth can give, must have known a high pleasure in the quiet self-restraint of the performance; and such a reader would probably have decided that the social situation in the piece was studied wholly from the outside, by an observer with special opportunities for knowing it, who was, as it were, surprised into final sympathy.

Now, however, it is known that the author of this story is of negro blood—diluted, indeed, in such measure that if he did not admit this descent few would imagine it, but still quite of that middle world which lies next, though wholly outside, our own. Since his first story appeared he has contributed several others to these pages, and he now makes a showing palpable to criticism in a volume called *The Wife of His Youth, and Other Stories of the Color Line* ⟨. . .⟩

William Dean Howells, "Mr. Charles W. Chesnutt's Stories," *Atlantic Monthly* 85, No. 5 (May 1900): 699–701

CHARLES W. CHESNUTT   The popular theory is that the future American race will consist of the harmonious fusion of the various European elements which now make up our heterogeneous population. The result is to be something infinitely superior to the best of the component elements. This perfection of type—for no good American could for a moment doubt that it will be as perfect as everything else American—is to be brought about by a combination of all the best characteristics of the different European races, and the elimination, by some strange alchemy, of all their undesirable traits—for even a good American will admit that European races, now and then, have some undesirable traits when they first come over. It is a beautiful, a hopeful, and to the eye of faith, a thrilling prospect. ⟨. . .⟩

By the eleventh census ⟨1890⟩, the ratios of which will probably not be changed materially by the census now under way, the total population of the United States was about 65,000,000, of which about seven million were black and colored, and something over 200,000 were of Indian blood. It is then in the three broad types—white, black and Indian—that the future American race will find the material for its formation. Any dream of a pure white race, of the Anglo-Saxon type, for the United States, may as well be abandoned as impossible, even if desirable. That such future race will be predominantly white may well be granted—unless the climate in the course of time should modify existing types; that it will call itself white is reasonably sure; that it will conform closely to the white type is likely; but that it will have absorbed and assimilated the blood of the other two races mentioned is as certain as the operation of any law well can be that deals with so uncertain a quantity as the human race.

There are no natural obstacles to such an amalgamation. The unity of the race is not only conceded but demonstrated by actual crossing. Any theory of sterility due to race crossing may as well be abandoned; it is founded mainly on prejudice and cannot be proved by the facts. If it come from Northern or European sources, it is likely to be weakened by lack of knowledge; if from Southern sources it is sure to be colored by prejudice. My own observation is that in a majority of cases people of mixed blood are very prolific and very long-lived. The admixture of races in the United States has never taken place under conditions likely to produce the best results; but there have nevertheless been enough conspicuous instances to the contrary in this country, to say nothing of a long and honorable list in other lands, to disprove the theory that people of mixed blood, other things being equal, are less virile, prolific or able than those of purer strains. But whether this be true or not is apart from this argument. Admitting that races may mix, and that they are thrown together under conditions which permit their admixture, the controlling motive will be not abstract considerations with regard to a remote posterity, but present interest and inclination.

Charles W. Chesnutt, "The Future American" (1900), MELUS 15, No. 3 (Fall 1988): 96–98

WILLIAM STANLEY BRAITHWAITE   The development of fiction among Negro authors has been, I might almost say, one of the repressed activities of our literary life. A fair start was made the last decade of the nineteenth century when Chestnutt and Dunbar were turning out both short stories and novels. In Dunbar's case, had he lived, I think his literary growth would have been in the evolution of the Race novel as indicated in The Uncalled and Sport of the Gods. ⟨. . .⟩ His contemporary, Charles W. Chestnutt, was concerned more primarily with the fiction of the Color Line and the contacts and conflicts of its two worlds. He was in a way more successful. In the five volumes to his credit, he has revealed himself as a fiction writer of a very high order. But after all Mr. Chestnutt is a story-teller of genius transformed by racial earnestness into the novelist of talent. His natural gift would have found freer vent in a flow of short stories like Bret Harte's, to judge from the facility and power of his two volumes of short stories, The Wife of His Youth and Other Stories and The Conjure Woman. But Mr. Chestnutt's serious effort was in the field of the novel, where he made a brave and partially successful effort to correct the distortions of Reconstruction fiction and offset the school of Page and Cable. Two of these novels, The Marrow of Tradition and The House Behind the Cedars, must be reckoned among the representative period novels of their time. But the situation was not ripe for the great Negro novelist. The American public preferred spurious values to the genuine; the coinage of the Confederacy was at literary par. Where Dunbar, the sentimentalist, was welcome, Chestnutt, the realist, was barred. In 1905 Mr. Chestnutt wrote *The Colonel's Dream*, and thereafter silence fell upon him.

William Stanley Braithwaite, "The Negro in American Literature," *The New Negro: An Interpretation*, ed. Alain Locke (New York: Albert & Charles Boni, 1925), pp. 42–43

HELEN M. CHESNUTT   Chesnutt's love of life was so great, his interest in the world and its problems so vital that he seemed to those who loved him perennially young. His gallant humor, his love for people, his keen enjoyment of all the little things in life never grew less. A passion for human justice possessed him; for justice he worked throughout his life.

His conception of human rights was simple. Rights are fundamental. Man does not have to earn them; does not have to struggle to be worthy of gaining them at some far-off future time. Rights are given by God and are inalienable, and any human being that does not demand his rights, all of them, is lacking in integrity and is something less than a man.

His philosophy for himself and his family was characteristic:

"We are normal human beings with all the natural desires of normal individuals. We acknowledge no inherent inferiority and resent any denial of rights and opportunities based on racial discrimination. We believe in equality and all that it implies. We shall live our lives as Americans pure and simple, and whatever experiences we encounter shall be borne with forbearance, and fortitude, and amusement if possible."

His children were nurtured on this philosophy which became a part of their mental and spiritual inheritance.

Chesnutt enjoyed a rich, full life. Starting out at the age of fourteen to earn his living, he had been able by his own efforts, with the assistance of what tutors he could find, to acquire a fine liberal education. He was an ardent reader and loved all kinds of books. In his later years the books on his bedside table showed his wide range of interest. *The Odes of Horace*, the latest French book, a mystery story, a current best-seller; the *Story of Philosophy*, the *Atlantic*, the *Crisis*, *Opportunity*, the *Nation*, the *New Republic*—all gave him interest and pleasure. He loved music and the theatre and, until his health became too poor, attended with his wife and daughters the many concerts and plays that have enriched the lives of Clevelanders. He loved beauty and was able to store his mind with the beauties of nature by extensive travel in America and parts of Europe.

But he was human and had his weaknesses. He was not a good business man. His real-estate ventures were always a hazard because of his forbearance—some of his tenants exploited him outrageously. He, like many others, suffered serious financial losses in the crash of the stock market in 1929. But he never grew cynical. Life to him was a beautiful thing.

He experienced in abundance the things that make life beautiful—aspiration, high endeavor, noted achievement, and widespread recognition; then disillusion, readjustment, service to mankind, the respect and affection of all who knew him, abiding love and devotion from every member of his family.

Helen M. Chesnutt, *Charles Waddell Chesnutt: Pioneer of the Color Line* (Chapel Hill: University of North Carolina Press, 1952), pp. 311–12

NIKKI GIOVANNI   *The Conjure Woman* puts Joel Chandler Harris and Stephen Foster and all those dudes up to and including ⟨William⟩ Styron in their places. Uncle Julius is out to win. And he does. He convinces the cracker that the grapes have a spell on them and are therefore better left alone. He shows what would happen if the white man had to live in the Black man's shoes in "Mars Jeems's Nightmare." And he keeps his nephew's job for him. He uses the white woman's natural curiosity about Black men to his advantage. She always sympathizes with him while her husband is prone to back off. He is a good Black politician. The cracker gives the lumber that is "Po'Sandy" to the Black church. Uncle Julius is one of Black literature's most exciting characters precisely because he is so definite about his aims. He intends to see his people come out on top. John, the white voice, thought he could use Julius while it was the other way around. And Chesnutt drops a few gems on us dispelling the romantic theory about slavery's charms.

Nikki Giovanni, *Gemini: An Extended Autobiographical Statement on My First Twenty-five Years of Being a Black Poet* (Indianapolis: Bobbs-Merrill, 1971), pp. 100–101

J. NOEL HEERMANCE   The skeletal structure of *The Colonel's Dream* is a kind of missionary travel novel, which operates on the framework of a national allegory, as Colonel French travels South with Northern ideas and attempts an economic conversion. French himself is a national American hero "type": a figure of military bearing who is also a successful businessman. He is also a man who represents the "whole country," coupling a Southern past with a Northern present and attempting to unite the two under the banner of his industrial Northern way of life. The geographic movement and semiallegorical characterization are essential elements of the plot structure: both are important, not only for the traditional elements contained, but also for the innovations which Chesnutt added.

The Colonel's Dream uses a "visiting narrator," travel novel technique, the sort that was so widely in use at the end of the nineteenth century in this country. Because of its value for bringing two sets of cultural ideas and ways of life together, almost all of America's novelists of the period employed it. Henry James, Mark Twain, William Dean Howells all worked extensively within its framework. It was likewise used as the format for the local color writers of the period, both North and South. ⟨. . .⟩

What is of equal importance to us is the fact that most of the novels in this subgenre were barefacedly unrealistic in their basic structure. They were "vacation" novels in which the narrator had little real motivation for the trip and just seemed to appear somehow on the scene with only the barest of structural mechanics to assist our belief in him. In one way *The Colonel's Dream* shares some of this artificiality in order to establish its national allegory. For French is really too young, handsome, rich, and free from entanglements to be realistically believable. Moreover, his son Phil is also overdrawn in fairytale fashion, having a perpetual "sweet temper" and "loving disposition." Yet we need only look at the characterization of French to see how hard Chesnutt has worked to break the stereotype feeling which often accompanies a symbolic national allegory. We note first how French faints at the end of the tense opening chapter, thereby destroying the rugged, successful, nonchalant American hero who everyone from Cooper to James had symbolically delineated before Chesnutt. In fact, not only does he faint, but he then loses his allegorical aura by sheepishly trying to joke his way out of it. Finally, even more realism creeps in when French's partner, in an explanatory aside, tells us how hard the latter has worked and how little sleep he has had. Clearly this hero is a real man.

Equally significant is the fact that French is a man with a tragic flaw stemming from his personality, and not just an allegorical hero who is defeated by a hostile, looming society. While he is partially the storybook hero of wealth, charm, money, ideals, and leisure, he is also the realistic product of his own past. Thus he brings to his crusade to the heathen South the same traits that made him successful in New York, and for that reason he is defeated. In the South he is pushing against an ingrown society that values prejudice and petty revenge even more than it does money, whereas in New York's business world French has been accustomed to hand-to-hand combat among single individuals or corporations who all shared the same monetary values. Therefore the persistence and drive which have made French successful in the North now greatly harm him in Clarendon; and he is too insensitive to realize this fact. As Chesnutt realistically portrays him, the Colonel is not only too weak to be victorious everywhere, but he is even blind at times.

> J. Noel Heermance, *Charles W. Chesnutt: America's First Great Black Novelist* (Hamden, CT: Archon/Shoestring Press, 1974), pp. 185–86

WILLIAM L. ANDREWS   One reason why "Baxter's Procrustes" epitomizes Chesnutt's work in the short story is that it revives and refines some of the most distinctive satiric techniques of his conjure and color line stories. Describing Chesnutt's last *Atlantic* story as one in which a hoax is perpetrated on a group of self-assured but self-deluded gentlemen helps to place "Baxter's Procrustes" in a tradition which embraces such works as "The Conjurer's Revenge," "A Matter of Principle," and "The Passing of Grandison." In each of these earlier stories an ostensibly innocuous but unexpectedly cunning subordinate—a handyman, an office assistant, and a slave—exposes the prejudices of his patron and supposed superior, by playing false roles and manipulating illusory situations so as to capitalize upon his superior's inability to look below the surface of things. The trickster triumphs simply by allowing the deceived to deceive themselves. Thus at the end of such diverse stories as "Baxter's Procrustes," "A Matter of Principle," or "The Passing of Grandison," the reader learns a good deal about deception though (and probably because) the duped does not. Similar to its predecessors, "Baxter's Procrustes" uses an irony mixed with pathos to elicit from the reader an Horatian smile of amusement at the follies of men. The reader is encouraged to laugh, but not too loudly or too long, for, like Chesnutt, his feeling of superiority to the Bodleians' investment-consciousness or the Blue Veins' social exclusivism will be tempered by a poignant recognition of his own sympathies with the now-questionable "principles" of these "best people" of American and Afro-American society.

What marks "Baxter's Procrustes" as an advancement over its forebears in Chesnutt's fiction is its attention to the character of the confidence man himself. Usually hardly more than a device or an authorial mouthpiece, the hoaxer in "Baxter's Procrustes" is characterized in almost as much detail as the hoaxed. Chesnutt seems at pains to individualize his hoaxer, even to the point of hinting at his past, his personal circumstances, his motives, and his "philosophy" of life. Apparently Chesnutt wanted his reader to pay as much attention to the hoaxer as to the effect of his hoax. The reason for this attempt to establish a bond of sympathy between Baxter and the reader becomes clearer as one examines the character of Baxter. For this is no ordinary hoaxer, not merely an instrument by which Chesnutt took his mocking revenge on the delusions of the socially pretentious and the racially "superior." Baxter is Chesnutt's most elaborate self-dramatization, the most transparent and close-fitting of the many masks the author assumed in his fiction. Baxter's satirical purpose derives from Chesnutt's apparent presentation of his own artistic situation in 1904 through that of Baxter, an unsuccessful author who is patronized, summarized, and categorized by an ignorant, commercially minded, pseudo-literary readership.

William L. Andrews, *The Literary Career of Charles W. Chesnutt* (Baton Rouge: Louisiana State University Press, 1980), pp. 213–14.

DONALD B. GIBSON   In his diary of July 31, 1875, Chesnutt made the following observation:

> Twice today, or oftener, I have been taken for "white." At the pond this morning one fellow said he'd "be damned if there was any nigger blood in me." At Coleman's I passed. On the road an old chap, seeing the trunks, took me for a student coming from school. I believe I'll leave here and pass anyhow, for I am as white as any of them. One old fellow said today, "Look here, Tom. Here's a black as white as you are."

Chesnutt expresses a paradox here, a paradox touching upon the essence of his self-conception. He indicates the disparity between illusion and reality, perception and knowledge. He deals with the enigma of the thing that is what it is not, and is not what it is: "Here's a black as white as you are." His "I am as white as any of them" is only meaningful in context coming from a person who does not conceive of himself as white. Although Chesnutt indicates the attitude that it is better to be white than black, his own personal decision when he confronted the possibility of passing was not to pass. His decision was not so much to be black as not to have distinguished between himself as mulatto and individuals more purely Negro. Speaking at the time of his reception of the NAACP's Spingarn Medal in 1928, Chesnutt says,

> . . . substantially all of my writings, with the exception of *The Conjure Woman*, have dealt with the problems of people of mixed blood, which, while in the main the same as those of the true Negro, are in some instances and in some respects more complex and difficult of treatment, in fiction as in life.

He sometimes refers indirectly to himself as "Negro" or "colored" but never directly. At one time he refers to himself as "an American of acknowledged African descent," but he follows that with, "In this case the infusion of African blood is very small—is not in fact a visible admixture."

At work in Chesnutt's paradoxical, multifaceted attitudes about his racial identity (and about his identity generally since race is an integral part of identity) is a particular habit of mind that allowed (or perhaps caused?) him to hold contradictory ideas at the same moment. It is what I would call the dialectical habit of mind, a way of perceiving the world in terms of ideas standing in opposing relation. In Chesnutt's case, opposing ideas may stand in diametrical opposition, but the opposing elements are not of equal weight; hence an idea or belief that Chesnutt strongly holds will be pitted against a contradictory idea, also within his scheme of values, of lesser weight or strength. Concretely expressed, Dr. Miller in *The Marrow of Tradition* embodies a great number of Chesnutt's own values, beliefs, and feelings, but Chesnutt's doubt about the validity of those values, beliefs, and feelings finds an objectification in the character of Josh Green. The two characters exist in thesis-antithesis relation.

Again to express concretely the dialectical character of his thought, we may take Chesnutt's expression of optimism and pessimism as an example.

On the one hand, Chesnutt's characters (and the man himself as the diary indicates) are usually optimistic and hopeful of the accomplishment of some desired end. On the other, they are thwarted so frequently and so completely as to suggest the impossibility of achieving anything resembling human happiness. A third turn of the screw suggests that some force, some agency outside human experience, in some measure rights things. Hence murderers are usually punished; evil is frequently revenged as the imbalance caused by the commission of wrong-doing is frequently restored, betokening an ordered world. These attitudes, the optimistic and the pessimistic, find expression within the same contexts. At the end of his darkest tale, "The Web of Circumstance," Chesnutt attempts to relieve the gloom by appending a paragraph in which he, as author, speaks:

> Some time, we are told, when the cycle of years has rolled
> around, there is to be another golden age, when all men will
> dwell together in love and harmony, and when peace and
> righteousness shall prevail for a thousand years. God speed the day
> and . . . give us here and there, and now and then, some little
> foretaste of this golden age, that we may the more patiently and
> hopefully await its coming!

This paragraph was necessary in order to counteract the meaning of the tale itself. Although inclined to believe that life as lived is essentially tragic, Chesnutt never intends to go so far as to suggest that life (and ultimately history) is without meaning, as the tale indeed suggests. No "foretaste of a golden age" is visible there; so Chesnutt, in the final passage of the tale and of the book, makes a statement entirely contrary to the meaning of this particular tale, as well as to the implications of some of the others. Once again in his fiction, antithesis undercuts and hence qualifies thesis.

The tension resulting from opposing elements forms the center of nearly all his fiction. Irony, paradox (of character and situation, not language and style), and ambivalence are his stock in trade. In his most complex work, theses, countertheses, subtheses, and countersubtheses play off against one another, revealing a subtlety of mind easily obscured by his formal style, diction, and traditional technique. This subtle play of mind, the awareness and expression of myriad gradations of thought and feeling, is another element distinguishing Chesnutt from the majority of his contemporaries.

Donald B. Gibson, "Charles W. Chesnutt: The Anatomy of a Dream," *The Politics of Literary Expression: A Study of Major Black Writers* (Westport, CT: Greenwood Press), 1981, pp. 125–28

SALLYANN H. FERGUSON   Scholarship on novelist and short story writer Charles W. Chesnutt stagnates in recent years because his critics have failed to address substantively the controversial issues raised by his essays. Indeed, many scholars either minimize or ignore the fact that these writings complement his fiction and, more importantly, that they often reveal unflattering aspects of Chesnutt the social reformer and artist. In a much-quoted journal entry of 16 March 1880, Chesnutt himself explicitly links his literary art with social reform, saying he would write for a "high, holy purpose," "not so much [for] the elevation of the colored people as the elevation of the whites." Using the most sophisticated artistic skills at his command, he ultimately hopes to expose the latter to a variety of positive and non-stereotypic images of the "colored people" and thereby mitigate white racism. As he remarks in a 29 May 1880 entry, "it is the province of literature to open the way for him [the colored person] to get it [equality]— to accustom the public mind to the idea; and while amusing them [whites], to lead people out, imperceptibly, unconsciously, step by step, to the desired state of feeling." Throughout his entire literary career, Chesnutt never strays far from these basic reasons for writing, in fiction and nonfiction alike.

It is in his essays, however, that Chesnutt most clearly reveals the limited nature of his social and literary goals. Armed with such familiar journal passages as those cited above, scholars have incorrectly presumed that this writer seeks to use literature primarily as a means for alleviating white color prejudice against *all* black people in this country. But, while the critics romantically hail him as a black artist championing the cause of his people, Chesnutt, as his essays show, is essentially a social and literary accommodationist who pointedly and repeatedly confines his reformist impulses to the "colored people"—a term that he almost always applies either to color-line blacks or those of mixed races. This self-imposed limitation probably stems from the fact that he wrote during a time of intense color hatred in America, when the masses of blacks, because of their dark skin, could not unobtrusively be assimilated into the mainstream culture. Chesnutt was well aware that the dismal plight of these "genuine negro[es]" (as he calls dark-skinned blacks in a 30 May 1889 *New York Independent* essay entitled "What Is a White Man?") was not amenable to his kind of artistic stealth and subtlety and required more aggression. In his "White Man" essay, therefore, the pacifist author stresses the futility of such a measure, arguing that force can have little effect in bringing about equal citizenship for black people of any hue. After discarding both force and non-violence as potential remedies for the predicament of "genuine Negroes" in America, Chesnutt must have viewed their plight as virtually insoluble. Thus, it is not surprising that the author deliberately limits his goals to that which he believed he could reasonably accomplish—to improving the lot of the "colored people," as he indicates very early in his career. ⟨. . .⟩

The "Future American" series and other essays by Chesnutt reveal how his self-imposed social and literary mission is essentially at odds with racial realities, a dilemma that accounts for his often contradictory views. For instance, in the "White Man" article discussed earlier, he is forced to criticize Southern whites for failing to enforce conflicting miscegenation laws, which he despises, in order to protect the rights of the "colored people" these laws might benefit. Perhaps his daughter Helen, who subtitled the first biography of her father, *Pioneer of the Color Line* (1952), understood best the purpose of her father's life and work. Present-day scholars may attain similar understanding if we begin to re-examine Chesnutt's fiction in light of his nonfiction. It may be that after blackness came into vogue, we grew too content with merely celebrating black literary achievement. Nonetheless, before African-American literature gains a solid footing in academe, it must undergo the same kind of tough critical scrutiny to which other literatures have been subjected. Although disputed by others, Chesnutt's published essays indicate that he was among the first "African-American" literary artists to break ranks with the race and openly advocate miscegenation. In his quest to bring racial peace and a taste of the good life to the light-skinned segment of the black population, he did not hesitate to sacrifice the interests of dark-skinned people. In this latter respect, Charles W. Chesnutt is oddly callous for an otherwise sensitive man—and, ironically enough, not very different from the white founding fathers of America.

SallyAnn H. Ferguson, "Chesnutt's Genuine Blacks and Future Americans," *MELUS* 15, No. 3 (Fall 1988): 109–10, 117–18

HENRY LOUIS GATES, JR.   Between 1899, when he published *The Conjure Woman*, a collection of short stories, and 1905 Chesnutt published six books, including five works of fiction and a short biography of Frederick Douglass. Of these, the work that for many scholars stands as his greatest achievement is his novel *The Marrow of Tradition*. Based upon the 1989 race riot at Wilmington, North Carolina, which Chesnutt researched for two years, *The Marrow of Tradition* is one of the earliest explorations of literary naturalism in the black tradition. Here, character and fate are determined by heredity and custom. Post-Reconstruction southern social conventions, customs, and mores, Chesnutt shows us, were not as they had been represented in the neoplantation fictions so popular in the last two decades of the nineteenth century, which sought to rewrite the history of slavery with nostalgia and romanticism, through a hazy filter of "moonbeams and magnolia blossoms." No, the South that emerged after Reconstruction was just as corrupt, dishonest, and racist as southern society had been before the war. While the forms of a supposedly "new" South might differ in outward appearance from the old, in substance the two were fundamentally the same.

Indeed, the book is profoundly pessimistic ⟨. . .⟩ And yet Chesnutt's narrative skill enables him to limn this world with nuance and intelligence.

Henry Louis Gates, Jr., "Introduction," Three Classic African American Novels (New York: Vintage Classics, 1990), pp. xv–xvi

---

ERIC SELINGER   Charles Chesnutt claimed the order of stories in *The Conjure Woman* was "not essential." The volume has another tale to tell. While indeed "not, strictly, a novel," the collection unfolds by an ominous logic: a sequence of stories, a series of frames, through which we can see Chesnutt confronting, subverting, but ultimately underwriting certain powerful images, not just of slavery or of African-Americans, in general, but of that figure peculiarly threatening to whites of the post-Reconstruction era, the black man. Readers have, of course, noted the gender division of the work's inscribed audience, the skeptical transplanted Ohian John and his sickly, sympathetic wife Annie—indeed, John himself comments upon it several times within the text. But sexual dynamics are central to the stories Julius tells as well, in his representation of black families and romances disrupted or destroyed by slavery, and in his remarkably contrasting portrayals of conjure women (Aunt Peggy and Tenie) and equally powerful, but more dangerous conjure men. An exploration of the threefold sexual politics of the book—in Julius's stories, in the world of their telling, and the crossroads of frame and tale—reveals the coherence of the *The Conjure Woman*, a strategic structure of overplot to the book as a whole. Increasingly capable, signifying and significant through the first five stories, manipulating John's and or Annie's generic expectations—what such a storyteller will talk to them about, and how he will do so—, Julius is symbolically castrated at the end of "The Gray Wolf's Ha'nt." And in "Hot-Foot Hannibal," the closing piece, after enabling the reconciliation of North and South in the persons of Annie's younger sister Mabel and the local gentleman Malcolm Murchison, he softly and silently vanishes.

That the collection's structure should involve issues of genre as much as gender issues should come as no surprise. As Richard Yarborough has argued, "much of the fiction produced by Afro-Americans before World War I" displays "not a desire to render black life as accurately and honestly as possible," but a similar manipulation of reader response: "a willingness to dissemble, to overemphasize, even to misrepresent—that is, to write with the aim of soliciting sympathy from the white reader." But the price of such sympathy, at least for male characters, involves a sacrifice of certain "manly" virtues, most notably the willingness to use violence in self-defense, in favor of those "feminine" values of self-sacrifice, nonviolence, and family preservation which undergird the sentimental novel in general, and the troublesome but influential model of Stowe's *Uncle Tom's Cabin* in particular. ". . . rage, bitterness, and a desire for revenge on the part of positively portrayed black figures," Yarborough explains, "must be curbed in order to establish them as self-controlled, all-forgiving, and eminently acceptable candidates for membership in the American mainstream." This is doubly true when these figures are male. Such restraint risks relying on "the antebellum stereotype of blacks as loyal, faithful retainers," never agitated except when provoked by outsiders; but any hint to the contrary risks invoking in white readers' minds the notion of African-American "savagery," with its implications of riot and rape, that lynch mobs claimed to be on guard against.

As Chesnutt demonstrates in Julius's shifting narrative fortunes, the more a tale departs from sentimental norms, the less interest it provokes in, and the less power it has over, its intended white audience. (The one apparent exception, "The Conjuror's Revenge," when read in context, proves the rule.) If, as Richard Baldwin contends, Chesnutt set himself the task in this volume of changing white perceptions of blacks, and not simply of touching white sentiments, we must admit that by the end of the collection this project has been abandoned as a failure. While Uncle Julius is not exactly the sort of black male heroine available since Stowe as a white-acceptable stereotype—his association with conjure, and not Christianity, complicates the issue—, the collection closes with a decisive move toward sentimentality in the plantation-story idiom that defuses the racial and sexual issues that seem to be building toward an explosion in certain earlier tales. The otherwise troubling, unimpressive end to the collection can be read, not as an artistic lapse, but as a strategic comment on the limits authors like Chesnutt worked within and against—including, perhaps, the definitions of masculinity and femininity his conjure figures suggest.

> Eric Selinger, "Aunts, Uncles, Audience: Gender and Genre in Charles Chesnutt's *The Conjure Woman*," *Black American Literature Forum* 25, No. 4 (Winter 1991): 665–67

◈ *Bibliography*

Frederick Douglass. 1899.

The Wife of His Youth and Other Stories of the Color Line. 1899.

The Conjure Woman. 1899.

The House Behind the Cedars. 1900.

The Marrow of Tradition. 1901.

The Colonel's Dream. 1905.

Short Fiction. Ed. Sylvia Lyons Render. 1974.

Countee Cullen
1903–1946

COUNTEE CULLEN was born Countee Leroy Porter on May 30, 1903. He was probably born in Louisville, Kentucky, although both New York City and Baltimore have been cited as his birthplace. Orphaned in childhood, he was raised by a Mrs. Porter, who was probably his grandmother. In his teens he was adopted by African Methodist Episcopal Church minister Frederick Asbury Cullen and his wife Carolyn, who encouraged Countee to write. Cullen's poetry was already seeing regular publication by the time he graduated from New York University in 1925. His first book, *Color*, appeared that same year; Cullen won the Harmon Gold Award and critical praise for his Keatsian verse and his frank depiction of racial prejudice.

Cullen received an M.A. from Harvard in 1926, then became assistant editor of the National Urban League journal *Opportunity*. In 1927 he published the acclaimed *Copper Sun* and *The Ballad of the Brown Girl*, and edited *Caroling Dusk*, a historic anthology of work by black poets. The following year he married Yolande Du Bois, daughter of W. E. B. Du Bois, and traveled to Paris on a Guggenheim Fellowship. Yolande filed for divorce before he returned; their relationship inspired the tortured love poetry of *The Black Christ and Other Poems* (1929).

Back in the United States, Cullen published a novel of life in Harlem, *One Way to Heaven* (1932), and a verse adaptation of Euripides' *Medea* (1935). From 1932 to 1945 Cullen settled into a teaching position at a junior high school in New York City. In 1940 he married Ida Mae Roberson and published a children's book of verse entitled *The Lost Zoo (A Rhyme for the Young, but Not Too Young)*, sharing the bylines with his pet, Christopher Cat. Two years later he published a prose work for children, *My Lives and How I Lost Them* (1942), which purported to be Christopher's autobiography. Cullen authored and coauthored a number of plays, most of which were not published; his own selection of his best poems was published posthumously as *On These I Stand: An Anthology of the Best Poems of Countee Cullen* (1947). Countee Cullen died on January 9, 1946. Gerald Early has now assembled Cullen's collected writings under the title *My Soul's High Song* (1991).

◈ *Critical Extracts*

CARL VAN VECHTEN   What the colored race needs to break its bonds is a few more men and women of genius. This is a theory recently promulgated by the Negro intelligentsia. Providence, apparently, is willing to test the theory, for genius, or talent, is pouring prodigally out of Harlem, and out of other cities' Black Belts as well. Such young writers as Jean Toomer, Jessie Fauset, Walter White, Claude McKay, Eric Walrond, Langston Hughes, Rudolph Fisher, and Alain Locke; such young musicians, actors, and dancers as Roland Hayes, Paul Robeson, Julius Bledsoe, Laurence Brown, Eddie Rector, Florence Mills, and Johnny Hudgins (I am naming only a few of the many) are sufficient earnest of what the "gift of black folk" (to employ Dr. Du Bois's poetic phrase) will be in the immediate future.

One of the best of the Negro writers, Countee Cullen, is the youngest of them all. He was barely twenty-one when "The Shroud of Color" (published in the November 1924 issue of the *American Mercury*) created a sensation analogous to that created by the appearance of Edna St. Vincent Millay's "Renascence" in 1912, lifting its author at once to a position in the front rank of contemporary American poets, white or black. "The Shroud of Color" was emotional in its passionate eloquence, but Countee Cullen sometimes ⟨. . .⟩ strikes the strings of his inspirational lyre more lightly, although a satiric or bitter aftertaste is likely to linger in his most ostensibly flippant verse. All his poetry is characterized by a suave, unpretentious, brittle, intellectual elegance; some of it—"To John Keats, Poet, at Spring Time" is an excellent example—by a haunting, lyric loveliness. It is to be noted that, like any distinguished artist of any race, he is able to write stanzas which have no bearing on the problems of his own race. In this respect his only Negro forebear, so far as I can recall at the moment, is the poet Pushkin, whose verses dwelt on Russian history and folklore, although he was the great-grandson of a slave.

Carl Van Vechten, "Countee Cullen: A Note by Carl Van Vechten," *Vanity Fair* 24, No. 4 (June 1925): 62

JESSIE FAUSET   *Color* is the name of Mr. Cullen's book and color is, rightly, in every sense its prevailing characteristic. For not only does every bright glancing line abound in color but it is also in another sense the yard-stick by which all the work in this volume is measured. Thus his poems fall into three categories: Those, and these are very few, in which no mention is made of color; those in which the adjectives "black" or "brown" or "ebony" are deliberately introduced to show that the type which the author had in mind was not white; and thirdly the poems which arise out of the conscious of being a "Negro in a day like this" in America.

These last are not only the most beautifully done but they are by far the most significant group in the book. I refer especially to poems of the type of "Yet Do I Marvel", "The Shroud of Color", "Heritage" and "Pagan Prayer". It is in such work as this that the peculiar and valuable contribution of the American colored man is to be made to American literature. For any genuine poet black or white might have written "Oh for a Little While Be Kind" or the lines to "John Keats"; the idea contained in a "Song of Praise" was used long ago by an old English poet and has since been set to music by Roger Quilter. But to pour forth poignantly and sincerely the feelings which make plain to the world the innerness of the life which black men live calls for special understanding. Cullen has packed into four illuminating lines the psychology of colored Americans, that strange extra dimension which totally artificial conditions have forced into sharp reality. He writes:

> All day long and all night through,
> One thing only must I do:
> Quench my pride and cool my blood,
> Lest I perish in the flood.

That is the new expression of the struggle now centuries old. Here I am convinced is Mr. Cullen's forte; he has the feeling and the gift to express colored-ness in a world of whiteness. I hope he will not be deflected from continuing to do that of which he has made such a brave and beautiful beginning. I hope that no one crying down "special treatment" will turn him from his native and valuable genre. There *is* no "universal treatment"; it is all specialized. When Kipling spoke of having the artist to

> paint the thing as he sees it
> For the God of things as they are,

he set the one infallible rule by which all workmanship should be conceived, achieved and judged. In a time when it is the vogue to make much of the

Negro's aptitude for clownishness or to depict him objectively as a serio-comic figure, it is a fine and praiseworthy act for Mr. Cullen to show through the interpretation of his own subjectivity the inner workings of the Negro soul and mind.

Jessie Fauset, [Review of *Color*], *Crisis* 31, No. 5 (March 1926): 238–39

RUDOLPH FISHER   The danger of falling below expectations is especially great in the case of the poet who turns novelist. Mr. Cullen, whose poetry is admired by so many, and whose danger therefore is the greater, has nevertheless challenged fate successfully. His first novel ⟨*One Way to Heaven*⟩ goes over. ⟨. . .⟩

Be not misled by the announcement that "this is a mad and witty modern picture of high life in Harlem." That part of it which portrays the "high life" of Harlem is not important and seems even less important than it might, because its effect is completely submerged in the larger and simpler realities of the rest of the book. This is because Mr. Cullen has chosen to change his method and his viewpoint in dealing with the upper level. Here he becomes a caricaturist, suppressing all his sympathies, sketching with a sharp and ungracious pen. But the less pretentious folk he has treated gently and delicately, in color. This juxtaposition of two so different subjects so differently handled is somehow like exhibiting a lovely pastel and a cartoon in the same frame.

But the pastel has in it such clear beauty as has escaped the eye and hand of most other portrayers of darkskinned America. Aunt Mandy, devout Christian and equally devout believer in fortune-telling cards; Mattie, simple child, torn between love for her Sam and love for her Jesus, and Sam, beloved rascal wiping the slate clean with a last splendid lie—these are real people who, for all the author's lightness of touch, live, breathe, and con-vince. Their creator, however, has achieved more than that. He has given them a beauty which his predecessors have been reluctant to dwell upon—a black beauty. And this beauty emanates so unmistakably from within these characters that it should never again be necessary for anyone to insist that fine souls are really white inside.

Rudolph Fisher, "Revealing a Beauty That Is Black," *New York Herald Tribune Books*, 28 February 1932, p. 3

J. SAUNDERS REDDING   Now undoubtedly the biggest, single unalterable circumstance in the life of Mr. Cullen is his color. Most of the life he has lived has been influenced by it. And when he writes by it, he *writes*; but when this does not guide him, his pen trails faded ink across his pages.

To argue long about Countee Cullen—his ideas, his poetic creed, and the results he obtains—is to come face to face with the poet's own confusion. It is not a matter of words or language merely, as it was with Dunbar: it is a matter of ideas and feelings. Once Mr. Cullen wrote: "Negro verse (as a designation, that is) would be more confusing than accurate. Negro poetry, it seems to me, in the sense that we speak of Russian, French, or Chinese poetry, must emanate from some country other than this in some language other than our own."

At another time: "Somehow or other I find my poetry of itself treating of the Negro, of his joys and his sorrows—mostly of the latter—, and of the heights and depths of emotion which I feel as a Negro."

And still another:

> Then call me traitor if you must,
> Shout treason and default!
> Saying I betray a sacred trust
> Aching beyond this vault.
> I'll bear your censure as your praise,
> For never shall the clan
> Confine my singing to its ways
> Beyond the ways of man.

The answer to all this seems to be: Chinese poetry translated into English remains Chinese poetry—Chinese in feeling, in ideas.

But there is no confusion in Mr. Cullen's first volume, *Color*, which is far and away his best. Here his poetry (nearly all of it on racial subjects, or definitely and frankly conditioned by race) helps to balance the savage poetic outbursts of Claude McKay. Countee Cullen is decidedly a gentle poet, a schoolroom poet whose vision of life is interestingly distorted by too much of the vicarious. This lends rather than detracts. It is as though he saw life through the eyes of a woman who is at once shrinking and bold, sweet and bitter. His province is the nuance, the finer shades of feeling, subtility and finesse of emotion and expression. Often however, with feline slyness, he bares the pointed talons of a coolly ironic and deliberate humor which is his way of expressing his resentment at the racial necessities.

J. Saunders Redding, *To Make a Poet Black* (Chapel Hill: University of North Carolina Press, 1939), pp. 109–10

BERTRAM L. WOODRUFF   The poet, ⟨. . .⟩ by using his creative power to change sadness into gladness, is able to offer consolation to men. With the healing force of its high ideals of Love, Beauty, Faith in Man, and Christian Belief, poetry is a balm for the evils and frustrations of life. Cullen tells of the confidence in the healing power of poetry possessed by the Irish poets whom he met at Padraic Colum's:

> I walked in a room where Irish poets were;
> I saw the muse enthroned, heard how they worshipped her,
> Felt men nor gods could never so envenon them
> That Poetry could pass and they not grasp her hem,
> Not cry on her for healing. ⟨"After a Visit"⟩

Inasmuch as Cullen confesses in the same poem that there had been a gulf between his aesthetic theory and his experience, there is no doubt of the intellectual and emotional dissension within his being concerning the meaning of life. As he himself acknowledges,

> There is a thorn forever in his breast,
> Who cannot take his world for what it seems.
> ⟨"A Thorn Forever in the Breast"⟩

Cullen, as a Negro, cannot take life in America for what it seems to him. Writing once of the race conflict in America and the natural beauty of the South, he exclaimed, "If only the South loved the Negro as he is capable of loving her—there is no end to what might be." He yearns for an abiding place in America where, as in France, "fair and kindly" folk may offer "what was denied my hungry heart at home." But the tie with America is too "taut to be undone." Cullen has posed the question, "This ground and I are we not one?"

All in all, Cullen's philosophy is a tentative ordering of what is inchoate in his experience. If his poetic intuition fails to bring order out of chaos, it is not because he is a victim of self-deception. His poetry reveals his sincere attempt to discern whatever spiritual adjustment there may be for suffering, passionate, and weak souls in a hostile world. In the treatment of his poetic themes he sifts minutely the wheat from the chaff of human ideals, leaving as hoped-for verities his faith in Love, Beauty, Mankind, the Sacrifice of Christ, and Poetry. In his moments of weakness and doubt, he feels too keenly the everlasting strife and frustration in the world and the awesome mystery of Death.

The thorn forever in his breast has prevented Countee Cullen from maintaining in his poetry the spiritual serenity and strength that may be felt, at times, in the core of his writings. Instead of sentimentalizing the anguish created by the thorn, he would do well to resolve the problem by holding fast to his "Faith the canny conjuror." Some day, perhaps, he may write fully of his "own soul's ecstasy," since he has already written what might be adopted as a personal and poetic creed:

> I count it little being barred
> From those who undervalue me.
> I have my own soul's ecstasy.
> Men may not bind the summer sea,
> Nor set a limit to the stars;
> The sun seeps through all iron bars;
> The moon is ever manifest.
> These things my heart always possessed.
> And more than this (and here's the crown)
> No man, my son, can batter down
> The star-flung ramparts of the mind.
> ⟨The Black Christ⟩

Bertram L. Woodruff, "The Poetic Philosophy of Countee Cullen," *Phylon* 1, No. 3 (September 1940): 222–23

WILLIAM STANLEY BRAITHWAITE   Countee Cullen as a poet was a traditionalist in line with the great English poets, and an apostle of beauty with the fountainhead of his inspiration in the poetic philosophy of John Keats. If his imagination was scorched by the injustice and oppression of a people with whom his lot was thrown, like Keats whose sensitive nature was also wounded, he soared, not by way of escape, but by precept and counsel, into the abstract realm of the spirit. He caught the complexities and contradictions in the net of this idealism, as is attested to in this stanza from "More Than a Fool's Song"—

> The world's a curious riddle thrown
> Water-wise from heaven's cup;
> The souls we think are hurtling down
> Perhaps are climbing up.

No poet we have as yet produced was so complete and spontaneous a master of the poetic technique as Countee Cullen. His octosyllabic line has not been more skilfully handled by any modern poet. He has used the sonnet for many moods and themes and carved its fourteen lines of varied temper and structure with a lyrical unity that earns him a place in the company of Wordsworth, Rossetti and Bridges. He possessed an epigramatic gift and turn of wit that gave uncommon delight as witnessed in the series of "Epitaphs" among which the one "For a Mouthy Woman" is a masterpiece. His translations from Baudelaire, especially the sinuous felinity of cats, rank with those of Swinburne, Arthur Symons and George Dillon, in the rendering of that feverish and fantastic French poet into English. The fantasy of the "Wakeupworld" from the mythical narrative of "The Lost Zoo," established his poetic kinship in imaginative humor to the delightful foolery of Richard H. Barham's *Ingoldsby Legends*.

No one will deny that Countee Cullen escaped the aches that come to a sensitive spirit aware of racial prejudice and insult, but he did not allow them to distort or distemper the ideals and visions which endowed him as an artist and poet. He had as deep a sensibility for the human denials and aches which absorbed the lesser racial ones, and strove through the exquisite creation of imagery and music to evoke and communicate the spirit of Beauty as a solacing and restorative power. Time will, I think, accept him on the spiritual terms he set for himself in the poem "To John Keats, the Poet at Spring Time," and know that though he could sing a "Ballad for a Brown Girl" and make a "Litany of the Dark People" the blood and soul of mankind were alike in its passions and aspirations.

William Stanley Braithwaite, "On These I Stand," *Opportunity* 25, No. 3 (July–September 1947): 170

ROBERT BONE   Countee Cullen has often been described as one of the more "respectable" Renaissance novelists, with the implication that he avoided the "sordid" subject matter of the Harlem School. Nothing could be farther from the truth. Cullen neither exploited low-life material for its own sake nor avoided it when it served his artistic ends. Though distinctly not of a Bohemian temperament, neither did he value respectability above art. His mischievous sense of humor and his penchant for satire differentiated him from those Renaissance novelists who were forever defending the race before the bar of white opinion. Countee Cullen had a lighter and truer touch, which speaks for itself in *One Way to Heaven*. ⟨. . .⟩

The aesthetic design of the novel consists of variations on a theme. The moral ambiguity of Sam's life and death is echoed in the lives of the other characters. Both the evangelist and the Reverend Drummond are sincere men of God, but neither is above a little showmanship for the Lord's sake. The devout but worldly wise Aunt Mandy takes a practical view of Mattie's marital difficulties: "Sometimes when the angels is too busy to help you, you have to fight the devil with his own tools." Even Mattie, "the gentle servitor of the gentlest of all the gods," abandons her Jesus for a conjure-woman and nearly murders her husband's mistress. The author's point is clear: he that is without sin among you, let him cast the first stone at Sam Lucas.

Sam's cards and razor provide an appropriate symbol for Cullen's theme. Like people, the cards and razor contain potentialities for either good or evil. In Sam's hands, they are the tools of deceit, yet they are no less the instruments of Mattie's salvation. In Mattie's possession, they are the sacred tokens of her conversion, but in her extremity she uses them as a voodoo charm. When Sam asks Aunt Mandy, "Don't you think that cards is evil?" she replies, "It all depends on the kind of cards you have and what you do with them." In Cullen's view the moral universe is infinitely complex. Form is unimportant; there is more than one way to heaven.

Robert Bone, *The Negro Novel in America* (New Haven: Yale University Press, 1958), pp. 78–79

DARWIN T. TURNER   Cullen had given credit for coauthorship of *The Lost Zoo* to Christopher, a cat who recited stories which he had heard from his father. In his final book ⟨*My Lives and How I Lost Them*⟩, Cullen, identified merely as the amanuensis of Christopher, created a work possibly superior stylistically and structurally to his earlier novel. In Chris, Countee Cullen found a *persona* he could enjoy. Confident of the innate superiority of his species, as he informs the reader in his first words, Christopher suffers neither the frustration nor the inhibitions of his human scribe; consequently, he is relaxed and self-assured as he explains to his dull-witted human amanuensis how he lost his first eight lives.

Comparison of the two individuals emphasizes the fact that Cullen escaped into a character free from the restrictions which had limited his own life. Christopher's father was a distinguished aristocrat: he traced his lineage to Noah's ark. His mother, though a commoner, provided all the love a growing kitten needs. With two brothers, three sisters, and a patient father determined to educate his kittens in proper "cateristics," Christopher, even during his first life, enjoyed family security which the human Cullen lacked until he was in his teens. Furthermore, not harassed by fellow cats urging him to be realistic or imagistic or chauvinistic or atavistic, or to write about this or that (Cullen did not dare to prescribe Chris's subjects), Chris was free to tell his story as he wished—sentimentally, suspensefully, digressively.

Reared with his brothers, and sisters—intellectual Claude, vain Claudia, lazy Carlos and Carole, and his twin Christobelle, young Chris learns the lessons essential to an educated cat: how to lap milk, how to wash, how to purr, and how to arch. He also learns that fathers sometimes err. Having been warned to avoid Rat, who is not a respectable companion for a cat, Chris meets Rufus the Ritten (if a young cat is a "kitten," then surely a young rat is a "ritten"; so Chris reasons with Humpty-Dumpty's logic). Similarly, Rufus's father has warned him against cats. Despite their prejudiced parents, Chris and Rufus become friends when they discover that they have identical habits and interests. ⟨. . .⟩

Even in these books for children, however, Cullen never persuades a reader that he has evaded consciousness of the discriminations against blacks. Christopher is a "catitarian" (and perhaps more sensitive than a "humanitarian"); consequently, in *The Lost Zoo*, he expresses chagrin that his ancestor had signed the petition against Sammie Skunk. Sammie's only fault was that, at times, he smelled bad; as Cullen reminded readers in *One Way to Heaven*, the allegedly offensive odor of blacks is a reason which bigots have used to justify the segregation of blacks and whites. Furthermore, in *My Lives and How I Lost Them*, Christopher Senior's explanation of why Chris must avoid rittens directly echoes bigots' pronouncements of the inferiority of black people.

Darwin T. Turner, "Countee Cullen: The Lost Ariel," *In a Minor Chord: Three Afro-American Writers and Their Search for Identity* (Carbondale: Southern Illinois University Press, 1971), pp. 85–87

ARTHUR P. DAVIS   Countee Cullen's single novel, *One Way to Heaven* (1932), belongs to that group of Harlem novels—among them *Nigger Heaven*, by Van Vechten, and *Home to Harlem*, by McKay—which sprang up during the Renaissance. The works of McKay and Van Vechten played up the more sensational aspects of the black ghetto and were obviously written to cater to the new taste in America for the exotic and primitive. Cullen's novel is more of an "inside" book than McKay's. It was designed to appeal primarily to a Negro audience. As a result, Cullen's picture of Harlem, covering not just the lower-class but the middle-class "intellectuals" as well, is closer to the *real* Harlem than McKay's, though certainly not as colorful. Some critics have blamed Cullen for his twofold approach, claiming that he wrote *two* novellas rather than *one* novel. The charge is not wholly warranted because the two plots do touch *naturally*—that is, they are not forced beyond plausibility.

Cullen was trying to tell a story about the religious life of the ordinary Harlemites, a story of their church life and what it meant to them. Knowing that this would be a one-sided account, he used contrapuntally the activities of the class to which he belonged to sharpen the focus on both groups. One must remember that Cullen was a part of both the worlds he delineated. Reared in the parsonage of one of Harlem's largest churches, Cullen, even though he was an intellectual, learned to respect the function of the church in Negro life. On the other hand, he was one of the First Fruits of the Harlem Renaissance, but he was never too close to the movement not to see that it too had its charlatans who were just as phony as Sam Lucas the "religious" hustler. Cullen is satirizing both groups, but it is not a strong attack; it is rather the gentle "ribbing" of one who sees the foibles but appreciates the essential worth of both segments of Harlem life.

Arthur P. Davis, *From the Dark Tower: Afro-American Writers 1900–1960* (Washington, DC: Howard University Press, 1974), pp. 81–82

ALAN R. SHUCARD   The first relatively important poem Cullen composed was the long *Ballad of the Brown Girl*, published as a separate volume in 1927. He wrote it as a sophomore at New York University, and it won second prize in the national Witter Bynner poetry contest for undergraduates, an award by the Poetry Society of America. It is undisputably racial—in terms of the definition effective here, "black poetry." To begin with, Cullen failed to discover until much later that the term "brown girl" as it was used in the old English ballad upon which his version was based had no racial connotation at all, but was only a designation for a peasant girl. In the Cullen poem the love triangle of the original, a gory ballad in which the man and his two lovers all perish, is transformed so that the following occurs: a peer named Lord Thomas is in love with "the lily-white maid," an appellation used interchangeably with "Fair London" and "pride"—of all possible sections of the country—"of all the south." Prodded by his grasping mother, though, the white man chooses to marry instead "the dark Brown Girl who knows / No more defining name." This decision is taken solely for economic reasons and despite Lord Thomas's awareness that "bitter tongues have worn their tips / In sneering at her shame." After the white peer marries the Brown Girl for material gain, Fair London plays a scene at the reception during which she wears her bitter tongue berating miscegenation: "only the rose and the rosee should mate, / Oh, never the hare and the hound." True, the Brown Girl mortally stabs the lily-white maid, but only after her new white husband has failed to defend her against the verbal abuse; before this, she has succeeded in keeping "her passions underfoot / Because she comes of kings." The theme of high African lineage concealed by menial blacks in an ambient white environment ⟨. . .⟩ appears elsewhere in Cullen. Where Lord Thomas is slow to avenge the insult to his brown wife, he is unhesitatingly brutal in punishing the Brown Girl for the murder of the white one; he throttles her with her own long hair. Only his own death inevitably remains to be brought about, and the explicit moral is that because he has permitted his mother to convince him to barter "love / For gold or fertile land," he has brought disaster upon one and all. Of special interest here is that while the sacrifice of love for economics is important to the ballad, the racial dimension is measurable also: love, for the lord, is white, as he is; riches are personified in black, as are also the forces of passion and vitality (that is, Fair London is poor and insipid by comparison with the Brown Girl). At the end of the poem, "The Brown Girl sleeps at her true lord's feet, / Fair London by his side"—a noteworthy positioning of the two women in relation to the lord.

There is a group of racial sub-themes in Cullen directly suggested by *The Ballad of the Brown Girl* or related to the racial ideas found there. Arthur P. Davis long ago referred to Cullen's absorption with Africa as "the alien-and-exile theme," a useful expression in the examination of Afro-American literature. He defines the term well as "an implied contrast between the Negro's present state as an oppressed alien and that happy existence long, long ago in his native land." *Color*, Cullen's first volume and, in terms of critical acclaim and his own sensibility, his best, provides a number of representative poems that reflect many of the racial sub-themes. It is fair to say "representative" because even shortly before his death, as he selected the poems that he wished to be remembered by in the volume *On These I Stand*, Cullen chose an inordinately large number of poems from *Color*. Touching directly on the matter of African heritage alluded to in the case of the Brown Girl are such verses as "A Song of Praise" in which he describes his dark love, whose walk is the replica of a barbaric African dance, as more desirable than the reader's white one; "Fruit of the Flower," in which he speaks of racial memories; and notably "Atlantic City Waiter" and "Heritage." In the former, the waiter must disavow half his pride and wear an acquiescent mask, though his dexterity embodies the history of "Ten thousand years on jungle clues." The longer "Heritage" is an attempt to determine what Africa means to the speaker: finally, he realizes that it is his essential soul that must be suppressed in a civilization that is inimical to it. ⟨. . .⟩ In the very beat is the tension between the coolness of the civilization in which he must live externally and the smoldering racial force that Cullen believes he carries within.

Alan R. Shucard, *Countee Cullen* (Boston: Twayne, 1984), pp. 22–24

HOUSTON A. BAKER, JR.   The space ascribed to Cullen seems describable as a dimly lit and seldom-visited chamber where genteel souls stare forth in benign solicitude. Darwin Turner, for example, calls him "the lost Ariel," and Nathan Huggins speaks of Cullen clinging "quite tenaciously to the genteel tradition." Such phrases indicate only that Cullen did not march to the beat of the drummer who has "boomlay, boomlay, boomlayed" us into the 1970s. But critics are often embarrassed by the poet who is out of step with the age, as though someone had brought out a picture of a nonpartisan ancestor and shown it to their most committed colleagues. There follow tacit dismissals, vague apologies, and overweening defenses. ⟨. . .⟩

The mode, or preshaping impulse, of his work is in harmony with his overall conception of the poet as a man who dwells above mundane realities; for Cullen, the poet is the dream keeper, the "man . . . endowed with more lively sensibility, more enthusiasm and tenderness," the individual who is "certain of nothing but of the holiness of the Heart's affection and the truth of Imagination." These quotations from Wordsworth and Keats are descriptive; they capture in brief the a priori mandates of the romantic poet. In *"Cor Cordium," "*To John Keats, Poet. At Springtime," "For a Poet,"

"To an Unknown Poet," and "That Bright Chimeric Beast," Cullen defines the poet as a creator of immortal beauty, a man still in harmony with the mysterious and the ideal in an age "cold to the core, undeified," a person who wraps his dreams in "a silken cloth" and lays them away in "a box of gold." Such an author is far removed from the ideal social artist and can hardly be compared to many of today's black artists, who compose as though our lived realities were contingent upon their next quatrain. What we have, then, is a difference not in degree but in kind. To apply the standards of a socially oriented criticism to Countee Cullen and dismiss him is to achieve no more than a pyrrhic victory. To expect the majority of his work to consist of the type of idiomatic, foot-tapping, and right-on stanzas that mark much of the work of Langston Hughes and Don Lee is not only naive but also disappointing. Moreover, to search always for the racial import in the writings of an artist who believed the poet dealt (or, at least, should be able to deal) above the realm of simple earthly distinctions is to find little. To examine the writings of Countee Cullen in detail, however, and attempt to understand both his aesthetic standpoint and the major ideas in his poetry is to move closer to an intelligent interpretation of both the man and the tradition to which he belongs. ⟨. . .⟩

Most often criticized is Cullen's choice of the romantic mode and his reliance on a long-standing poetical tradition. And if his detractors stuck to these charges, there would be little conflict. Most, however, go beyond them and assume that, say, Langston Hughes and Jean Toomer were more forthright, "modern," and independent than Cullen. To do so is to forget that the publication of Hughes's first book was contingent upon the kind offices of Vachel Lindsay, and that Toomer was—according to Marjorie Content Toomer—a man who disavowed all allegiance to the Black Renaissance. The artistic independence of the black author was an implied goal rather than a tangible fact of the Renaissance, and one suspects that Cullen was not the only author who told Hughes that he wanted to be just a writer, not a "Negro" writer.

Houston A. Baker, Jr., "A Many-Colored Coat of Dreams: The Poetry of Countee Cullen," *Afro-American Poetics: Revisions of Harlem and the Black Aesthetic* (Madison: University of Wisconsin Press, 1988), pp. 52–54, 59

GERALD EARLY   Perhaps Countee Cullen was never fully understood as a poet or a writer because he has never been understood fully as a man. There is, and always has been, a quality of unknowableness, sheer inscrutability, that surrounds Cullen and is no more better symbolized, in a small yet telling way, than by the official, but varied accounts of his height. His passport of both 1934 and 1938 gives his height as 5' 3", his selective service registration card of 1942 lists him as 5' 10" and his war ration book number 3, issued when Cullen was forty years old, gives his height as 5' 7".

We still do not know where Cullen was born. In James W. Tuttleton's extremely useful essay "Countee Cullen at 'The Heights,' " which provides a detailed account of Cullen's undergraduate years at New York University, we learn that Cullen's college transcript, for which he himself provided the information, lists his place of birth as Louisville, Kentucky. This transcript was dated 1922. In the biographical headnote which Cullen wrote for his selections of poetry—contained in his own anthology of black poetry, *Caroling Dusk*—Cullen says he was born in New York City. ⟨. . .⟩ Whatever the reasons for Cullen changing the place of his birth, one inescapable fact is that in 1922 he was a relatively obscure but well-regarded black student with some poetic inclination and ability. By 1927 only Edna St. Vincent Millay surpassed him in American poetry circles in critical and press attention. Here with the whole business of birthplaces, we have the difference between the public and private Cullen. ⟨. . .⟩ Around the time of Cullen's death, stories began to circulate that he was born in Baltimore (one writer even says that Mrs. ⟨Ida⟩ Cullen confirms this). But there is little evidence for this ⟨. . .⟩ Oddly Beulah Reimherr, who had done the most extensive research into Cullen's childhood and young life, finds no record of anything about him in either the Louisville or Baltimore Bureau of Vital Statistics. There is, moreover, no birth record for Cullen in New York City. The mystery remains unsolved. ⟨. . .⟩

⟨. . .⟩ Cullen was very taken with the art of lying or why else did he have his cat tell tall tales in *The Lost Zoo* and in *My Lives and How I Lost Them*, or why else did he translate *The Medea*, which is all about the lying of two lovers, or why write a novel where the central character lies about his conversion? The entire scope of Cullen's 1930s career seems a long philosophical and aesthetic examination of the many creative and nefarious dimensions of lying, deception, and hypocrisy. Also the interest in lying as art explains the character Sam Lucas in *One Way to Heaven*. Many critics have felt that Cullen named the character Lucas because his own real name may have been Lucas. What makes a great deal more sense is that the con man character of Cullen's novel is named after the great black stage minstrel of the same name who was very popular in the early 1900s. As the novel turns on Lucas's ability to act, to play out a conversion that he does not feel convincingly, both in the beginning of the novel and at the novel's end, we see instantly that the book centers on the art of lying, and what black person was a better professional liar than a minstrel with his degrading, low, stereotypical comedy? In fact, the connection between the novel's character and the minstrel is made even more explicit by the symbols of the playing cards and razor, which Sam tosses away at every conversion. These are of course the props of the stereotypical black minstrel.

Gerald Early, "Introduction," *My Soul's High Song: The Collected Writings of Countee Cullen, Voice of the Harlem Renaissance,* ·ed. Gerald Early (New York: Doubleday, 1991), pp. 6–8, 59

MICHEL FABRE   How can one evaluate the impact of French culture and Parisian life on the works of "the greatest francophile" of the Harlem Renaissance? Besides, how far did his presence in Paris help establish links between Afro-American writers and the French-speaking world? Clearly, Cullen spent nearly as much time in France as Claude McKay, and although his acquaintance was less diverse than McKay's and largely restricted to Paris, Cullen's knowledge of the language and culture enabled him to appreciate France far more than Hughes, and clearly as much as McKay, did. But differences in class and ideological choice intervened: whereas McKay was impatient with polished circles and the literati and seemed to breathe more freely among "the folks," Cullen gives the impression that he felt he was slumming when he made the rounds of working-class dance halls or tried the exotic setting of the Bal Colonial. He enjoyed these deeply, but possibly owing to his puritanical upbringing, one side of his personality would hold his spontaneity in check. Or, when attending a performance of *Rigoletto*, he would feel compelled to apologize for liking bel canto. He was visibly torn: he sought refinement but craved more vital, lusty entertainment than romantic infatuation. Thus France could quench his thirst for culture and unbridled enjoyment alike. Paris was the City of Light, the repository of ancient traditions, and also the embodiment of sexually free and piquantly dissolute life to which a touch of Africa or the West Indies added spice.

Cullen also visualized France as a generous mother-country. In America, which was his home, he felt that much was denied him because of his color. As a result he projected France as a haven, a substitute mother, as he made clear in his sonnet "To France":

> Among a fair and kindly foreign folk
> There might I only breathe my latest days,
> With those rich accents falling on my ear
> That most have made me feel that freedom's rays
> Still have a shrine where they may leap and soar—
> Though I were palsied there, or halt, or blind,
> So were I there, I think I should not mind.

Michel Fabre, *From Harlem to Paris: Black American Writers in France 1840–1980* (Urbana: University of Illinois Press, 1991), pp. 88–89

◈ *Bibliography*

Color. 1925.

The Ballad of the Brown Girl: An Old Ballad Retold. 1927.

Copper Sun. 1927.

Caroling Dusk: An Anthology of Verse by Negro Poets (editor). 1927.

The Black Christ and Other Poems. 1929.

One Way to Heaven. 1932.

The Medea and Some Poems. 1935.

The Lost Zoo (A Rhyme for the Young, but Not Too Young). 1940.

My Lives and How I Lost Them. 1942.

On These I Stand: An Anthology of the Best Poems of Countee Cullen. 1947.

My Soul's High Song: The Collected Writings of Countee Cullen, Voice of the Harlem Renaissance. Ed. Gerald Early. 1991.

Frederick Douglass
1818–1895

FREDERICK DOUGLASS was born into slavery in February 1818 on a plantation in Maryland. The exact date of his birth and the identity of his father were never known to him. Though Douglass knew his mother, Harriet Bailey, he had little contact with her. He eluded the demands of slavery and lived in relative happiness with his maternal grandmother Betsey Bailey until 1824, when he was forced by his master Aaron Anthony to serve the Lloyd family, from whom Anthony rented a farm. On that day, he claims, his childhood ended. Douglass was introduced to the horrors of slavery during this period, as well as the ostentatious wealth of the Lloyd family. Douglass was the companion of Colonel Lloyd's son, Daniel, until 1826 when he was sent to Baltimore to serve the Auld family, in-laws of Aaron Anthony, where he became the companion of the Auld's newborn son, Thomas. Douglass also received the tutelage of Sophia Auld, who began to teach him how to read and write until forbidden to do so by her husband.

From 1827 to 1832 Douglass, who became the property of Thomas Auld upon the death of Aaron Anthony in 1826, remained with Hugh and Sophia Auld. During this time he continued to educate himself, met free blacks, and read abolitionist newspapers. He also helplessly watched the Aulds separate his family, selling many members south. Thomas Auld, discouraged by Douglass's worsening disposition, sent him to a slave breaker named Edward Covey. Douglass endured the worst of slavery—the fields and the whip—until he could stand no more and wrestled Covey for his dignity. His will strengthened by the victory over Covey, Douglass planned an escape. The escape, however, was discovered, and Douglass was returned to the Aulds.

From 1836 to 1838 Douglass worked as an apprentice ship caulker. His life around the docks brought him into contact with the outside world again, renewing his hope for freedom. On September 3, 1838, Douglass, in the guise of a sailor, boarded a train and rode without incident to the free states. Shortly thereafter, on September 15, he married Anna Murray, a free black woman from Baltimore. The couple moved from New York City to New Bedford, Massachusetts, where Douglass was invited by the prominent abolitionist William Lloyd Garrison to recount his life as a slave at abolitionist meetings. Douglass revealed a natural ability for oratory and became a powerful abolitionist speaker. Douglass's eloquence, in fact, caused many audiences to doubt that he was once a slave. In 1845, to substantiate his biographical speeches, he published *Narrative of the Life of Frederick Douglass, an American Slave: Written by Himself*. In exposing his identity, circumstances, and former owner, he exposed himself to recapture and therefore fled to Great Britain, where he continued speaking for the abolitionist cause while his book became a best-seller in Europe and America. Money was raised by his English friends to purchase his freedom, and in 1847 he returned to America as a freeman. Douglass began publishing a newspaper, the *North Star* (renamed *Frederick Douglass' Paper* in 1851), in which he published his only known work of fiction, "The Heroic Slave." In 1855 he published a revised edition of his autobiography entitled *My Bondage and My Freedom*, which was also well received, and still another version in 1881 entitled *Life and Times of Frederick Douglass*. Many of the speeches Douglass delivered over his long career as public speaker were published as pamphlets. These and his other writings were assembled by Philip S. Foner in *The Life and Writings of Frederick Douglass* (5 vols., 1950–75). A new edition of his works, under the title *The Frederick Douglass Papers*, is now being compiled under the editorship of John W. Blassingame.

In his later years Douglass received several political appointments: assistant secretary of the Santo Domingo Comission (1871), president of the Freedman's Bank (1874), marshall (1874–81) and recorder of deeds (1881–86) of the District of Columbia, and U.S. minister to Haiti (1889–91). He died on February 20, 1895, after attending a woman's suffrage meeting.

◈ *Critical Extracts*

WILLIAM LLOYD GARRISON   Mr. Douglass has very properly chosen to write his own Narrative, in his own style, and according to the best of his ability, rather than to employ someone else. It is, therefore, entirely his own production; and, considering how long and dark was the career he had to run as a slave,—how few have been his opportunities to improve his mind since he broke his iron fetters,—it is, in my judgement, highly creditable to his head and heart. He who can peruse without a tearful eye, a heaving breast, and afflicted spirit,—without being filled with an unutterable abhorrence of slavery and all its abettors, and animated with a determination to seek the immediate overthrow of that execrable system,— without trembling for the fate of his country in the hands of a righteous God, who is ever on the side of the oppressed, and whose arm is not shortened that it can not save,—must have a flinty heart, and be qualified to act the part of a trafficker "in slaves and the souls of men." I am confident that it is essentially true in all its statements; that nothing has been set down in malice, nothing exaggerated, nothing drawn from the imagination; that it comes short of the reality, rather than overstates a single fact in regard to SLAVERY AS IT IS. The experience of Frederick Douglass, as a slave, was not a peculiar one; his lot was not especially a hard one; his case may be regarded as a very fair specimen of the treatment of slaves in Maryland, in which state it is conceded that they are better fed and less cruelly treated than in Georgia, Alabama, or Louisiana. Many have suffered incomparably more, while very few on the plantations have suffered less, than himself. Yet how deplorable was his situation! what terrible chastise- ments were inflicted upon his person! what still more shocking outrages were perpetrated on his mind! with all his noble powers and sublime aspira- tions, how like a brute was he treated, even by those professing to have the same mind in them that was in Jesus Christ! to what dreadful liabilities was he continually subjected! how destitute of friendly counsel and aid, even in his greatest extremities! how heavy was the midnight of woe which shrouded in blackness the last ray of hope, and filled the future with terror and gloom! what longings after freedom took possession of his breast, and how misery augmented, in proportion as he grew reflective and intelligent,— thus demonstrating that a happy slave is an extinct man! how he thought, reasoned, felt, under the lash of the driver, with the chains upon his limbs! what perils he encountered in his endeavors to escape from his horrible doom! and how signal have been his deliverance and preservation in the midst of a nation of pitiless enemies!

William Lloyd Garrison, "Preface," *Narrative of the Life of Frederick Douglass, an American Slave: Written by Himself* (1845; rpt. Harmondsworth: Penguin, 1982), pp. 37–39

FREDERICK DOUGLASS   I have been frequently asked how I felt when I found myself in a free State. I have never been able to answer the question with any satisfaction to myself. It was a moment of the highest excitement I ever experienced. I suppose I felt as one may imagine the unarmed mariner to feel when he is rescued by a friendly man-of-war from the pursuit of a pirate. In writing to a dear friend, immediately after my arrival at New York, I said I felt like one who had escaped a den of hungry lions. This state of mind, however, very soon subsided; and I was again seized with a feeling of great insecurity and loneliness. I was yet liable to be taken back, and subjected to all the tortures of slavery. This in itself was enough to damp the ardor of my enthusiasm. But the loneliness overcame me. There I was in the midst of thousands, and yet a perfect stranger; without home and without friends, in the midst of thousands of my own brethren—children of a common Father, and yet I dared not to unfold to any of them my sad condition. I was afraid to speak to any one for fear of speaking to the wrong one, and thereby falling into the hands of money-loving kidnappers, whose business it was to lie in wait for the panting fugitive, as the ferocious beasts of the forest lie in wait for their prey. The motto which I adopted when I started from slavery was this—"Trust no man!" I saw in every white man an enemy, and in almost every colored man cause for distrust. It was a most painful situation; and, to understand it, one must needs experience it, or imagine himself in similar circumstances. Let him be a fugitive slave in a strange land—a land given up to be the hunting-ground for slaveholders—whose inhabitants are legalized kidnappers—where he is every moment subjected to the terrible liability of being seized upon by his fellow-men, as the hideous crocodile seizes upon his prey!—I say, let him place himself in my situation—without home or friends—without money or credit—wanting shelter, and no one to give it—wanting bread, and no money to buy it,—and at the same time let him feel that he is pursued by merciless men-hunters, and in total darkness as to what to do, where to go, or where to stay,—perfectly helpless both as to the means of defence and means of escape,—in the midst of plenty, yet suffering the terrible gnawings of hunger,—in the midst of houses, yet having no home,—among fellow-men, yet feeling as if in the midst of wild beasts, whose greediness to swallow up the trembling and half-famished fugitive is only equalled by that with which the monsters of the deep swallow up the helpless fish upon which they subsist,—I say, let him be placed in this most trying situation,—the situation in which I was placed,—then, and not till then, will he fully appreciate the hardships of, and know how to sympathize with, the toil-worn and whip-scarred fugitive slave.

Frederick Douglass, *Narrative of the Life of Frederick Douglass, an American Slave: Written by Himself* (1845; rpt. Harmondsworth: Penguin, 1982), pp. 143–44

CHARLES W. CHESNUTT   Douglass possessed in unusual degree the faculty of swaying his audience, sometimes against their maturer judgment. There is something in the argument from first principles which, if presented with force and eloquence, never fails to appeal to those who are not blinded by self-interest or deep-seated prejudice. Douglass's argument was that of the Declaration of Independence,—"that *all* men are created equal; that they are endowed by their Creator with certain inalienable rights; that among these are life, liberty, and the pursuit of happiness. That, to secure these rights, governments are instituted among men, deriving their just powers from the *consent of the governed.*" The writer may be pardoned for this quotation; for there are times when we seem to forget that now and here, no less than in ancient Rome, "eternal vigilance is the price of liberty." Douglass brushed aside all sophistries about Constitutional guarantees, and vested rights, and inferior races, and, having postulated the right of men to be free, maintained that negroes were men, and offered himself as a proof of his assertion,—an argument that few had the temerity to deny. If it were answered that he was only half a negro, he would reply that slavery made no such distinction, and as a still more irrefutable argument would point to his friend, Samuel R. Ward, who often accompanied him on the platform,—an eloquent and effective orator, of whom Wendell Phillips said that "he was so black that, if he would shut his eyes, one could not see him." It was difficult for an auditor to avoid assent to such arguments, presented with all the force and fire of genius, relieved by a ready wit, a contagious humor, and a tear-compelling power rarely excelled.

Charles W. Chesnutt, *Frederick Douglass* (Boston: Small, Maynard, 1899), pp. 110–11

J. SAUNDERS REDDING   In 1855 the autobiographical *My Bondage and My Freedom* was published. ⟨Douglass's⟩ style, still without tricks, proves surer. Considerably longer than his first book, its length is amply justified by its matter. Though the first part follows in general the simple plan of the *Narrative*, he acquaints us more intimately with slavery and expresses his more mature thoughts on the problems which he faced. It is evident, especially when he writes of his English trip, that his knowledge of men had grown. Equally evident in the logic and sincerity of his arguments is the growth of his knowledge of issues. ⟨. . .⟩ My *Bondage and My Freedom* is the high mark of the second stage of Douglass's career. Indeed, though for many years after 1865 he was active as both speaker and writer, and though his thoughts steadily matured, he did not exceed the emotional pitch of this second period. As his intellectual vigor increased (and became, it may be said, a little warped by the overdevelopment of his capacity for irony), his emotional and artistic powers fell off. By the 1880's he was not an orator speaking with a spontaneous overflow of emotion: he was a finished public speaker, more concerned with intellectual than emotional responses.

Douglass's aroused powers of thought made it possible for him to do a work that grew steadily in importance. Emotionally drunk, men had become intellectually blind to the true status of the Negro. A great many people seemed to think that abolition was a calm bay through which the black race would sail to some safe harbor. Few saw that harbors had yet to be constructed. It was this task that Douglass now engaged in. He accepted abolition as a future certainty and looked far beyond it. ⟨. . .⟩

The literary work of Douglass is first important as examples of a type and period of American literature. Many of his speeches rank with the best of all times and are included in collections of the finest oratorical art. That at least two of his books, My *Bondage and My Freedom* and the first *Life and Times*, have not been recognized for what they are is attributable more to neglect than to the judgment of honest inquiry. Certainly no American biographies rank above them in the literary qualities of simplicity, interest, and compression of style. They delineate from an exceptional point of view a period in the history of the United States than which no other is more fraught with drama and sociological significance. By any standard his work ranks high.

J. Saunders Redding, *To Make a Poet Black* (Chapel Hill: University of North Carolina Press, 1939), pp. 35–38

ARNA BONTEMPS   It was a daring thing to attempt. Perhaps it was even reckless, but by now Douglass had considered and rejected every alternative. To answer those people who had begun to doubt his story, to silence the whispering that threatened to destroy his value as an abolitionist agent, he would throw caution away, he would put the full account in writing. That was it. He would write a *book*. In his book he would tell the whole world just whose slave he had been, how he had squirmed and plotted in his chains, where and when he had escaped. The only detail he would withhold would be the manner of his getaway. Even that would not be concealed for his own sake. He would reveal everything and take his chances as a fugitive in Massachusetts. But to disclose the maneuver by which he gave his owners the slip would be to close that particular gate to other slaves. That he would not do. As for the rest, the lid was off. Next time he undertook a series of lectures, he would have an answer for those who accused him of inventing personal history for the sake of winning antislavery sympathizers.

> Arna Bontemps, *Free at Last: The Life of Frederick Douglass* (New York: Dodd, Mead, 1971), p. 95

ROBERT B. STEPTO   One reason Douglass wrote 'The Heroic Slave' is easy to come by. In 1845, in response to the taunting cries that he had never been a slave, Douglass was 'induced', as he put it ⟨in *My Bondage and My Freedom*⟩, 'to write out the leading facts connected with [his] experience in slavery, giving names of persons, places, and dates—thus putting it in the power of any who doubted, to ascertain the truth or falsehood of [his] story of being a fugitive slave'. Thus *The Narrative of the Life of Frederick Douglass, an American Slave, Written by Himself* came to life. And in 1847, while harassed by suggestions that his *place* was to speak, not to write, Douglass began the *North Star*, his mission being to demonstrate that a 'tolerably well conducted press, in the hands of persons of the despised race', could prove to be a 'most powerful means of removing prejudice, and of awakening an interest in them'. Then, in 1852, Douglass took a logical next step: he wrote a historical fiction about a heroic slave named Madison Washington who had led a slave revolt aboard a slave ship in 1841. All these *writing* activities, as opposed to speaking duties, are of a piece, each one bolder than the one preceding it, each a measure of Douglass's remove from acts of literacy involving merely spoken renditions of what Garrison and company alternately called Douglass's 'facts' or 'story' or simply 'narrative'. This suggests something of why Douglass would attempt a novella at this time ⟨. . .⟩

'The Heroic Slave' is not an altogether extraordinary piece of work. I'm not about to argue that it should take a place beside, say, *Benito Cereno* as a major short fiction of the day. Still, after dismissing the florid soliloquies which unfortunately besmirch this and too many other anti-slavery writings, we find that the novella is full of craft, especially of the sort that combines artfulness with a certain fabulistic usefulness. Appropriately enough, evidence of Douglass's craft is available in the novella's attention to both theme and character. In Part I of 'The Heroic Slave' we are told of the 'double state' of Virginia and introduced not only to Madison Washington but also to Mr Listwell, who figures as the model abolitionist in the story. The meticulous development of the Virginia theme and of the portrait of Mr Listwell, much more than the portrayal of Washington as a hero, is the stuff of useful art-making in Douglass's novella.

The theme of the duality or 'doubleness' of Virginia begins in the novella's very first sentence: 'The State of Virginia is famous in American annals for the multitudinous array of her statesmen and heroes.' The rest of the paragraph continues as follows:

> She has been dignified by some the mother of statesmen. History has not been sparing in recording their names, or in blazoning their deeds. Her high position in this respect, has given her enviable distinction among her sister States. With Virginia for his birth-place, even a man of ordinary parts, on account of the general partiality for her sons, easily rises to eminent stations. Men, not great enough to attract attention in their native States, have, like a certain distinguished citizen in the State of New York, sighed and repined that they were not born in Virginia. Yet not all the great ones of the Old Dominion have, by the fact of their birthplace, escaped undeserved obscurity. By some strange neglect, *one* of the truest, manliest, and bravest of her children,— one who, in after years, will, I think, command the pen of genius to set his merits forth—holds now no higher place in the records of that grand old Commonwealth than is held by a horse or an ox. Let those account for it who can, but there stands the fact, that a man who loved liberty as well as did Patrick Henry—who deserved it as much as Thomas Jefferson—and who fought for it with a valor as high, an arm as strong, and against odds as great as he who led all the armies of the American colonies through the great war for freedom and independence, lives now only in the chattel records of his native state.

At least two features here are worthy of note. The paragraph as a whole, but especially its initial sentences, can be seen as significant revoicing of the conventional opening of a slave narrative. Slave narratives usually begin with the phrase 'I was born'; this is true of Douglass's 1845 *Narrative* and true also, as James Olney reminds us, of the narratives of Henry Bibb, Henry 'Box' Brown, William Wells Brown, John Thompson, Samuel Ringgold Ward, James W. C. Pennington, Austin Steward, James Roberts, and many, many other former slaves. In 'The Heroic Slave', however, Douglass transforms 'I was born' into the broader assertion that in Virginia many heroes have been born. After that, he then works his way to the central point that a certain *one*—an unknown hero who lives now only in the chattel records and not the history books—has been born. Douglass knows the slave-narrative convention, partly because he has used it himself; but, more to the point, he seems to have an understanding of how to exploit its rhetorical usefulness in terms of proclaiming the existence and identity of an individual without merely employing it verbatim. This is clear evidence, I think, of a first step, albeit a small one, toward the creation of an Afro-American fiction based upon the conventions of the slave narratives. That Douglass himself was quite possibly thinking in these terms while writing is suggested by his persistent reference to the 'chattel records' which must, in effect, be transformed by 'the pen of genius' so that his hero's merits may be set forth—indeed, set free. If by this Douglass means that his hero's story must be liberated from the realm—the text—of brutal fact and, more, that texts must be created to compete with other texts, then it's safe to say that he brought to the creation of 'The Heroic Slave' all the intentions, if not all the skills, of the self-conscious *writer*.

Robert B. Stepto, "Storytelling in Early Afro-American Fiction: Frederick Douglass's 'The Heroic Slave,' " *Black Literature and Literary Theory*, ed. Henry Louis Gates, Jr. (New York: Methuen, 1984) pp. 177–80

WALDO E. MARTIN, JR.   In many ways, Frederick Douglass remains the prototypical black American hero: a peerless self-made man and symbol of success; a fearless and tireless spokesman; a thoroughgoing humanist. The most striking and enduring aspect of Douglass's heroic legacy in his day—its classic, even archetypal aura—has persisted down to the present. Although often viewed and used differently by others, the heroic and legendary Douglass clearly personifies the American success ethic. The key to his eminently evocative essence is twofold. First, he, like the American nation itself and its most enduring folk heroes, rose above seemingly overwhelming odds to achieve historical distinction. Second, he represents a model self-made man: an exemplary black version of uncommon achievement primarily through the agency of a resolute will and hard toil aided by moral law and divine providence. Not only did he succeed, but he did so in terms signifying mythic greatness: the uniquely gifted individual rising above anonymity and adversity to renown and good fortune largely through the force of superlative character and indefatigable effort. Douglass's life story exemplifies both the romance and the reality of heroic greatness.

Notwithstanding its universal appeal, Douglass's heroic and symbolic viability has had special meaning for black Americans. In 1908, Kelly Miller, Howard University sociologist and mathematician, gave his view of Douglass's particular importance for black Americans. "Frederick Douglass is the one commanding historic character of the colored race in America. He is the model of emulation of those who are struggling up through the trials and difficulties which he himself suffered and subdued. He is illustrative and exemplary of what they might become—the first fruit of promise of a dormant race. To the aspiring colored youth of this land Mr. Douglass is, at once, the inspiration of their hopes and the justification of their claims." While one may reasonably argue, especially today, with Miller's claim of Douglass's singular historical eminence, his claim for Douglass's prototypical heroic and symbolic preeminence is more cogent. Perhaps better than any other nineteenth-century black American, Douglass personified the travail and triumph of his people. A heroic and symbolic view of Douglass continues to be meaningful because his life struggle so vividly represented his people's struggle. In 1853, he remarked that "mine has been the experience of the colored people of America, both slave and free." Douglass saw himself and wanted to be seen as an example and an inspiration to all people, but especially to blacks.

Waldo E. Martin, Jr., *The Mind of Frederick Douglass* (Chapel Hill: University of North Carolina Press, 1984), p. 253

JOHN SEKORA   Because it is one of the most important books ever published in America, Frederick Douglass's *Narrative* of 1845 has justly received much attention. That attention has been increasing for a generation at a rate parallel to the growth in interest in autobiography as a literary genre, and the *Narrative* as autobiography has been the subject of several influential studies. Without denying the insights of such studies, I should like to suggest that in 1845 Douglass had no opportunity to write what (since the eighteenth century) we would call autobiography, that the achievement of the *Narrative* lies in another form. ⟨. . .⟩

The *Narrative,* I would contend, is the first comprehensive, personal history of American slavery. Autobiography would come a decade later, in *My Bondage and My Freedom.* If many readers prefer the earlier volume, the reasons are not so far to search. The *Narrative* is as tightly written as a sonnet, the work of years in the pulpit and on the lecture circuit. It comprehends all major aspects of slavery as Douglass knew it in a narrative that is as dramatically compassing as any first-person novel. It is at the same time a personal history of the struggle with and for language—against words that repress, for words that liberate. It is for author and reader alike a personalizing account of a system that would depersonalize everyone. It is the retelling of the most important Christian story, the Crucifixion, in the midst of the most important American civil crisis, the battle over slavery.

In *The Fugitive Blacksmith* ⟨James W. C.⟩ Pennington asked if a slave had no need of character. He answered the question in the following way: "Suppose insult, reproach, or slander, should render it necessary for him to appeal to the history of his family in vindication of his character, where does he find that history? He goes to his native state, to his native county, to his native town; but nowhere does he find any record of himself *as a man*." It is an acute question, one he is eager to raise, I believe, because of Douglass's example. Douglass renewed the conservative form of the slave narrative at a critical time. He gave record of himself as an antislavery man. And the magnitude of that achievement is difficult to overestimate. For in moral terms the slave narrative and its postbellum heirs are the only history of American slavery we have. Outside the narrative, slavery was a wordless, nameless, timeless time. It was time without history and time with imminence. Slaveholders sought to reduce existence to the duration of the psychological present and to mandate their records as the only reliable texts. Whatever the restrictions placed upon them, Douglass and the other narrators changed that forever. To recall one's personal history is to *renew* it. The *Narrative* is both instrument and inscription of that renewal.

John Sekora, "Comprehending Slavery: Language and Personal History in Douglass's *Narrative* of 1845," *CLA Journal* 29, No. 2 (December 1985): 157–58, 169–70

BLYDEN JACKSON   In terms of content, Douglass' *Narrative* abounds with episodes which are nothing more or less than case studies illustrative of the inhumanity of slavery to the slave and of this very slave's humanity in spite of his inhuman treatment by southern, and many northern, whites and in obvious contradiction to such pseudoscientists as Dr. Josiah Nott of Mobile, who would, by 1850, deny that blacks and whites even belonged to the same genus of the animal kingdom. Atrocities are committed, in the *Narrative*, as far as, allegedly, in at least five cases, the extreme of cold-blooded murder, by whites upon blacks. No atrocities are committed there in any way by negroes. Black women are preyed upon sexually, in the *Narrative*, by white men. Of course, no white women in the *Narrative* are subjected to the venery of black men. And while the slaves in the *Narrative* live meanly—poorly housed, poorly clothed, and poorly fed—instance after instance of their unquenchable propensity to care for one another in the role of a responsible parent or a grateful child or a loyal friend and to observe, in general, an especially magnanimous version of the golden rule toward all their fellow men, demonstrates their ability to rise above their circumstances and to practice those domestic and civic virtues which are the basic underpinnings of a human society in an advanced stage of man's elevation of himself from savagery. One thing more of special note appears in the *Narrative*, a series of pictures revealing the hypocrisy of white southern Christianity. Douglass' voice in the *Narrative* is never more charged with condemnation, contempt, and ire than when he shows some of his white neighbors at worship and then moves on to add, as tellingly as possible, vignettes of these same white neighbors, with their psalms and scriptures still ringing in their supposedly pious ears, abusing their slaves unmercifully. His voice in this regard is a voice found in all other abolitionist slave narratives, just as the case studies of slaves and their masters which supply the content of his *Narrative* are but duplicates of similar case studies distributed copiously throughout all other abolitionist slave narratives.

Once, however, Douglass' acquiescence in the habitual practices of writers associated with the abolitionist slave narrative is recognized, acknowledgement should then be made of what he does which, in his *Narrative*, redeems his resort to those practices from a mere hackneyed reproduction of a prevailing fashion. And what he does thereby constitutes a genuine tribute to his own original powers and his individual cultural growth. He pours, as it were, into old bottles representative of the customs to which he is deferring a fresh and often delightful vintage compounded from the effects directly attributable to aesthetic sensibilities which were his and his alone. As an orator he had held live audiences spellbound, not simply because of his appearance, much to the advantage of any public figure as that appearance was, or of his voice, a rich bass-baritone which he could inflect at will and project, without artificial aid, into the ears of hearers on the farther edge of the not infrequently large crowds that he addressed. But he was, sometimes while he spoke, among other things, a superb mime. He liked, for example, occasionally to turn his platform into a pulpit from which a southern white preacher, a lackey of the slaveholding South, could be seen and heard preaching to slaves, warning them to obey their masters and brandishing over their heads, like a would-be fiery sword, gospel verses in defense of slavery. When he became this preacher, an organic mixture of the real thing and of broad caricature, Douglass was availing himself of talents in his possession which a literary artist might well exactly so have used. It was of these same talents, involving, as they did, a genuinely artistic apprehension, re-creation, and enhancement of reality, that Douglass availed himself in his *Narrative*.

> Blyden Jackson, *A History of Afro-American Literature* (Baton Rouge: Louisiana State University Press, 1989), Vol. 1, pp. 111–12

▨ Bibliography

Narrative of the Life of Frederick Douglass, an American Slave: Written by Himself. 1845.

Abolition Fanaticism in New York: Speech of a Runaway Slave from Baltimore, at an Abolition Meeting in New York, Held May 11, 1847. 1847.

Farewell Speech, Previously to Embarking on Board the Cambria, upon His Return to America. 1847.

Letter to His Old Master. c. 1848.

Lectures on American Slavery. 1851.

Oration Delivered in Corinthian Hall, Rochester. 1852.

Arguments: Pro and Con, on the Case for a National Emigration Convention (with W. J. Watkins and J. M. Whitfield). 1854.

The Claims of the Negro Ethnologically Considered. 1854.

My Bondage and My Freedom. 1855.

Address Delivered at the Erection of the Wing Monument, at Mexico, Oswego, N.Y., September 11th, 1855. 1855.

The Anti-Slavery Monument: A Lecture Before the Rochester Ladies' Anti-Slavery Society. 1855.

Two Speeches. 1857.

Eulogy of the Late Hon. Wm. Jay. 1859.

The Constitution of the United States: Is It Pro-Slavery or Anti-Slavery? c. 1860.

Men of Color, to Arms! 1863.

Addresses at a Mass Meeting . . . for the Promotion of Colored Enlistments (with W. D. Kelley and Anna E. Dickinson). 1863.

The Equality of All Men Before the Law Claimed and Defended (with others). 1865.

U. S. Grant and the Colored People. 1872.

Address Delivered at the Third Annual Fair of the Tennessee Colored Agricultural and Mechanical Association. 1873.

Oration Delivered on the Occasion of the Unveiling of the Freedmen's Monument in Memory of Abraham Lincoln. 1876.

Speech on the Death of William Lloyd Garrison. c. 1879.

Life and Times of Frederick Douglass. 1881.

John Brown: An Address. 1881.

Address Delivered in the Congregational Church, Washington, D.C., April 16, 1883: On the Twenty-first Anniversary of Emancipation in the District of Columbia. 1883.

⟨*Address to*⟩ *National Convention of Colored Men, at Louisville, Ky., September 24, 1883.* 1883.

Proceedings of the Civil Rights Mass-Meeting Held in Lincoln Hall, Oct. 22, 1883 (with Robert G. Ingersoll). 1883.

Three Addresses on the Relations Subsisting Between the White and Colored People of the United States. 1886.

The Nation's Problem: A Speech, Delivered Before the Bethel Literary and Historical Society. 1889.

The Race Problem. 1890.

Lecture on Haiti. 1893.

The Reason Why the Colored American Is Not in the World's Columbian Exposition. 1893.

Address Delivered in the Metropolitan A.M.E. Church, Washington, D.C., Tuesday, January 9th, 1894, on the Lessons of the Hour. 1894.

A Defence of the Negro Race. 1894.

Why Is the Negro Lynched? 1895.

Negroes and the War Effort. 1942.

Selections from His Writings. Ed. Philip S. Foner. 1945.

Life and Writings. Ed. Philip S. Foner. 1950–75. 5 vols.

Frederick Douglass on Women's Rights. Ed. Philip S. Foner. 1976.

A Black Diplomat in Haiti: The Diplomatic Correspondence of U.S. Minister Frederick Douglass from Haiti, 1889–1891. Ed. Norma Brown. 1977. 2 vols.

The Frederick Douglass Papers. Ed. John W. Blassingame et al. 1979– . 4 vols. (to date).

The Narrative and Selected Writings. Ed. Michael Meyer. 1984.

W. E. B. Du Bois
1868–1963

WILLIAM EDWARD BURGHARDT DU BOIS was born in the village of Great Barrington, Massachusetts, on February 23, 1868. His father, Alfred, was born in Haiti, and after a stint in the Union army settled in the Berkshires, where he met and married Mary Burghardt, a descendant of a slave brought from West Africa. However, Alfred Du Bois drifted away from the family and never returned to his wife and son. Du Bois's mother, crippled by depression and a stroke, raised her son with the assistance of her brother and sisters.

Du Bois graduated from high school with honors and delivered a speech on the abolition of slavery. However, because of financial difficulties, Du Bois attended Fisk University instead of Harvard, his first choice. Du Bois later took his master's at Harvard, although by then he had shed most of his illusions about the university. He attended classes taught by George Santayana and William James and developed a close relationship with the latter. In 1892, after receiving his degree in history, Du Bois went to the University of Berlin to study. Although he had a deep distrust of orthodox religion, he nevertheless secured a position at the African Methodist Wilberforce College in Xenia, Ohio, and published his dissertation for Harvard, *The Suppression of the African Slave-Trade to the United States of America, 1638–1870* (1896). He then accepted a position to study the black neighborhoods of Philadelphia and compiled the first sociological text on a black American community in the United States: *The Philadelphia Negro* (1899).

At Atlanta University, where he began to teach history and economics in 1897, Du Bois laid the foundations for the field of black sociology. He established annual conferences devoted to "efforts of American Negroes for their own social betterment," and edited its proceedings from 1896 to 1913. He also founded the journals the *Crisis* and, later, *Phylon*. This work, along with his prolific writing, established Du Bois as the leading black literary, educational, and political figure of the early twentieth century.

Du Bois achieved tremendous fame for a collection of essays, *The Souls of Black Folk* (1903), which went through many editions. In 1909 he published a substantial biography of John Brown. His seminal work, *The Negro* (1915), is important in that its theoretical departure was Pan-African: the study of African writing and culture could no longer ignore slavery, as well as the extended links between the peoples of Africa and those of the Caribbean and the Americas. Other important volumes of essays are *Darkwater: Voices from within the Veil* (1920), *The Gift of Black Folk* (1924), *Black Reconstruction* (1935), *Dusk of Dawn* (1940), and many others.

In addition to his nonfiction, Du Bois published several novels over his long literary career. His first was *The Quest of the Silver Fleece* (1911). *Dark Princess* followed in 1928, and after many years Du Bois wrote a trilogy collectively titled *Black Flame*, consisting of *The Ordeal of Mansart* (1957), *Mansart Builds a School* (1959), and *Worlds of Color* (1961).

With the passing of years Du Bois became a problematic leader; his closest disciples found him cold and arrogant and such figures as Claude McKay and Marcus Garvey challenged his achievements and socialist ideology. He was dismissed from the NAACP as its director of special research in 1948; he became a target of domestic anticommunism, being tried in 1951 for being an "unregistered foreign agent" and acquitted by a federal grand jury. In 1961, at the invitation of President Kwame Nkrumah of Ghana, Du Bois traveled to this Western African nation and began to direct the *Encyclopedia Africana* project, joining the U.S. Communist party as well. Denied a U.S. passport because of his political beliefs, Du Bois became a citizen of Ghana and died there on August 27, 1963, at the age of ninety-five. His *Autobiography* was published in 1968, and an edition of his *Complete Published Works* is being compiled by Herbert Aptheker. His wife, Shirley Graham Du Bois, has written a memoir of her life with him, *His Day Is Marching On* (1971).

▧ *Critical Extracts*

W. E. B. DU BOIS   High in the tower, where I sit above the loud complaining of the human sea, I know many souls that toss and whirl and pass, but none there are that intrigue me more than the Souls of White Folk.

Of them I am singularly clairvoyant. I see in and through them. I view them from unusual points of vantage. Not as a foreigner do I come, for I am native, not foreign, bone of their thought and flesh of their language. Mine is not the knowledge of the traveler or the colonial composite of dear memories, words and wonder. Nor yet is my knowledge that which servants have of masters, or mass of class, or capitalist of artisan. Rather I see these souls undressed and from the back and side. I see the working of their entrails. I know their thoughts and they know that I know. This knowledge makes them now embarrassed, now furious! They deny my right to live and be and call me misbirth! My word is to them mere bitterness and my soul, pessimism. And yet as they preach and strut and shout and threaten, crouching as they clutch at rags of facts and fancies to hide their nakedness, they go twisting, flying by my tired eyes and I see them ever stripped,— ugly, human. ⟨. . .⟩

A true and worthy ideal frees and uplifts a people; a false ideal imprisons and lowers. Say to men, earnestly and repeatedly: "Honesty is best, knowledge is power; do unto others as you would be done by." Say this and act it and the nation must move toward it, if not to it. But say to a people: "The one virtue is to be white," and the people rush to the inevitable conclusion, "Kill the 'nigger'!"

Is this not the record of present America? Is not this its headlong progress? Are we not coming more and more, day by day, to making the statement "I am white," the one fundamental tenet of our practical morality? Only when this basic, iron rule is involved is our defense of right nation-wide and prompt. Murder may swagger, theft may rule and prostitution may flourish and the nation gives but spasmodic, intermittent and lukewarm attention. But let the murderer be black or the thief brown or the violator of womanhood have a drop of Negro blood, and the righteousness of indignation sweeps the world. Nor would this fact make the indignation less justifiable did not we all know that it was blackness that was condemned and not crime. ⟨. . .⟩

Here is a civilization that has boasted much. Neither Roman nor Arab, Greek nor Egyptian, Persian nor Mongol ever took himself and his own perfectness with such disconcerting seriousness as the modern white man. We whose shame, humiliation, and deep insult his aggrandizement so often involved were never deceived. We looked at him clearly, with world-old eyes, and saw simply a human being, weak and pitiable and cruel, even as we are and were.

These super-men and world-mastering demi-gods listened, however, to no low tongues of ours, even when we pointed silently to their feet of clay. Perhaps we, as folk of simpler soul and more primitive type, have been most struck in the welter of recent years by the utter failure of white religion. We have curled our lips in something like contempt as we have witnessed glib apology and weary explanation. Nothing of the sort deceived us. A nation's religion is its life, and as such white Christianity is a miserable failure.

Nor would we be unfair in this criticism: We know that we, too, have failed, as you have, and have rejected many a Buddha, even as you have denied Christ; but we acknowledge our human frailty, while you, claiming super-humanity, scoff endlessly at our shortcomings.

The number of white individuals who are practising with even reasonable approximation the democracy and unselfishness of Jesus Christ is so small and unimportant as to be fit subject for jest in Sunday supplements and in *Punch, Life, Le Rire,* and *Fliegende Blätter.* In her foreign mission work the extraordinary self-deception of white religion is epitomized: solemnly the white world sends five million dollars worth of missionary propaganda to Africa each year and in the same twelve months adds twenty-five million dollars worth of the vilest gin manufactured. Peace to the augurs of Rome!

W. E. B. Du Bois, "The Souls of White Folk," *Darkwater: Voices from Within the Veil* (New York: Harcourt, Brace & Howe, 1920), pp. 29, 34–36

AUGUST MEIER   Of the great trio of Negro leaders, Douglass was the orator, Du Bois the polished writer, and Washington the practical man of affairs. Like Douglass, Du Bois has been known primarily as a protest leader, though he was not as consistent in this role as Douglass. Like Douglass, too, he exhibited a marked oscillation in his ideologies—in fact his was more marked than that of Douglass. Like Douglass he clearly stated the ultimate goals which Washington obscured. Yet Du Bois displayed more of a sense of racial solidarity than Douglass usually did. Nor did he envisage the degree of amalgamation and loss of racial consciousness that Douglass regarded as the *summum bonum.* On the contrary he, like Washington, emphasized race pride and solidarity and economic chauvinism, though after 1905 he no longer championed support of the individualist entrepreneur but favored instead a co-operative economy. Where Washington wanted to make Negroes entrepreneurs and captains of industry in accordance with the American economic dream (a dream shared with less emphasis by Douglass), Du Bois stressed the role of the college-educated elite and later developed a vision of a world largely dominated by the colored races which would combine with the white workers in overthrowing the domination of white capital and thus secure social justice under socialism. All three emphasized the moral values in American culture and the necessity of justice for the Negro if the promise of American life were to be fulfilled. But of the three men it was Douglass who was pre-eminently the moralist, while Washington and Du Bois expressed sharply divergent economic interpretations. Where Douglass and Washington were primarily petit-bourgeois in their outlook, Du Bois played the role of the Marxist intelligentsia. Where the interest of Douglass and Washington in Africa was largely perfunctory, Du Bois exhibited a deep sense of racial identity with Africans. Above all, though only Douglass favored amalgamation, all three had as their goal the integration of Negroes into American society.

Scholar and prophet; mystic and materialist; ardent agitator for political rights and propagandist for economic co-operation; one who espoused an economic interpretation of politics and yet emphasized the necessity of political rights for economic advancement; one who denounced segregation and called for integration into American society in accordance with the principles of human brotherhood and the ideals of democracy, and at the same time one who favored the maintenance of racial solidarity and integrity and a feeling of identity with Negroes elsewhere in the world; an equalitarian who apparently believed in innate racial differences; a Marxist who was fundamentally a middle-class intellectual, Du Bois becomes the epitome of the paradoxes in American Negro thought. In fact, despite his early tendencies toward an accommodating viewpoint, and despite his strong sense of race solidarity and integrity, Du Bois expressed more effectively than any of his contemporaries the protest tendency in Negro thought, and the desire for citizenship rights and integration into American society.

August Meier, "The Paradox of W. E. B. Du Bois," *Negro Thought in America, 1880–1915: Racial Ideologies in the Age of Booker T. Washington* (Ann Arbor: University of Michigan Press, 1963), pp. 205–6

JOHN OLIVER KILLENS   It was early morning of the March on Washington. We stood in the busy lobby of the Willard Hotel. I believe there were among those with me, chatting quietly, excitedly, nervously, James Baldwin and Sidney Poitier. Outside, Washington, D.C. was like an occupied city, with police and helmeted soldiers everywhere. There were very few civilians on the streets that memorable morning. By air, busses, automobiles, on foot, people were gathering on the outskirts of the city by the tens of thousands. The downtown government district was hushed and awesomely white as only Washington can be. Our group was waiting for transportation to the National Airport, where we were to participate in a press conference before the March began.

Some one walked over to our group and said, "The old man died." Just that. And not one of us asked, "What old man?" We all knew who the old man was, because he was our old man. He belonged to every one of us. And we belonged to him. To some of us he was our patron saint, our teacher and our major prophet. He was Big Daddy? No. He was Big Grand Daddy. More than any other single human being, he, through the sheer power of his vast and profound intelligence, his tireless scholarship and his fierce dedication to the cause of black liberation, had brought us and the other two hundred and fifty thousand souls to this place, to this moment in time and space.

> John Oliver Killens, "An Introduction," *The ABC of Color: Selections Chosen by the Author from Over a Half Century of His Writings* by W. E. B. Du Bois (New York: International Publishers, 1969), p. 9

ARNOLD RAMPERSAD   In the years since Du Bois' death in 1963, the memory of his gifts as a poet, scholar, and fighter has stayed alive among the majority of thinking black Americans. For others, though, his contribution has sunk to the status of a footnote in the long history of race relations in the United States. This decline has come in spite of the decades of brilliant political crusading, the beauty and cultural significance of *The Souls of Black Folk*, the power of historical imagination represented by such works as *The Suppression of the African Slave-Trade*, *The Negro*, and *Black Reconstruction in America*, and the innovative and thorough social science of *The Philadelphia Negro*.

But in a way both modest and extraordinary, Du Bois was a maker of history. Although he sometimes raged, he achieved success through his long, slow influence on the thinkers of black America and their white sympathizers and allies. If the history of ideas in Afro-America is ever written, Du Bois should occupy the most conspicuous place. If—even more unlikely—the full history of the impact of blacks on the American mind is ever charted, his education of the whole nation will be seen as significant indeed.

His works have not received the study they deserve, and his modest reputation now rests on grounds that he would not wholly appreciate. He is remembered for his strategy in controversies not always properly understood, and for slogans and concepts that inadequately represent the range of his mind. His words appear to support a variety of contradictory causes and, in common with great bodies of art and literature, are susceptible to such a large number of interpretations that the casual reader is sometimes bewildered.

These inexact views of the man occur because Du Bois' vision was filtered through a variety of experiences possible only in America. He was a product of black and white, poverty and privilege, love and hate. He was of New England and of the South, an alien and an American, a provincial and a cosmopolite, nationalist and communist, Victorian and modern. With the soul of a poet and the intellect of a scientist, he lived at least a double life, continually compelled to respond to the challenge of reconciling opposites. ⟨. . .⟩

His final achievement was in his service to his folk, his nation, and to all those who could comprehend the fuller human significance of the lessons of his life. More than any other individual, he was responsible for the conversion of the facts and episodes of Afro-American history into that coherent, though necessarily diffuse, mythology on which collective self-respect and self-love must inevitably be founded. And far more powerfully than any other American intellectual, he explicated the mysteries of race in a nation which, proud of its racial pluralism, has just begun to show remorse for crimes inspired by racism.

Arnold Rampersad, *The Art and Imagination of W. E. B. Du Bois* (Cambridge, MA: Harvard University Press, 1976), pp. 291–93

MARION BERGHAHN   It is not unimportant that DuBois's painful experience of the racism in his country came relatively late when his self-confidence had become sufficiently consolidated and could no longer be profoundly shaken. As he himself reports, he experienced hardly any

racial problems at school. There were few Afro-Americans in Great Barrington, and it was therefore not necessary to draw a clear line separating
blacks from whites, even though such a line existed unofficially. The general
contempt for the 'poor, drunken and sloven' Irish and South Germans living
in the slums—which the black population shared—helped to obscure the
'color line'. DuBois's schoolmates were often the sons of affluent whites
whom he outstripped in intelligence and performance at school and who
frequently chose him to be their leader at play. Because of this he thought
of himself as belonging to the 'rich and well-to-do', although his own family
lived in modest circumstances. ⟨Harold R.⟩ Isaacs thinks that 'his natural
impulse was to gravitate to the top'. The older DuBois grew, however, the
clearer it became that this 'impulse' was not quite so 'natural'; rather it
seems to have originated in a psychological compensating mechanism. For
gradually DuBois did grow conscious of the fact that his darker skin and
his slightly negroid physiognomy were regarded as a blemish by a number
of whites and that 'some human beings even thought it a crime'. But he
refused to be disconcerted by this attitude, '. . . although, of course, there
were some days of secret tears; rather I was spurred to tireless effort. If they
beat me at anything, I was grimly determined to make them sweat for it!'
And indeed he succeeded, through diligence and energy, in turning his
negroid appearance into an advantage; it set him visibly apart from his peers
and helped to emphasise his above-average intelligence all the more clearly.
He won the respect of his schoolmates, and this led him to assume that
'the secret of life and the losing of the color bar, then, lay in excellence,
in accomplishment . . . There was no real discrimination on account of
color—it was all a matter of ability and hard work.' This ethic of work and
accomplishment governed his whole life: 'God is Work', one of his fictional
characters says. Nor did he ever abandon his childhood belief in the power
and superiority of knowledge above all other human activities.

DuBois developed yet another, very characteristic, attitude toward his
early youth: in order to avoid being humiliated he never sought contact
with whites himself. This meant that his schoolmates were never given an
opportunity 'to refuse me invitations; they must seek me out and urge me
to come, as indeed they often did. When my presence was not wanted
they had only to refrain from asking.' Even when, later, after some initial
difficulties, he had won a place at Harvard, he was too proud to seek
associations with white students. He even boasted of not having known

most of his contemporaries, some of whom became very well known later. Yet he is frank enough to admit that

> something of a certain inferiority complex was possibly a cause of this. I was desperately afraid of intruding where I was not wanted; . . . I should in fact have been pleased if most of my fellow students had wanted to associate with me; if I had been popular and envied. But the absence of this made me neither unhappy nor morose. I had my 'island within' and it was a fair country.

Above all he avoided white or very light-skinned 'black' women and for the same reason rejected any thought of racial mixing: 'I resented the assumption that we desired it.' These and similar statements show how deeply DuBois's pride was hurt by any actual or potential threat of being rejected by the whites. 'He wanted recognition, acceptance, eminence, a life among peers. When he was denied, he cut himself off' (Harold R. Isaacs). Thus DuBois—who had spent his early youth primarily in the company of whites—developed into a passionate black nationalist; it was among blacks that he would find the satisfaction of his pride which the whites had denied him. This need 'to show it to the whites', to prove to them that blacks are equal or even superior to them which grew out of humiliations is one—maybe even the most important—root of his later cultural nationalism, and it explains as well as any other reason his fixation with white culture.

Marion Berghahn, "Pan-Africa as a Myth in the Literary Work of DuBois," *Images of Africa in Black American Literature* (Totowa, NJ: Rowman & Littlefield, 1977), pp. 69–71

KEITH E. BYERMAN   The first essay in W. E. B. Du Bois's collection, *The Souls of Black Folk* (1903), offers a classic statement of the psychological meaning of being black in America:

> It is a peculiar sensation, this double-consciousness, this sense of always looking at one's self through the eyes of others, of measuring one's soul by the tape of a world that looks on in amused contempt and pity. One ever feels his twoness,—an American, a Negro; two souls, two thoughts, two unreconciled strivings; two warring ideals in one dark body, whose dogged strength alone keeps it from being torn asunder.

The duality described here has been a common theme in black literature from Paul Laurence Dunbar's "We Wear the Mask" (1895) to Toni Morrison's *Song of Solomon* (1977). Du Bois articulated an ambiguity that clearly has significance for black writers, and his book has been recognized for years for its insight. Shortly after publication, Jessie Fauset commended the author of *Souls* as "a man of fine sensibilities" who voiced "the intricacies of the blind maze of thought and action along which the modern, educated colored man or woman struggles." Later commentators have noted the specific image, the veil, that Du Bois used to express the division of the world for blacks and have also identified his basic optimism in arguing that a healing of the split can occur if only his political and moral ideas are accepted.

What has been ignored in all these observations is the fact that Du Bois, in at least two of his essays in the book—"Of the Meaning of Progress" and "Of the Passing of the First-Born"—creates narrators who express a far more ambivalent attitude toward the possibility of ending the war of the two ideals. Though these particular essays are usually seen as autobiographical, careful analysis reveals narrative voices that are very different from the rational, morally confident Du Bois of the more expository chapters. These uncertain speakers, in the process of presenting their stories, show us rather than tell us the deep psychological implication of living the life of double-consciousness. The implicit suggestion is that the reformist arguments of most of *Souls* do not deal with the deeper consequences of racism. The author who juxtaposes such arguments with unresolved psychological dramas is clearly a man who is himself of two minds about the nature of racism and the possibilities for its eradication. He argues for a rational approach, but his subtler efforts, as in the creation of narrators, indicate a recognition that the psychological and moral effects of the problem raise serious doubts about his reform proposals. Significantly, he does not attempt to resolve this conflict of optimism and pessimism; instead he explores its dramatic possibilities. By analyzing the narrators through which he presents this drama, it becomes possible to see the greater literary significance and moral complexity of a work that is a major contribution to black literature specifically but also to American literature in general. ⟨. . .⟩

"Of the Meaning of Progress" and "Of the Passing of the First-Born" are generally taken as the autobiographical essays in a work that uses many different disciplines and forms to communicate its egalitarian ideology. The "facts" of the essays certainly correspond to the facts of Du Bois's life. But more important than those facts are the means by which they are expressed.

Du Bois creates narrative characters who reveal themselves as far more complex than the narrative facts would lead us to believe. They show us, in the process of telling their tales, the deeper and more serious impact that racism has on even those blacks who are relatively sophisticated and successful. They are figures who have had their idealism destroyed and, in the case of the father, their instincts distorted. Though they both are carrying on their lives at the end of their stories, they no longer have vitality or certainty.

The success of such creations suggests that the real literary achievement of *The Souls of Black Folk* is not in the genteel and often archaic nature of its language, nor in the fortuitous selection of the image of the veil, nor even in the rhetorical power of its combination of a significant theme with a range of classical literary devices. Instead, its achievement can be found in Du Bois's ability to dramatize the meaning of being black in America. It is in effectively showing as well as telling that he communicates the deeper significance of racism. He shows the impact of prejudices on the black mind and clearly understands that this impact will not be removed by his reform proposals. At its most insidious, racism destroys both the meaning of life and the desire to live. Du Bois's recognition of such a dark reality and his creation of narrators to express it make *The Souls of Black Folk* a major literary achievement.

Keith E. Byerman, "Hearts of Darkness: Narrative Voices in *The Souls of Black Folk*," *American Literary Realism* 14, No. 1 (Spring 1981): 43–44, 50–51

JANE CAMPBELL   As the only romancer of post-Reconstruction to lay bare the plight of lower-class blacks, Du Bois (in *The Quest of the Silver Fleece*) reveals the sharecropping system to be very little different from slavery. The Christmas season illustrates the system's duplicity. Colonel Creswell, one of "the lords of the soil," converses with his clerks about the proper way to distribute the wages to one sharecropper: "Well, he's a good nigger and needs encouragement; cancel his debt and give him ten dollars for Christmas." Creswell perceives that another farmer, having raised a bountiful crop, is trying to move away from the plantation. To ensure his servitude, Creswell advises, "Keep him in debt, but let him draw what he wants." Similarly, when Zora and Bles, the romance's protagonists, raise a good crop, Harry Creswell cheats Zora out of her money and leaves her

twenty-five dollars in debt. Through these and other scenes, Du Bois fiction-
alizes the manipulation of the sharecroppers that takes place in part because
the landlords are dishonest, in part because the workers themselves are too
ignorant to understand the system and too acculturated to question it. Only
through the "talented tenth's" messianic power that Du Bois celebrates in
The Souls of Black Folk (1903) can the uneducated be saved from such
exploitation. Therefore, when Bles and Zora return from Washington, they
organize the people to fight against the sharecropping system.

In contrast, the political corruption that Bles and Zora confront in Washington appears indomitable. Du Bois goes further than Griggs and Chesnutt
in depicting the horror and complexity of post-Reconstruction politics. His
distance from his material is such that he achieves an almost naturalistic
work; unlike Griggs and Chesnutt he rarely editorializes but simply presents
scenes and characters responsible for the corruption. On a quest for wealth,
power, and status, all are enmeshed in a web of intrigue and backstabbing
that coolly dispenses with those incapable of playing by the rules. Caroline
Wynn, an educated mulatta, has become a senator's mistress to further her
own interests. Eager to marry a politician, she suggests to the senator that
Bles, her suitor, be given an office. Mrs. Vanderpool, a wealthy and influential
woman, agrees to promote Bles for treasurer, in hopes of securing the French
ambassadorship for her husband. When Bles speaks against the Republican
party for refusing to support an education bill, however, the position of
treasurer goes to Sam Stillings, a former friend of Bles. Seeing her chance,
Caroline jilts Bles to marry Sam. Further complicating the unbelievable
tangle of coincidence, Mary Taylor Creswell, whose husband Harry has
been suggested for the French ambassadorship instead of the dissolute Vanderpool, is in turn framed by Mrs. Vanderpool for having deliberately given
a prize to a sculpture submitted by Caroline. When the press discovers that
the prize has gone to a black, Creswell loses the appointment.

In all these machinations, Du Bois reveals that he, like Chesnutt, sees
historical process as resulting from human needs for security, wealth, and
status and from humanity's ability to learn the methods to satisfy those
needs. ⟨Herbert⟩ Aptheker delineates the positive aspect of this view of
history when he summarizes Du Bois's essay "Mr. Sorokin's Systems." "The
historian," Du Bois held, ". . . must believe that creative human initiative,
working outside mechanical sequence, directs and changes the course of
human action and so history . . . it is man who causes movement and
change." And for Du Bois, as for Griggs and Chesnutt, education represents

the primary means for the individual to effect change. But the type of education acquired is of great significance. To analyze the educational situation for black America during post-Reconstruction one must acknowledge Booker T. Washington. Chesnutt and Washington were good friends. Although Chesnutt disagreed with Washington's insistence on industrial education, their friendship prevented Chesnutt in his published writings from disparaging Washington's ideas. Both Chesnutt and Griggs reacted to Washington's rejection of higher educational aims, his elevation of industrial work, but neither openly denounced him as did Du Bois. In "Of Mr. Booker T. Washington and Others," Du Bois enunciates his view that not only had Washington's educational and political theories sped disenfranchisement and withdrawal of aid to black colleges, but these same blacks could not survive without the voting privileges Washington discounted. Furthermore, Washington's insistence on self-respect conflicted with his insistence on silent submission. Finally, though Washington deprecated black colleges and supported common-schools, neither his own Tuskegee Institute nor the common-schools could stay open without teachers, who had to attend black colleges. Du Bois thus exposes the fundamental contradictions of Washington's thought. Accordingly, he organized the Niagara Movement in 1905 to fight discrimination, segregation, and Washington's accommodationist policies.

Jane Campbell, "Visions of Transcendence in W. E. B. Du Bois's *The Quest of the Silver Fleece* and William Attaway's *Blood on the Forge*," *Mythic Black Fiction: The Transformation of History* (Knoxville: University of Tennessee Press, 1986), pp. 66–68

NELLIE Y. McKAY   ⟨. . .⟩ while it is true that Du Bois's autobiographies are about "ideas" and do not represent the archetypal "journey" of the man, the extent to which he includes the influences of women's experience, and especially those of black women, on his thinking; his recognition of gender oppression; and his acceptance of the worth of his emotional and spiritual feelings makes his work distinctive. More than any other black man in our history, his three autobiographies demonstrate that black women have been central to the development of his intellectual thought. In his old age he would say that he had always had more friends among black women than among black men; that he was less attracted to relationships with the men of the race because many of them "imitated an American culture which [he] did not share." Using the criteria of inclusiveness of experience, and an awareness of race and gender oppression as aspects of the composition of feminist autobiography, Du Bois comes closer to consciously repudiating the intellectual/emotional, mind/body split than many other writers of intellectual autobiography.

To begin at the beginning, we know that Du Bois had a perception that black folk have "souls" that not only understand the problems of the Veil, but also embody peculiarly transcending sensibilities that enhance their humanity. We also know that he was aware that the folk were not all men. If anything can be said about his views on the souls of black women folk, it is that he felt that they had struggled through to an even higher plane than black men had. He was not afraid to acknowledge his own spiritual-emotional feelings, and he was not afraid to acknowledge their manifestations in the lives of others, including women. In like manner, he was not afraid to recognize the more concrete elements of human experience. It is this kind of inclusive perspective on experience that makes his autobiographies stand out for me. ⟨. . .⟩

There is little doubt that the souls of black women folk were close to Du Bois's consciousness throughout his life—that is, that the importance of women, beyond their socially defined roles of subordination to men, was a matter that he took very seriously.

Nellie Y. McKay, "The Souls of Black Women Folk in the Writings of W. E. B. Du Bois," *Reading Black, Reading Feminist: A Critical Anthology*, ed. Henry Louis Gates, Jr. (New York: Meridian, 1990), pp. 227–28

RICHARD KOSTELANETZ   In the end, although Du Bois's novels were published over a span of fifty years, their attitudes on politics are nearly all of a single piece. In *The Quest of the Silver Fleece*, the possibilities of individual African-American independence within the South are tested and found wanting; yet opportunities in the North are hardly better. Among the politically favorable portraits are, first, the few kindly whites who teach Southern blacks and, second, the agitators for a well-organized communal settlement that would only compete with the white South. In *Dark Princess*, not only the South but also the North is rejected, as the novel's protagonist expatriates to India; and the novel predicts that all colored people will claim as their own the land they now occupy. In the *Black Flame* trilogy, nearly all Afro-American possibilities in America are tested and, finally, rejected; and again expatriation, particularly to Africa, is favored, in addition to alliances with international Communism. Du Bois's novels, in addition to posing general questions, also define a range of options that Richard Wright and Ralph Ellison, political novelists both, subsequently incorporated into their own fictions.

Richard Kostelanetz, "W. E. B. Du Bois," *Politics in the African-American Novel* (Westport, CT: Greenwood Press, 1991), p. 66

DAVID LEVERING LEWIS   The African-American "ever feels his two-ness—an American, a Negro; two souls, two thoughts, two unreconciled strivings," Du Bois wrote ⟨in "Of Our Spiritual Strivings"⟩, echoing almost surely his beloved Goethe's words in *Faust* and even possibly those of Ralph Waldo Emerson in "The Transcendentalist." "Two warring ideals in one dark body, whose dogged strength alone keeps it from being torn asunder," he continues, repeating word for word the ardent prose of his *Atlantic Monthly* essay. "The history of the American Negro is the history of this strife—this longing to attain self-conscious manhood, to merge his double self into a better and truer self." Others brooding over the outcast status of their people ultimately wished it away in visions of future racial harmony or heavenly rewards, or, like Douglass, put their faith in full assimilation. A few—Garnet, Delany, Holly—had chosen the path of cultural separatism and expatriation. Debate about what African-Americans were and what they should become had been like a zero-sum game, shuttlecocking between the Integrated Society and the Black Zion. The genius of *The Souls of Black Folk* was that it transcended this dialectic in the most obvious way—by affirming it in a permanent tension. Henceforth, the destiny of the race could be conceived as leading neither to assimilation nor separatism but to proud, enduring hyphenation.

It was a revolutionary conception. It was not just revolutionary; the concept of the divided self was profoundly mystical, for Du Bois invested this double consciousness with a capacity to see incomparably farther and deeper. The African-American—seventh son after the Egyptian and Indian, the Greek and Roman, the Teuton and Mongolian—possessed the gift of "second-sight in this American world," an intuitive faculty (prelogical in a sense) enabling him/her to see and say things about American society that possessed heightened moral validity. Because he dwelt equally in the mind and heart of his oppressor as in his own beset psyche, the African-American embraced a vision of the commonweal at its best. But the gift was also double-edged—always potentially enervating—because the African-American only saw him/herself reflected from a white surface, "a world which yields him no true self-consciousness, but only lets him see himself through the revelation of the other world." If it was true that large numbers (perhaps even a majority) of the race had never thought of themselves as having such a convoluted, refractive existence, Du Bois's foray into group psychology was certainly valid for those African-Americans (like himself) whose cultural backgrounds predisposed them to hold fast to the values of the dominant class of the dominant society. In all probability, Sam Hose had had a simpler self-concept, one uninfluenced by Hegel and more fixed by a common identity based on color and raw oppression. It is not certain what he would have made of Du Bois's confident prescription—"This, then, is the end of his striving: to be a co-worker in the kingdom of culture." Even as Du Bois assumed the role as its premier advocate, a definite tension (not quite a contradiction) existed, therefore, in the Du Boisian affirmation of the race's soul.

David Levering Lewis, "*The Souls of Black Folk*," *W. E. B. Du Bois: Biography of a Race 1868–1919* (New York: Henry Holt, 1993), pp. 281–82

◈ Bibliography

The Suppression of the African Slave-Trade to the United States of America, 1638–1870. 1896.

Mortality among Negroes in Cities (editor). 1896.

Social and Physical Condition of Negroes in Cities (editor). 1897.

The Conservation of Races. 1897.

Some Efforts of American Negroes for Their Own Social Betterment (editor). 1898.

Careers Open to Young Negro-Americans. 1898.

The College-Bred Negro. c. 1898.

The Negro in Business (editor). 1899.

The Philadelphia Negro (with Isabel Eaton). 1899.

Memorial to the Legislature of Georgia on the Hardwick Bill (with others). 1899.

The College-Bred Negro (editor). 1900.

The Negro Common School (editor). 1901.

Results of Ten Tuskegee Negro Conferences. 1901.

A Select Bibliography of the American Negro. 1901.

The Negro Artisan (editor). 1902.

The Negro Church (editor). 1903.

Some Notes on the Negroes in New York City. 1903.

The Souls of Black Folk: Essays and Sketches. 1903.

A Bibliography of Negro Folk Songs. 1903.

Heredity and the Public Schools: A Lecture Delivered under the Auspices of the Principals' Association of the Colored Schools of Washington. 1904.

Some Notes on Negro Crime, Particularly in Georgia (editor). 1904.

A Select Bibliography of the Negro American (editor). 1905.

Niagara Movement—Declaration of Principles (with others). 1905.

The Health and Physique of the Negro American (editor). 1906.

Economic Co-operation among Negro Americans (editor). 1907.

The Negro American Family (editor). 1908.

Efforts for Social Betterment among Negro Americans (editor). 1909.

John Brown. 1909.

The College-Bred Negro American (editor; with Augustus Granville Dill). 1910.

College-Bred Negro Communities: Address at Brookline, Massachusetts. 1910.

Race Relations in the United States: An Appeal to England (with others). 1910.

The Common School and the Negro American (editor; with Augustus Granville Dill). 1911.

The Quest of the Silver Fleece. 1911.

The Social Evolution of the Black South. 1911.

The Negro American Artisan (editor; with Augustus Granville Dill). 1912.

Disenfranchisement. 1912.

Morals and Manners among Negro Americans (editor; with Augustus Granville Dill). 1914.

A Half Century of Freedom. 1914.

The Negro. 1915.

Darkwater: Voices from within the Veil. 1920.

The Gift of Black Folk: The Negroes in the Making of America. 1924.

The Amenia Conference: An Historic Negro Gathering. 1925.

Dark Princess: A Romance. 1928.

Notes on the Negro in City Politics. 1929.

Africa—Its Place in Modern History. 1930.

Africa: Its Geography, People and Products. 1930.

A Study of the Atlanta University Federal Housing Area. 1934.

Black Reconstruction: An Essay toward a History of the Part Which Black Folk Played in the Attempt to Reconstruct Democracy in America, 1860–1880. 1935.

What the Negro Has Done for the United States and Texas. 1936.

Race Philosophy and Policies for Negro Life in the North. 1936.

A Pageant in Seven Decades, 1868–1938: An Address Delivered on the Occasion of His Seventieth Birthday at the University Convocation of Atlanta University, Morehouse College, and Spelman College. 1938.

Black Folk, Then and Now: An Essay in the History and Sociology of the Negro Race. 1939.

Dusk of Dawn: An Essay toward an Autobiography of a Race Concept. 1940.

Conference of Negro Land Grant Colleges for Coordinating a Program of Cooperative Social Studies (editor). 1943.

Conference of Negro Land Grant Colleges for Coordinating a Program of Cooperative Social Studies (editor). 1944.

Color and Democracy: Colonies and Peace. 1945.

Encyclopedia of the Negro (with others). 1945, 1946.

Human Rights for All Minorities. 1945.

The World and Africa: An Inquiry into the Part Which Africa Has Played in World History. 1947.

An Appeal to the World (editor). 1947.

Peace Is Dangerous. 1951.

In Battle for Peace: The Story of My 83rd Birthday. 1952.

What Is Wrong with the United States. 1954.

The Story of Benjamin Franklin. 1956.

The Ordeal of Mansart. 1957.

Mansart Builds a School. 1959.

Socialism Today. 1959.

Africa in Battle against Colonialism, Racialism, Imperialism. 1960.

Worlds of Color. 1961.

An ABC of Color: Selections from Over a Half Century of the Writings of W. E. B. Du Bois. 1963, 1969.

The Autobiography of W. E. B. Du Bois: A Soliloquy on Viewing My Life from the Last Decade of Its First Century. 1968.

W. E. B. Du Bois: A Reader. Ed. Meyer Weinberg. 1970.

W. E. B. Du Bois Speaks: Speeches and Addresses. Ed. Philip S. Foner. 1970. 2 vols.

A W. E. B. Du Bois Reader. Ed. Andrew G. Paschal. 1971.

The Seventh Son: The Thought and Writings of W. E. B. Du Bois. Ed. Julius Lester. 1971.

The Crisis *Writings*. Ed. Daniel Walden. 1972.

The Education of Black People: Ten Critiques, 1906–1960. Ed. Herbert Aptheker. 1973.

Du Bois on the Importance of Africa in World History. 1978.

Complete Published Works. Ed. Herbert Aptheker. 1980– .

Against Racism: Unpublished Essays, Papers, Addresses, 1887–1961. Ed. Herbert Aptheker. 1985.

Writings. 1986.

W. E. B. Du Bois on Sociology and the Black Community. Ed. Dan S. Green and Edwin D. Driver. 1987.

The Atlanta Conference. n.d.

The Damnation of Women. n.d.

The Immortal Child: Background on Crises in Education. n.d.

❈ ❈ ❈

Paul Laurence Dunbar
1872–1906

PAUL LAURENCE DUNBAR was born in Dayton, Ohio, on June 27, 1872, the son of former slaves. He attended a local high school where he was the only black enrolled and was the editor of the school paper. After school Dunbar worked as an elevator boy in Dayton but also began to contribute poems and stories to local newspapers. He met Charles Thatcher, a lawyer from Toledo who gave substantial support in launching his literary career. Dunbar also worked as a clerk in the Haitian Pavilion at the World's Columbian Exposition in Chicago, where he met Frederick Douglass and other prominent black figures.

Dunbar published poems in Dayton newspapers and brought out two verse collections, *Oak and Ivy* and *Majors and Minors*, privately printed in 1893 and 1895, respectively. William Dean Howells's influential review of the latter in *Harper's Weekly* marked the beginning of Dunbar's fame as a poet on a national level. Howells also wrote the introduction to Dunbar's next collection, *Lyrics of Lowly Life* (1896), which was well received. In 1897 Dunbar ventured to England for public readings and met and collaborated with composer Samuel Coleridge-Taylor. Later that year he became employed as reading room assistant in the Library of Congress in Washington, D.C.

In 1898 Dunbar married Alice Ruth Moore, herself a noted poet and short story writer. In that same year he published his first novel, *The Uncalled*, followed by three others in rapid succession: *The Love of Landry* (1900), *The Fanatics* (1901), and *The Sport of the Gods* (1902). In 1899 he participated with Booker T. Washington and W. E. B. Du Bois in readings to raise funds for the Tuskegee Institute, a Southern college for black American students; the following year he took part in Du Bois's conferences on black American issues at Atlanta University. Dunbar also retained a fondness for the Republican party, and in particular Theodore Roosevelt; he participated in this president's inaugural parades, and in 1905 he wrote a poem for the candidate's campaign.

Dunbar's health began to fail around 1900 and he died of tuberculosis on February 8, 1906. His *Complete Poems* was published in 1913. Dunbar was most admired in his own time, and is best remembered today, for his poems and stories written in black dialect. He was the first black author to employ this device, and was inspired, in part, by the example of Robert Burns.

◈ Critical Extracts

W. D. HOWELLS   What struck me in reading Mr. Dunbar's poetry was what had already struck his friends in Ohio and Indiana, in Kentucky and Illinois. They had felt, as I felt, that however gifted his race had proven itself in music, in oratory, in several of the other arts, here was the first instance of an American negro who had evinced innate distinction in literature. In my criticism of his book ⟨*Majors and Minors*⟩ I had alleged Dumas in France, and I had forgetfully failed to allege the far greater Pushkin in Russia; but these were both mulattoes, who might have been supposed to derive their qualities from white blood vastly more artistic than ours, and who were the creatures of an environment more favorable to their literary development. So far as I could remember, Paul Dunbar was the only man of pure African blood and of American civilization to feel the negro life aesthetically and express it lyrically. It seemed to me that this had come to its most modern consciousness in him, and that his brilliant and unique achievement was to have studied the American negro objectively, and to have represented him as he found him to be, with humor, with sympathy, and yet with what the reader must instinctively feel to be entire truthfulness. I said that a race which had come to this effect in any member of it, had attained civilization in him, and I permitted myself the imaginative prophecy that the hostilities and the prejudices which had so long constrained his race were destined to vanish in the arts; that these were to be the final proof that God had made of one blood all nations of men. I thought his merits positive and not comparative; and I held that if his black poems had been written by a white man, I should not have found them less admirable. I accepted them as an evidence of the essential unity of the human race, which does not think or feel black in one and white in another, but humanly in all.

Yet it appeared to me then, and it appears to me now, that there is a precious difference of temperament between the races which it would be a great pity ever to lose, and that this is best preserved and most charmingly suggested by Mr. Dunbar in those pieces of his where he studies the moods and traits of his race in its own accent of our English. We call such pieces dialect pieces for want of some closer phrase, but they are really not dialect so much as delightful personal attempts and failures for the written and spoken language. In nothing is his essentially refined and delicate art so well shown as in these pieces, which, as I ventured to say, described the range between appetite and emotion, with certain lifts far beyond and above it, which is the range of the race. He reveals in these a finely ironical perception of the negro's limitations, with a tenderness for them which I think so very rare as to be almost quite new. I should say, perhaps, that it was this humorous quality which Mr. Dunbar had added to our literature, and it would be this which would most distinguish him, now and hereafter.

W. D. Howells, "Introduction" (1896), *The Complete Poems of Paul Lawrence Dunbar* (New York: Dodd, Mead, 1913), pp. viii–x

---

ROBERT T. KERLIN   Dunbar is a fact, as Burns, as Whittier, as Riley, are facts—a fact of great moment to a people and for a people. ⟨. . .⟩ I mention Dunbar here only to draw attention to my theme, that theme being, not one poet, but a multitude animated by one spirit though characterized by diversity of talent, all spokesmen of their race in its new era. Dunbar does indeed appear to sustain a definite relation to these black singers of the new day. For one thing, he revealed to the Negro youth of our land the latent literary powers of their race, and, not less important, he revealed also the poetic materials at hand in the Negro people, lowly or distinguished. He may therefore be thought of as the fecundating genius of their muses. But I think they are born, as he was, of the creative zeitgeist, sent of heaven.

But to give my assertion regarding Dunbar its proper significance, I must remark, for white people, that there were two Dunbars, and that they know but one. There is the Dunbar of "the jingle in a broken tongue," whom Howells with gracious but imperfect sympathy and understanding brought to the knowledge of the world, and whom the public readers, white and black alike (the sin is upon both), have found it delightful to present, to the entire eclipse of the other Dunbar. That other Dunbar was the poet of the flaming "Ode to Ethiopia," the pathetic lyric, "We Wear the Mask," and a score of other pieces in which, using their speech, he matches himself with the poets who shine as stars in the firmament of our admiration. This Dunbar, I say, Howells failed to appreciate, and ignorance of him has been fostered by professional readers and writers. The first Dunbar, the generally accepted one, was, as Howells pointed out, the artistic interpreter of the old fashioned, vanishing generation of black folk—the generation that was maimed and scarred by slavery, that presented so many ludicrous and pathetic, abject and lovable aspects in strange mixture. The second Dunbar was the prophet robed in a mantle of austerity, shod with fire, bowed with sorrow, as every true prophet has been, in whatever time, among whatever people. He was the prophet, I say, of a new generation, a coming generation, as he was the poet of a vanishing generation. The generation of which he was the prophet-herald has arrived. Its most authentic representatives are the poets to whom I have referred.

> Robert T. Kerlin, *Contemporary Poetry of the Negro* (Hampton, VA: Hampton Norman & Agricultural Institute, 1921), pp. 6–7

BENJAMIN BRAWLEY   Dunbar's conception of his art was based on his theory of life. He felt that he was first of all a man, then an American, and incidentally a Negro. To a world that looked upon him primarily as a Negro and wanted to hear from him simply in his capacity as a Negro, he was thus a little difficult to understand. He never regarded the dialect poems as his best work, and, as he said in the eight lines entitled "The Poet," when one tried to sing of the greatest themes in life, it was hard to have the world praise only "a jingle in a broken tongue." His position was debatable, of course, but that was the way he felt. At the meeting at the Waldorf-Astoria a reporter asked about the quality of the poetry written by Negroes as compared with that of white people. Dunbar replied, "The predominating power of the African race is lyric. In that I should expect the writers of my race to excel. But, broadly speaking, their poetry will not be exotic or differ much from that of the whites. . . . For two hundred and fifty years the environment of the Negro has been American, in every respect the same as that of all other Americans." "But isn't there," continued the interviewer, "a certain tropic warmth, a cast of temperament that belongs of right to the African race?" "Ah," said the poet, "what you speak of is going to be a loss. It is inevitable. We must write like the white men. I do not mean imitate them; but our life is now the same." Then he added: "I hope you are not one of those who would hold the Negro down to a certain kind of poetry—dialect and concerning only scenes on plantations in the South?"

To a later school of Negro writers, one more definitely conscious of race, Dunbar thus appears as somewhat artificial. The difference is that wrought by the World War. About the close of that conflict Marcus Garvey, by a positively radical program, made black a fashionable color. It was something not to be apologized for, but exploited. Thenceforth one heard much about "the new Negro," and for a while Harlem was a literary capital. In Dunbar's time, however, black was not fashionable. The burden still rested upon the Negro to prove that he could do what any other man could do, and in America that meant to use the white man's technique and meet the white man's standard of excellence. It was to this task that Dunbar addressed himself. This was the test that he felt he had to satisfy, and not many will doubt that he met it admirably.

Benjamin Brawley, *Paul Laurence Dunbar: Poet of His People* (Chapel Hill: University of North Carolina Press, 1936), pp. 76–77

STERLING A. BROWN   As has been pointed out, Dunbar was not the first Negro poet to use dialect, although his predecessors had not realized the possibilities of the medium. The influential work of white authors in Negro dialect, from Stephen Foster and the minstrel song writers through local colorists such as Erwin Russell, J. A. Macon, Joel Chandler Harris and Thomas Nelson Page, will be our concern in the concluding chapters devoted to poetry. In spite of these forerunners, however, Dunbar was not only the first American Negro to "feel the Negro life aesthetically and express it lyrically," as William Dean Howells wrote, but also the first American poet to handle Negro folklife with any degree of fullness. As a portrayal of Negro life, Dunbar's picture has undoubted limitations, but they are by no means so grave as those of Russell and Page. ⟨. . .⟩

Dunbar's best qualities are clear. Such early poems as "Accountability" and "An Antebellum Sermon" show flashes of the unforced gay humor that was to be with him even to the last. With a few well-turned folk phrases he calls up a scene as in "Song of Summer," or

> Tu'key gobbler gwine 'roun' blowin'
> Gwine 'roun' gibbin' sass an' slack
> Keep on talkin' Mistah Tu'key
> You ain't seed no almanac. ("Signs of the Times")

> Tek a cool night, good an' cleah
> Skiff o' snow upon de groun' ("Hunting Song")

Except when unexplainably urged to write Irish dialect or imitate Riley's "Orphant Annie," or to cross misspelling with moralizing as in "Keep A Pluggin' Away," his grasp upon folk-speech is generally sure. His rhythms almost never stumble and are frequently catchy: at times as in "Itching Heels" he gets the syncopation of a folk dance. Most of all he took up the Negro peasant as a clown, and made him a likeable person.

Sterling A. Brown, *Negro Poetry and Drama* (Washington, DC: Associates in Negro Folk Education, 1937), pp. 32, 35

THEODORA W. DANIEL   Dunbar's prose stories were yet another channel through which he called attention to the failings of American democracy as applied to his race. His resentment of the old, old custom of assigning a "place" to the Negro beyond which he should not advance, ability and initiative notwithstanding, is evident in "The Scapegoat." The scapegoat is a Negro political boss who is sacrificed upon the altar of political reform by his party. Old Judge Davis, a prominent party man, is spokesman for his kind of racial bigot everywhere and for all time.

"Asbury," he said, "you are—you are—well, you ought to be white, that's all. When we find a black man like you we send him to State's prison. If you were white, you'd go to the Senate."

According to democratic theory, the accused is presumed to be innocent until guilt is definitely established. All too often, however, when a Negro is suspect the principle is reversed and guilt is automatically assumed. The violation of this tenet of democracy is subjected to a subtle but searching criticism in "The Lynching of Jube Benson." Here the narrator, Dr. Melville, entertains a group of friends with the revolting details of a lynching which followed the murder of his fiancée. As the innocent black man-of-all-work gasped his last, the real murderer is discovered—a white man with a blackened face. The doctor, who had always loved old Jube and been convinced of the old Negro's love for him and "Miss Annie," thus accounts for his readiness to believe Jube guilty:

"A false education, I reckon, one false from the beginning. I saw his black face glooming there in the half light and I could only think of him as a monster. It's tradition. At first I was told that the black man would catch me, and when I got over that, they taught me that the devil was black, and when I had recovered from the sickness of that belief, here was Jube and his fellows with faces of menacing blackness. There was only one conclusion: This black man stood for all the powers of evil, the result of whose machinations had been gathering in my mind from childhood up. . . ."

Theodora W. Daniel, "Paul Laurence Dunbar and the Democratic Ideal," *Negro History Bulletin* 6, No. 9 (June 1943): 207–8

DARWIN TURNER   Even if Dunbar had been completely free to write scathing protest about the South, he could not have written it, or would have written it ineptly. His experiences and those of his family had not compelled him to hate white people as a group or the South as a region. After Dunbar was twenty, every major job he secured, every publication, and all national recognition resulted directly from the assistance of white benefactors. It is not remarkable that Dunbar assumed that successful Negroes need such help or that, knowing the actuality of Northern benefactors, he believed in the existence of their Southern counterparts. Dunbar was not a unique disciple of such a creed. In *The Ordeal of Mansart*, the militant W. E. B. Du Bois has described the manner in which intelligent freedmen sought salvation with the assistance of Southern aristocrats.

As his personal experiences freed him from bitterness towards Caucasians as a group, so his family's experiences relieved bitterness towards the South. The experiences of his parents in slavery probably had been milder than most. His father had been trained in a trade and had been taught to read, write, and compute. As a semi-skilled worker occasionally hired out, he fared better than the average field hand. Irony rather than bitterness is the dominant tone in "The Ingrate," a story Dunbar based on his father's life. Although Dunbar's mother had experienced unpleasantness (as what slave did not), her life as a house slave in Kentucky undoubtedly was easier than that of a slave in the deeper South.

Even had his experiences prompted protest against the South, his social and economic philosophies would have militated against it. Believing that America would prosper only if all citizens recognized their interdependence, he sought to win respect for Negroes by showing that, instead of sulking about the past, they were ready to participate in the joint effort to create a new America. In the poems of *Majors and Minors* (1895) and the stories of *Folks from Dixie* (1898), he repeatedly emphasized the ability and willingness of Negroes to forgive white Americans for previous injustices.

Dunbar's noble sentiments and protagonists reveal not only a naive political philosophy but also a romantic and idealized concept of society. He believed in right rule by an aristocracy based on birth and blood which assured culture, good breeding, and all the virtues appropriate to a gentleman. He further believed that Negroes, instead of condemning such a society, must prove themselves worthy of a place in it by showing that they had civilized themselves to a level above the savagery which he assumed to be characteristic of Africa. Furthermore, having been reared in Dayton, Ohio, he distrusted big cities and industrialization. Provincially, he assumed the good life for the uneducated to be the life of a farmer in a small western or mid-western settlement or the life of a sharecropper for a benevolent Southern aristocrat. Neither a scholar, political scientist, nor economist, he naively offered an agrarian myth as a shield against the painful reality of discrimination in cities. ⟨. . .⟩

In summary, Dunbar's experiences, his social and economic philosophies, and his artistic ideals limited his criticism of the South. This fact, however, should not imply, as some suppose, that Dunbar accepted the total myth of the plantation tradition. In reality, he was no more willing to assume the romanticized plantation to be characteristic of the entire South than he was willing to deny that some slaves had loved their masters or had behaved foolishly.

> Darwin Turner, "Paul Laurence Dunbar: The Rejected Symbol," *Journal of Negro History* 52, No. 1 (January 1967): 2–4

CHARLES R. LARSON   That the protest is missing from much of his earlier writing there can be little doubt. It will be the premise of this article, however, to illustrate that in his novels, at least, Dunbar was becoming more and more concerned with racial issues during the course of his brief, five-year novelistic career; and, further, as illustrated in his four novels, that this social concern coupled with a slow but increasing move in the direction of literary naturalism is clearly apparent by the time of Dunbar's early death. Had he lived another ten or fifteen years—or even five—had he not died at thirty-four, there are indications that the term *Uncle Tom* might never have been applied to his writing. ⟨. . .⟩

In his biography of Dunbar, Brawley has said, "Dunbar's conception of his art was based on his theory of life. He felt that he was first of all a man, then an American, and incidentally a Negro." It is in this quotation, I believe, that the key to Dunbar's novelistic achievement may be seen. It seems unfair to criticize him for being an Uncle Tom simply because he was writing primarily for a white audience. In no way could he have been a financial success had he written solely for the Negro reading audience of his day. Neither does it seem fair to criticize his early novels because they fail to take a conscious stand against the social atrocities leveled on the Negro race. The protest is there, be it latent and somewhat hidden, even in the first two novels. The remaining two take a much more direct stand against the problems which were undoubtedly eating at Dunbar's conscience throughout his entire lifetime. From these last two novels, it seems almost certain that had Paul Laurence Dunbar lived a few more years, his protest would probably have been vitriolic enough to eradicate all the derogatory terms which have since been leveled against his work.

Charles R. Larson, "The Novels of Paul Laurence Dunbar," *Phylon* 29, No. 3 (Fall 1968): 257, 270–71

ADDISON GAYLE, JR.   Despite the importance of *A Career* to Dunbar's development as a poet, few of his biographers have realized its full implication. Had they done so, they might have noted that Dunbar's most serious poems in *Oak and Ivy* were written in standard English and that the poet himself was less than pleased with the success of his dialect pieces. ⟨. . .⟩

Dunbar never took these poems seriously. For him they were humorous ditties written to entertain white audiences. Few black people could afford to spend a dollar for his book. Therefore, he was able to sell enough copies to repay his debt three weeks after publication only because of the book's popularity with whites. They bought copies for themselves and sent others to their friends. Some, like Attorney Thatcher and Dr. Tobey, were sophisticated men who differentiated between the humorous poems and the more serious ones. As for the others, he tried to instruct them. His title was his way of choosing between his poems in dialect and those in standard English. He thought of a tree with ivy growing all about it. The tree was more important than the ivy, for the ivy was neither strong nor functional, but merely useless ornamentation. So, too, was the ivy of his book—the dialect poems—ornamentation to the sturdy oak—the poems in standard English. Only later in life was he to learn that within this title he had planted the seeds of a truer metaphor; that of the ivy engulfing the oak, strangling the life out of it, so that in time what was at first ornament replaced the dominant element, and was admired as if it had always been the more important of the two.

Addison Gayle, Jr., *Oak and Ivy: A Biography of Paul Laurence Dunbar* (Garden City, NY: Doubleday, 1971), pp. 29–31

ROBERT BONE   Throughout Dunbar's fiction, the Northern city is depicted as a repository of false ideals. Anti-heroes, or negative exemplars, are created to embody these false values and illusory goals. Typically they are youthful migrants who succumb to the temptations of gambling, drinking, street crime, disease, or promiscuity. "Silas Jackson" is the purest story of its kind. It deals with a Virginia farmboy who becomes a waiter at a resort hotel. Eventually he is corrupted and destroyed by an opportunity to join a troupe of Negro singers in New York. Like Silas Bollender, he returns from his excursion in disgrace: ". . . spent, broken, hopeless, all contentment and simplicity gone, he turned his face toward his native fields."

A variation on the theme of false ambition is what might be called the carpetbagger theme. Here the protagonist is tempted by a get-rich-quick scheme which promises to bring success without the trouble of hard work. Such a scheme might involve political patronage ("Mr. Cornelius Johnson, Office Seeker"), real estate manipulation ("The Promoter"), or the policy game ("The Trustfulness of Polly"), but always the protagonist falls victim to his own avarice. In the end his Eldorado vanishes, and he is brought low. The moral of these tales is Washingtonian: only through hard work and sacrifice can the black man hope to improve his lot.

Some of Dunbar's overly ambitious blacks are undone by their own pretentiousness and pride. These are the boastful ones, who insist on flaunting their prosperity. Success turns their heads; they put on airs, become pompous, and adopt a condescending attitude toward their less fortunate brothers. In imitation of the white aristocracy they buy expensive clothes, assume fancy names, cultivate impressive manners, and in short become dandified. Such stories as "The Wisdom of Silence," "Johnsonham, Jr." and "The Home-Coming of 'Rastus Smith" warn the blacks to keep a low profile and do nothing to arouse the envy of their enemies.

Robert Bone, Down Home: A History of Afro-American Short Fiction from Its Beginnings to the End of the Harlem Renaissance (New York: G. P. Putnam's Sons, 1975), p. 65

KENNY J. WILLIAMS   Those who condemn him for his lack of involvement must permit him the right to select his personal view of the role of the writer. His literary creed was certainly an expedient one for the closing years of the nineteenth century. Yet, through his sometimes "race-less" novels Dunbar was able to demonstrate implicitly—although he too was not the most skillful craftsman—that there are some human values which transcend race. For example, in his first novel, *The Uncalled*, the relationship between Freddie Brent and his guardian is a basic relationship and illustrates the conflicts which frequently arise when one person of an older generation attempts to superimpose his will upon one of the younger generation. The novel also demonstrates Dunbar's negative attitude toward the city, an attitude which he was to express time and time again and which was fully explored in his last novel, *The Sport of the Gods*. Romanticist that he was, he dealt with the small-town environment and looked at the city— as had other romantics—as a place of potential evil and degradation for the individual. But as he viewed the conflict between the agrarian values of American life and the rising interest in the city, Dunbar's novels evince a growing awareness not only of the realistic method but also of the hypocrisy of American society. Thus one can see even before *The Sport of the Gods* that Dunbar did indeed deal with social issues and with the racial struggles of this nation.

Interestingly enough, Dunbar frequently relied rather heavily upon his own experiences for his novels. In *The Uncalled* he expanded his own interest in the ministry in order to tell the story of a youngster adopted by a prudish woman of a small-town community and then literally forced by her into the ministry. While decidedly not the great American novel, it does present some realistic conflicts between characters in addition to being a sentimental story in the nineteenth-century tradition. In *The Love of Landry* his search for health in Colorado became the basis for the story of Mildred Osborne, who also goes to Colorado to seek health and who becomes greater by virtue of her association with nature. Commenting on the purpose for Mildred's trip, Dunbar muses rather pathetically in the novel:

> With all the faith one may have in one's self, with all the strong hopefulness of youth, it is yet a terrible thing to be forced away from home, from all one loves, to an unknown, uncared-for country, there to fight, hand to hand with death, an uncertain fight. There is none of the rush and clamour of battle that keeps up the soldier's courage. There is no clang of the instruments of war. The panting warrior hears no loud huzzas, and yet the deadly combat goes on; in the still night, when all the world's asleep, in the gray day, in the pale morning, it goes on, and no one knows it save himself and death. Then if he goes down, he knows no hero's honors; if he wins, he has no special praise. And yet, it is a terrible, lone, still fight.

Kenny J. Williams, "The Masking of the Novelist," *A Singer in the Dawn: Reinterpretations of Paul Laurence Dunbar*, ed. Jay Martin (New York: Dodd, Mead, 1975), pp. 168–69

CHIDI IKONNÉ   Paul Laurence Dunbar's complaints about being compelled to write dialect poems are well known. So also is the lament of his autobiographical poem "The Poet" about the world closing its eyes on the good things he has written only "to praise / A jingle in a broken tongue." The frequency with which he employed either literary English or a language that is nonliterary only in appearance, his rejection of the Whitman of *Leaves of Grass* (1855) and adoption of conventional poetic formats even in dialect pieces, his treatment of some of his Negro folk material à la Erwin Russell, James Whitcomb Riley, and Thomas Nelson Page all show his great desire to be numbered among the mainstream American writers of his age. Yet it will be wrong either to interpret his apparent reluctance to be remembered mainly by his dialect poetry as his disapproval of that part of his work or to regard the pieces themselves as a bunch of insincerity. The legitimacy of dialect as a medium of literary representation of folkways is not in question. What Dunbar complains about is being forced to write nothing but dialect: "I am tired, so tired of dialect, . . . I send out graceful little poems, suited for any of the magazines, but they are returned to me by editors who say, 'We would be very glad to have a dialect poem, Mr. Dunbar, but we do not care for the language composition.' "

In a letter dated 13 July 1895 and addressed to his friend Henry A. Tobey he confesses how his earlier ambition to be a lawyer had "died out before the all-absorbing desire to be a worthy singer of the songs of God and nature." He wishes "to be able to interpret my own people through song and story, and to prove to the many that after all we are more human than African." Most of his "people" at that time were "lowly" folk; dialect provided him with a more effective means (compared with his poetry in literary English) of demonstrating and, by extension, defending their life-style.

Chidi Ikonné, *From Du Bois to Van Vechten: The Early New Negro Literature 1903–1926* (Westport, CT: Greenwood Press, 1981), p. 51

HOUSTON A. BAKER, JR.   The title ⟨of *The Sport of the Gods*⟩ finds its meaning, not in the historically documented betrayals and confusions of American Reconstructions, but in the domain of literature. The blinded and deceived Gloucester of Shakespeare's drama *King Lear* remarks: "As flies to wanton boys are we to the Gods; / They kill us for their sport." The origin and nature of the world, this utterance implies, are functions of capricious supernaturals. The mythic universe of discourse is thus invoked in explanation of man's failings: Man is nothing special. He is a toy in the ludic world of the gods. While the title alone suggests *The Sport of the Gods'* association with Gloucester's mythic view of human events, the concluding line of the novel's narrator suggests an even more direct parallel. The novel ends as follows: "It was not a happy life [that of the black servant Berry Hamilton and his wife, who have returned to the South], but it was all that was left to them, and they took it up without complaint for they knew they were powerless against some Will infinitely stronger than their own." An apotheosized Will "infinitely stronger" than human powers can only exist in a world of myth.

The "limitless" freedom of myth and its efficacy as a causal explanation in human affairs, however, exist in the works of both the Renaissance dramatist and the Afro-American novelist as ironic postulates. There may well be powerful, invisible beings in the wings, but the reader of *King Lear* is aware that the play's sufferings and deaths have more to do with distinctively human shortcomings than with the ludic wielding of authority by immortals. That Gloucester, whose incredible folly is matched only by that of his aged counterpart Lear, is the character who offers "the sport of the Gods" as explanation reinforces a reader's decision to concentrate on human agents and actions in understanding Shakespeare's drama. Similarly, having followed the controlling voice of the narrator from the first to the concluding line of *The Sport of the Gods*, a reader knows there is little need to summon incomprehensible supernatural powers to explain the human affairs represented in the novel.

The characters of Dunbar's work are, finally, victims of their own individual modes of processing reality. Their failings are paradoxical results of their peculiarly human ability (and inclination) to form theories of knowledge, to construct what Walter Pater calls in *The Renaissance* "habits of thought." The narrator's recourse to what seems a mythic dimension (an invincible "Will"), therefore, like Gloucester's evocation of the Gods in *Lear*, not only stands in ironic contrast to the novel's representations of a mundane reality but also suggests ⟨. . .⟩ an authorial awareness on Dunbar's part crucial to a full, blues understanding of his narrative. ⟨. . .⟩

The Sport of the Gods ⟨. . .⟩ is Dunbar's symbolic "acting out" of the effects of American life and letters of a supreme, revelatory fiction that will enable human beings to see life steadily and whole, enabling them to break free from both their "artistic" and "ordinary" modes of structuring experience. The novel thus captures in subtly energetic ways a dream of American form. It specifically explores the proposition that a literary tradition governed by plantation and coon-show images of Afro-Americans can be altered through an ironic, symbolic, fictive (blues) manipulation of such images and the tradition of which they are a formative part.

The Plantation Tradition and its images (like the coon show) did not spring, ab nihilo, from Dunbar's mind. Both were intrinsic to the world of artistic discourse institutionalized in the society of his era. Hence, while he was at liberty to suggest in *The Sport of the Gods* a radical alteration of the prevailing universe of fictive discourse, Dunbar was at the same time hedged round by the conventions—the social existence, as it were—of that very universe. His own fictive discourse could imply a nontraditional fiction, but since his novel was not intended or designed as a utilitarian, communicative, or historical text, he knew that it was not likely to be taken as an injunction to act. He could propose a shattering of old icons, and he could even represent such iconoclasm in literary form. Ultimately, however, it was men and women governed by traditional images who had the power to dispose.

Though Dunbar's freedom in creating *The Sport of the Gods* was shaped by the conventions of the "institution of literature," his novel's rich implications suggest a need for modes of interpretation that go beyond traditional historico-social critical approaches to narrative. In order to apprehend the turn-of-the-century Afro-American narrative as an act of fictive discourse which initiates, in energetic blues ways, a dream of American form, one must engage the freedom of an adequate critical mythology. One's mode of explaining the novel's meanings (and, indeed, the meanings of Afro-American literary texts in general) must transcend, that is to say, a customary, sharply limiting critical strategy that yokes the analysis of works of verbal art to acts of historical interpretation.

Houston A. Baker, Jr., "The 'Limitless' Freedom of Myth: Paul Laurence Dunbar's *The Sport of the Gods* and the Criticism of Afro-American Literature," *Blues, Ideology, and Afro-American Literature: A Vernacular Theory* (Chicago: University of Chicago Press, 1984), pp. 124–25, 137–38

JOANNE M. BRAXTON   Throughout the Harlem Renaissance, Dunbar remained a model for writers as diverse as Countee Cullen and Langston Hughes, both of whom considered Dunbar a great poet. Langston Hughes wrote his first "Dunbarstyle" folk poem when he was still in high school and published it later in his collection *The Dream Keeper*. Likewise, Cullen eulogized Dunbar with the poem "To Paul Laurence Dunbar," published in his first collection of poetry, *Color* (1925): Indeed, there was much to bind Dunbar's legacy with the spirit of what some would call "these bad New Negroes." To begin with, there was what James A. Emanuel calls Dunbar's "racial fire," his pride in his blackness and his outcry against the oppression of his people, his well-directed if sometimes too understated anger. Then there is Dunbar's appreciation of the significance of his racial and cultural heritage, his loving depiction of the black man and woman farthest down, and his musical rendition of musical black folk language: in short, his daring creation of something completely original, new and unique—an Afrocentric poetic diction that transcended the racist heritage of the plantation tradition and did more than strive to imitate the Anglo-Saxon literary past. The more avant-garde of the Harlem Renaissance artists especially were to identify with and build upon these Dunbar innovations. Likewise, they would struggle with the demands of a predominantly white readership and its insistence on illustrations of black life that were at times more in keeping with its own taste than with the black writer's quest for the artistic freedom and authenticity.

In the final analysis, it is difficult to answer the question of whether Dunbar *unconsciously* acquiesced to racist stereotypes. One could argue that because the dialect tradition Dunbar inherited was so completely and fully invested with negative and demeaning images of blackness, it was not possible for him to be successful, in every instance, in inverting these associations to "signify" on his received linguistic heritage. Perhaps what Dunbar attempted to do, in the words of contemporary black poet Audre Lorde, was "to dismantle the master's house using the master's tools," an extremely difficult if not impossible task. Despite Dunbar's success in writing dialect poetry, he was rightly uncomfortable with the approval he garnered from mainstream white critics, because he knew that they were deaf to his voice of protest and that they misread his work and praised it for the wrong reasons; they did not possess Dunbar's cultural background, his keen ear, or his sympathetic racial sensibility.

Joanne M. Braxton, "Introduction," *The Collected Poetry of Paul Laurence Dunbar* (Charlottesville: University of Virginia Press, 1993), pp. xxix–xxx

Bibliography

Oak and Ivy. 1893.
Majors and Minors. 1895.
Lyrics of Lowly Life. 1896.
African Romances (with Samuel Coleridge-Taylor). 1897.
Folks from Dixie. 1898.

The Uncalled. 1898.

Dream Lovers. 1898.

Lyrics of the Hearthside. 1899.

Poems of Cabin and Field. 1899.

The Strength of Gideon and Other Stories. 1900.

The Love of Landry. 1900.

Uncle Eph's Christmas: A One Act Negro Musical Sketch (with Will Marion Cook). 1900.

The Fanatics. 1901.

Candle-Lightin' Time. 1901.

The Sport of the Gods. 1902.

Lyrics of Love and Laughter. 1902.

In Old Plantation Days. 1903.

When Malindy Sings. 1903.

The Heart of Happy Hollow. 1904.

Li'l' Gal. 1904.

Lyrics of Sunshine and Shadow. 1905.

Howdy, Honey, Howdy. 1905.

A Plantation Portrait. 1905.

Joggin' Erlong. 1906.

Chris'mus Is a'Comin' and Other Poems. 1907.

Life and Works. Ed. Lina Keck Wiggins. 1907.

Complete Poems. 1913.

Speakin' o' Christmas and Other Christmas and Special Poems. 1914.

Best Stories. Ed. Benjamin Brawley. 1938.

Little Brown Baby: Poems for Young People. Ed. Bertha Rodgers. 1940.

The Paul Laurence Dunbar Reader. Ed. Jay Martin and Gossie H. Hudson. 1975.

I Greet the Dawn. Ed. Ashley Bryan. 1978.

Collected Poetry. Ed. Joanne M. Braxton. 1993.

Langston Hughes
1902–1967

JAMES LANGSTON HUGHES was born in Joplin, Missouri, on February 1, 1902. His mother, Carrie Langston Hughes, had been a schoolteacher; his father, James Nathaniel Hughes, was a storekeeper. James left for Mexico while his son was still an infant, and the latter was raised mostly by his grandmother, Mary Langston. Hughes lived for a time in Illinois with his mother, who remarried, and went to high school in Cleveland. He spent the summer of 1919 in Mexico with his father, then taught for a year in Mexican schools. He entered Columbia University in September 1921, a few months after his poem, "The Negro Speaks of Rivers," appeared in the *Crisis* for June 1921.

After a year of schooling, Hughes took on various jobs in New York, on trans-Atlantic ships, and in Paris. He returned to America in 1925, and while working as a busboy in Washington, D.C., he slipped three poems beside Vachel Lindsay's plate. Lindsay was impressed and began promoting the young poet. In 1925 Hughes won a literary contest in *Opportunity*, and his writing career was launched. His first collection of poems, *The Weary Blues*, was published in 1926. Another volume, *Fine Clothes to the Jew*, appeared the next year. A benefactor sent Hughes to Lincoln University, from which he received a B.A. in 1929.

Hughes subsequently supported himself as a poet, novelist, and writer of stories, screenplays, articles, children's books, and songs. His first novel, *Not without Laughter*, appeared in 1930. His first short-story collection was *The Ways of White Folks* (1934). He wrote a children's book in collaboration with Arna Bontemps, *Popo and Fifina, Children of Haiti* (1932), based on a trip Hughes took to Haiti in 1931. He also collaborated with Zora Neale Hurston on a folk comedy, *Mule Bone*, but it was not published until 1991.

Having received several literary awards and fellowships in the 1930s, including a Guggenheim Fellowship in 1935, Hughes was able to write without financial worries. He promoted black theatre in both Harlem and Los Angeles, and himself wrote a number of plays, the most famous of which is *Tambourines to Glory* (1958). In 1940 he published his first autobiography, *The Big Sea*.

Hughes moved to California in 1939, settling in Hollow Hills Farm near Monterey. Two years later he moved to Chicago, and from 1942 onward he lived in Harlem. Such volumes as *Shakespeare in Harlem* (1942) and *Fields of Wonder* (1947) established him as the leading black poet in America. Hughes's Communist leanings, initially triggered by a trip to the Soviet Union in 1931, caused him to be summoned before the House Un-American Activities Committee (HUAC), where, fearful of being imprisoned or black-balled, he repudiated any Communist or socialist tendencies and maintained that his repeated calls for social justice for black Americans, expressed in his earlier work, were not incompatible with American political ideals.

In the 1950s and 1960s, Hughes gained popularity through the recurring protagonist of his stories, Jesse B. Semple, or "Simple." These stories were collected in four volumes: *Simple Speaks His Mind* (1950), *Simple Takes a Wife* (1953), *Simple Stakes a Claim* (1957), and *Simple's Uncle Sam* (1965). A selection, *The Best of Simple*, appeared in 1961. Story collections not involving Simple are *Laughing to Keep from Crying* (1952) and *Something in Common and Other Stories* (1963). A second autobiography, *I Wonder as I Wander*, was published in 1956.

In his later years Hughes devoted himself to promoting black literature by compiling anthologies of black American poetry, fiction, and folklore, and by writing nonfiction books for children, including *The First Book of Negroes* (1952), *The First Book of Jazz* (1955), and *The First Book of Africa* (1960). He received the NAACP's Spingarn Medal in 1960 and was elected to the National Institute of Arts and Letters in 1961. Hughes never married. He died of congestive heart failure in New York City on May 22, 1967.

▨ *Critical Extracts*

LANGSTON HUGHES   ⟨. . .⟩ there is, for the American Negro artist who can escape the restrictions the more advanced among his own group would put upon him, a great field of unused material ready for his art. Without going outside his race, and even among the better classes with their "white" culture and conscious American manners, but still Negro enough to be different, there is sufficient matter to furnish a black artist with a lifetime of creative work. And when he chooses to touch on the relations between Negroes and whites in this country with their innumerable overtones and undertones, surely, and especially for literature and the drama, there is an inexhaustible supply of themes at hand. To these the Negro artist can give his racial individuality, his heritage of rhythm and warmth, and his incongruous humor that so often, as in the Blues, becomes ironic laughter mixed with tears. But let us look again at the mountain.

A prominent Negro clubwoman in Philadelphia paid eleven dollars to hear Raquel Meller sing Andalusian popular songs. But she told me a few weeks before she would not think of going to hear "that woman," Clara Smith, a great black artist, sing Negro folksongs. And many an upper-class Negro church, even now, would not dream of employing a spiritual in its services. The drab melodies in white folks' hymnbooks are much to be preferred. "We want to worship the Lord correctly and quietly. We don't believe in 'shouting.' Let's be dull like the Nordics," they say, in effect.

The road for the serious black artist, then, who would produce a racial art is most certainly rocky and the mountain is high. Until recently he received almost no encouragement for his work from either white or colored people. The fine novels of Chesnutt go out of print with neither race noticing their passing. The quaint charm and humor of Dunbar's dialect verse brought to him, in his day, largely the same kind of encouragement one would give a sideshow freak (A colored man writing poetry! How odd!) or a clown (How amusing!).

The present vogue in things Negro, although it may do as much harm as good for the budding colored artist, has at least done this: it has brought him forcibly to the attention of his own people among whom for so long, unless the other race had noticed him beforehand, he was a prophet with little honor. I understand that Charles Gilpin acted for years in Negro theaters without any special acclaim from his own, but when Broadway gave him eight curtain calls, Negroes, too, began to beat a tin pan in his honor. I know a young colored writer, a manual worker by day, who had been writing well for the colored magazines for some years, but it was not until he recently broke into the white publications and his first book was accepted by a prominent New York publisher that the "best" Negroes in his city took the trouble to discover that he lived there. Then almost immediately they decided to give a grand dinner for him. But the society ladies were careful to whisper to his mother that perhaps she'd better not come. They were not sure she would have an evening gown.

The Negro artist works against an undertow of sharp criticism and misunderstanding from his own group and unintentional bribes from the whites. "O, be respectable, write about nice people, show how good we are," say the Negroes. "Be stereotyped, don't go too far, don't shatter our illusions about you, don't amuse us too seriously. We will pay you," say the whites. Both would have told Jean Toomer not to write *Cane*. The colored people did not praise it. The white people did not buy it. Most of the colored people who did read *Cane* hate it. They are afraid of it. Although the critics gave it good reviews the public remained indifferent. Yet (excepting the work of Du Bois) *Cane* contains the finest prose written by a Negro in America. And like the singing of Robeson, it is truly racial. ⟨. . .⟩

Let the blare of Negro jazz bands and the bellowing voice of Bessie Smith singing Blues penetrate the closed ears of the colored near-intellectuals until they listen and perhaps understand. Let Paul Robeson singing Water Boy, and Rudolph Fisher writing about the streets of Harlem, and Jean Toomer holding the heart of Georgia in his hands, and Aaron Douglas drawing strange black fantasies cause the smug Negro middle class to turn from their white, respectable, ordinary books and papers to catch a glimmer of their own beauty. We younger Negro artists who create now intend to express our individual dark-skinned selves without fear or shame. If white people are pleased we are glad. If they are not, it doesn't matter. We know we are beautiful. And ugly too. The tom-tom cries and the tom-tom laughs. If colored people are pleased we are glad. If they are not, their displeasure doesn't matter either. We build our temples for tomorrow, strong as we know how, and we stand on top of the mountain, free within ourselves.

Langston Hughes, "The Negro Artist and the Racial Mountain" (1926), *Langston Hughes Review* 4, No. 1 (Spring 1985): 2–4

ALAIN LOCKE   Fine clothes may not make either the poet or the gentleman, but they certainly help; and it is a rare genius that can strip life to the buff and still poetize it. This, however, Langston Hughes has done, in a volume ⟨*Fine Clothes to the Jew*⟩ that is even more starkly realistic and colloquial than his first,—*The Weary Blues*. It is a current ambition in American poetry to take the common clay of life and fashion it to living beauty, but very few have succeeded, even Masters and Sandburg not invariably. They get their effects, but too often at the expense of poetry. Here, on the contrary, there is scarcely a prosaic note or a spiritual sag in spite of the fact that never has cruder colloquialism or more sordid life been put into the substance of poetry. The book is, therefore, notable as an achievement in poetic realism in addition to its particular value as a folk study in verse of Negro life.

The success of these poems owes much to the clever and apt device of taking folk-song forms and idioms as the mold into which the life of the plain people is descriptively poured. This gives not only an authentic background and the impression that it is the people themselves speaking, but the sordidness of common life is caught up in the lilt of its own poetry and without any sentimental propping attains something of the necessary elevation of art. Many of the poems are modelled in the exact metrical form of the Negro "Blues," now so suddenly popular, and in thought and style of expression are so close as scarcely to be distinguishable from the popular variety. But these poems are not transcriptions, every now and then one catches sight of the deft poetic touch that unostentatiously transforms them into folk portraits. ⟨. . .⟩ The author apparently loves the plain people in every aspect of their lives, their gin-drinking carousals, their street brawls, their tenement publicity, and their slum matings and partings, and reveals this segment of Negro life as it has never been shown before. Its open frankness will be a shock and a snare for the critic and moralist who cannot distinguish clay from mire. The poet has himself said elsewhere,—"The 'low-down' Negroes furnish a wealth of colorful, distinctive material for any artist, because they hold their individuality in the face of American standardizations. And perhaps these common people will give to the world its truly great Negro artist, the one who is not afraid to be himself." And as one watches Langston Hughes's own career, one wonders.

Alain Locke, "Common Clay and Poetry," *Nation*, 9 April 1927, p. 712

ARNA BONTEMPS   Few people have enjoyed being Negro as much as Langston Hughes. Despite the bitterness with which he has occasionally indicted those who mistreat him because of his color (and in this collection of sketches and stories ⟨*Laughing to Keep from Crying*⟩ he certainly does not let up), there has never been any question in this reader's mind about his basic attitude. He would not have missed the experience of being what he is for the world.

The story "Why, You Reckon?," which appeared originally in *The New Yorker*, is really a veiled expression of his own feeling. Disguised as a young Park Avenue bachelor who comes with a group of wealthy friends for a night of colorful, if not primitive, entertainment in a Harlem night club, the Langston Hughes of a couple of decades ago can be clearly detected. He too had come exploring and looking for fun in the unfamiliar territory north of 125th Street. The kidnapping and robbing of the visitor in the story is of course contrived, but the young man's reluctance to rejoin his friends or to go back to the safety of his home downtown reflects the author's own commentary. "This is the first exciting thing that's ever happened to me," he has the white victim say to the amazement of his abductors as he stands in a coal bin stripped of his overcoat and shoes, his wallet and studs. "This was real."

Over this tale, as over most of the others in *Laughing to Keep from Crying*, the depression of the Thirties hangs ominously, and it serves as more than just an indication of the dates of their writing. It provides a kind of continuity. After a while it begins to suggest the nameless dread which darkens human lives without reference to breadlines and relief agencies. ⟨. . .⟩

Langston Hughes has practiced the craft of the short story no more than he has practiced the forms of poetry. His is a spontaneous art which stands or falls by the sureness of his intuition, his mother wit. His stories, like his poems, are for readers who will judge them with their hearts as well as their heads. By that standard he has always measured well. He still does.

Arna Bontemps, "Black & Bubbling," Saturday Review, 5 April 1952, p. 17

WILLIAM MILES   Few writers have been as prolific in their attempt to describe and interpret Negro American life as Langston Hughes. Poet, novelist, short story writer, and dramatist, "he writes to express those truths he feels need expressing about characters he believes need to be recognized" ⟨Webster Smalley⟩. One such truth is the forced isolation of the majority of black people by the culture within which they are forced by circumstance to exist. The intensity and repressiveness of such isolation alienates the black person not only from the culture at large, but frequently from his own brothers as well. This is the theme of Hughes' powerful one-act play, *Soul*

Gone Home. In less than four pages of text he presents a tragic and poignant picture of a people so isolated from each other that the establishment of meaningful emotional relationship is no longer possible.

The theme of isolation is not, of course, original with Hughes. What is original in *Soul Gone Home,* however, is the manner in which this theme is treated. The play is a fantasy of both situation and structure. Reality as we commonly experience it is replaced by the unreal, the dreamlike; the usual physical laws governing life and death are suspended. Yet the emphasis of the play is clearly on things as they exist in actuality. The play is about a situation resulting from the condition of black people in America. The immediate situation explored within the fantastic world of the play is itself unreal: a conflict between an uncaring mother and the ghost of her dead son in which the latter condemns his mother ("You been a hell of a mamma! . . . I say you been a no-good mamma.") because she failed to provide him with the necessities of life, food, clothing, "manners and morals."

This internal conflict in the realm of fantasy forms the center of the drama, but the structural limits are defined by reality. *Soul Gone Home* begins with the mother grieving over her son's body and concludes with his removal by the ambulance drivers. However, Hughes has constructed even these apparently real incidents in such a way as to render them unreal. For example, the opening stage direction informs us that the mother is "loudly simulating grief" and the play ends on the same note with her again feigning grief in the presence of the indifferent ambulance drivers.

The importance of both this underlying structure and the unreality of the situation is that they immediately establish the fact of the isolated condition of the mother and son. The boy is, of course, apart from the real world in the sense that he is dead, and, likewise, the mother is removed by the very fact that she can openly converse with him. Indeed, the mother is actually doubly removed: her "real" life, or what glimpses we get of it, is characterized by a sense of unreality. Symbolically, therefore, she is not a part of the reality defined by the general society, and her being outside in large part is the result of her race. To emphasize this fact, Hughes underlines the isolated condition of both mother and son through their lack of relatedness to the white ambulance drivers. Both are completely oblivious and indifferent to the dead boy and the tears of the "grieving" mother, and their lack of responsiveness to the situation is a measure of the vast gulf separating black and white.

Structurally, therefore, fantasy functions to establish the complete physical isolation of the two main characters from the real world. The focal point of the play, the inability of mother and son to relate on the emotional level, exists in a cause-and-effect relationship with their isolation from the society: forced and repressive physical isolation of one group by another results in severe emotional alienation among members of the persecuted group. In developing and emphasizing this emotional element, Hughes superimposes upon his fantasy clear implications of stark reality. Thus the total effect of *Soul Gone Home* is realism, and while the central conflict may be internal, the implied commentary relates wholly to the external world. ⟨. . .⟩

Through the skillful combination of situation, structure, character and symbol, Hughes has produced a compact and powerful play of a people so isolated that even the ordinarily secure relationship between mother and son is impossible. And while this thematic consideration is immediately revelant to the Negro American, *Soul Gone Home* does achieve a sense of universality in that its social commentary relates to any oppressed minority.

William Miles, "Isolation in Langston Hughes' *Soul Gone Home*," *Five Black Writers: Essays on Wright, Ellison, Baldwin, Hughes, and Leroi Jones*, ed. Donald B. Gibson (New York: New York University Press, 1970), pp. 178–79, 182

JULIAN C. CAREY   Simple's greatest challenge to his *négritude* comes from his friend and bourgeois foil, "I." An articulate, sophisticated, educated Negro liberal, the antagonist questions Simple's militancy and simple solutions to his problem. Simple, for example, is amazed that "white folks is scared to come to Harlem," when it is he who should be afraid of them: "The white race drug me over from Africa, slaved me, freed me, lynched me, starved me during the depression, jim crowed me during the war—then they come talking about they is scared of me!" "I" reminds him that he sounds just like a Negro nationalist, "someone who wants Negroes to be on top." Simple replies, "when everybody else keeps me on the bottom, I don't see why I shouldn't want to be on top. I will, too, someday." The antagonist asks Simple to have an open mind about white people, to separate the good ones from the bad, to which he replies, "I have near about lost my mind worrying with them. . . . In fact, they have hurt my soul." "I" then reminds him that white people "blasted each other down with V-bombs during the war." However equally distributed the white man's brutality, "to be shot down is bad for the body," says Simple, "but to be Jim Crowed is worse for the spirit."

Simple, however, is not entirely antagonistic to white people. He would just like for them to experience and endure his life; he wants to "share and share alike." He believes that if the "good white friends" that "I" mentions would share a hot old half-baggage jim crow train car with him or use a "COLORED" toilet in a Southern town, they would stop resolving and start solving. "I" tells Simple that it is against the law for white people to use colored facilities down South and asks if he wants "decent white folks to get locked up just to prove they love [him]?" "I get locked up for going in their waiting rooms," responds Simple, "so why shouldn't they get locked up for going in mine." "Your explanation depresses me," "I" states. "Your nonsense depresses me," replies Simple.

There is yet another conflict involving his *négritude* that Simple has with "I," and it is an intellectual one. Being educated and "observing life for literary purposes," "I" finds fault with Simple's verse when the latter expresses himself poetically. It would seem that the antagonist is trying to make a poet out of a Negro, but Simple would just as soon remain a Negro poet. After spending a creative week-end at Orchard Beach, but being sure that the "violent rays" did not tamper with his complexion, Simple shows his "colleged" friend a poem: "Sitting under the trees / With the birds and the bees / Watching the girls go by." Recalling his literary training, "I" states that Simple "ought to have another rhyme. . . . 'By' ought to rhyme with 'sky' or something." Simple fails to see the reasoning behind the request, for he "was not looking up at no sky. . . . [He] was looking at the girls." When Simple tries to imitate Elizabethan verse (he pronounces it "Lizzie Beasley"), he is told his lyric is doggerel; but not discouraged by his friend's remarks, he reminds "I" that "you don't learn everything in books." Though the men, at times, strain the bonds of their friendship, their discussions, no matter how heated, usually end with Simple ordering "two beers for two steers" and then saying, "Pay for them, chum!"

Julian C. Carey, "Jesse B. Semple Revisited and Revised," *Phylon* 32, No. 2 (Summer 1971): 160–61.

FAITH BERRY   The House Un-American Activities Committee (HUAC) was reaching out like an octopus and, by 1950, was referring to Hughes in its documents. ⟨. . .⟩

Hughes did not know what the repercussions would be when he appeared before the McCarthy Committee on March 26, 1953. He did know that some witnesses, in order to save themselves, had destroyed others by "naming names," which he was determined not to do. He knew, too, that others who had taken the Fifth Amendment had ended up in jail or, worse, as suicides. Having seen enough careers broken, he could not be sure that the same would not happen to him. ⟨. . .⟩

When McCarthy sounded the gavel at the public hearing and came face to face with Hughes and his lawyer for this encounter, Frank D. Reeves, it appeared they were meeting for the first time. In fact, they had already met privately in executive session—first with ⟨Roy⟩ Cohn and ⟨G. David⟩ Schine, and then in the Senator's office. Cohn, a harsher interrogator than Schine, had grilled Hughes about some of his writings. McCarthy, however, was anxious that a renowned American author should not become a "hostile witness." He had worked out an arrangement whereby Hughes would not be asked to "name names" of known Communists, but only in order to admit tacitly his own pro-Communist sympathies and writings. Having been indecisive about whether he would testify at all, after much private discussion with Reeves, he finally agreed to cooperate in the McCarthy scenario. He feared the worst if he didn't. Raising his right hand, he said, "I do," when the Senator asked him, "Do you swear to tell the whole truth and nothing but the truth, so help you God?"

On the witness stand, Hughes confessed that "there was such a period" when Cohn asked whether he had been a believer in the Soviet form of government; and "I certainly did," when questioned whether he wrote poetry which reflected his feelings during that time; and "That is correct, sir," when Cohn added, "I understand your testimony to be that you never actually joined the Communist Party." But so hard did he try to tell the truth about his past Soviet sympathies and at the same time sound like a patriotic American that he was only a shadow of himself. "A complete reorientation of my thinking and feelings occurred roughly four or five years ago," he offered, but Cohn quickly interjected "I notice that in 1949 you made a statement in defense of the Communist leaders who were on trial, which was in the *Daily Worker*." Hughes said he believed "one can and does" get a fair trial in America. Pressed to defend "When a Man Sees Red" and other works, he got away with, "They do not represent my current thinking," and "I have more recent books I would prefer." Asked to explain his "complete change in ideology," he affirmed, "I have always been a believer in the American form of government." There were moments when, pulverized into submission, he did disparage the Soviet Union. Praised by Southern Senator John McClellan for his "refreshing and comforting testimony," Hughes finally asked McCarthy, after about an hour of the inquisition, "Am I excused now, sir?" McCarthy finally let him go, after announcing he had "included in the record, on request," Hughes's earlier poem, "Goodbye, Christ" "to show the type of thinking of Mr. Hughes at that time." To show he also had been a "friendly witness," he sought assurance from the poet that he had not been "in any way mistreated by the staff or by the Committee." The capitulation was complete, from beginning to end.

Faith Berry, *Langston Hughes: Before and Beyond Harlem* (Westport, CT: Lawrence Hill, 1983), pp. 317–19.

R. BAXTER MILLER   Though Hughes accepted explicitly the Marxist belief that history produces events and men—namely, the doctrine of Darwinian determinism—he believed as well that people determine their own fate, for he almost never minimized human will. When fiscal policies brought on the Great Depression of the United States in the 1930s and the subsequent aggression helped provoke World War II, he still dreamed.

Hughes, believing in Marxism more discursively than naturally, is ambiguous on the subject. Facing the basic conceptions of materialism and colonialism, he seeks to bridge the rupture between the material form of the English language and the ironic need to materialize through this very language those ideas that seem at odds with a Euro-American perspective. To him, writing becomes intellectual armament against colonialism throughout the world. While *A New Song* (1938) illustrates his inability at the age of thirty-six to analyze the complex flaws of liberal idealism, he is not naive about historical evil.

Hughes resists the Marxist tendency to repress conscience in order to make history evolve according to some preordained pattern. *Jim Crow's Last Stand* (1943) shows his intransigence to disillusion and his potential for self-recovery.

> Some folks think
> By burning books
> They burn freedom.
> . . . .

Some folks think
By lynching a Negro
They lynch freedom.
But freedom
Stands up and laughs
In their faces,
And says,
You'll *never kill me!* ["Freedom"]

Even in *Good Morning Revolution*, which lacks the structural and chronological unity of the other published works, the tension appears strongly. And
when Hughes subsequently confronts the social history of the years 1963–67,
including the deaths of martyrs, and seems sometimes to abandon all hope,
it is rarely for long. Where such psychological complexities recur in *Ask
Your Mama* (1961), memory and human consciousness take shape through
words. Hughes provides, finally, not the mere reflection of history but a
brilliant and metaphoric code by which to read the record profoundly. The
narrative conscience does threaten in *The Panther and the Lash* (1967) to
regress into inevitable brutality, as the counterpart to an even greater savagery imposed upon the Black self ⟨. . .⟩ Yet, the collapse remains incomplete.

Langston Hughes gives verbal shape to the political and psychological
struggle of humanity, particularly in American civilization. What is necessary
for a reassessment of his political imagination is a careful reading of the
developmental cycle that passes from direct didacticism (*A New Song*, 1938)
through a more liberal and lyrical kind of political statement (*Jim Crow's
Last Stand*, 1943) to a more symbolic rendition of the political world (*Good
Morning Revolution*, 1925–53, collected 1972) and finally to a great psychological complexity (*Ask Your Mama*, 1961). Near the end of Hughes' life
(*The Panther and the Lash*, 1967) his political imagination returns almost
to the tone with which it began, though with some lyrical qualification.

R. Baxter Miller, *The Art and Imagination of Langston Hughes* (Lexington: University
Press of Kentucky, 1989), pp. 67–69

KAREN JACKSON FORD   ⟨. . .⟩ "The Negro Speaks of Rivers"
is one of Hughes's most uncharacteristic poems, and yet it has defined his
reputation, along with a small but constant selection of other poems included
in anthologies. "The Negro Speaks of Rivers," "A House in Taos," "The
Weary Blues," "Montage of a Dream Deferred," "Theme for English B,"
"Refugee in America," and "I, Too"—these poems invariably comprise his

anthology repertoire despite the fact that none of them typifies his writing. What makes these poems atypical is exactly what makes them appealing and intelligible to the scholars who edit anthologies—their complexity. True, anthologies produced in the current market, which is hospitable to the African-American tradition and to canon reform, now include a brief selection of poems in black folk forms. But even though Hughes has fared better in anthologies than most African-American writers, only a small and predictable segment of his poetry has been preserved. A look back through the original volumes of poetry, and even through the severely redrawn *Selected Poems*, reveals a wealth of simpler poems we ought to be reading. ⟨. . .⟩

The repression of the great bulk of Hughes's poems is the result of chronic critical scorn for their simplicity. Throughout his long career, but especially after his first two volumes of poetry (readers were at first willing to assume that a youthful poet might grow to be more complex), his books received their harshest reviews for a variety of "flaws" that all originate in an aesthetics of simplicity. From his first book, *The Weary Blues* (1926), to his last one, *The Panther and the Lash* (1967), the reviews invoke a litany of faults: the poems are superficial, infantile, silly, small, unpoetic, common, jejune, iterative, and, of course, simple. Even his admirers reluctantly conclude that Hughes's poetics failed. Saunders Redding flatly opposes simplicity and artfulness: "While Hughes's rejection of his own growth shows an admirable loyalty to his self-commitment as the poet of the 'simple, Negro commonfolk' . . . it does a disservice to his art." James Baldwin, who recognizes the potential of simplicity as an artistic principle, faults the poems for "tak[ing] refuge . . . in a fake simplicity in order to avoid the very difficult simplicity of the experience."

Despite a lifetime of critical disappointments, then, Hughes remained loyal to the aesthetic program he had outlined in 1926 in his decisive poetic treatise, "The Negro Artist and the Racial Mountain." There he had predicted that the common people would "give to this world its truly great Negro artist, the one who is not afraid to be himself," a poet who would explore the "great field of unused [folk] material ready for his art" and recognize that this source would provide "sufficient matter to furnish a black artist with a lifetime of creative work." This is clearly a portrait of the poet Hughes would become, and he maintained his fidelity to this ideal at great cost to his literary reputation.

Karen Jackson Ford, "Do Right to Write Right: Langston Hughes's Aesthetics of Simplicity," *Twentieth Century Literature* 38, No. 4 (Winter 1992): 436–38

HANS OSTROM   ⟨. . .⟩ Hughes's stories implicitly define a kind of story that is different from modernist modes crafted by James Joyce, Katherine Mansfield, Ernest Hemingway, and others. In this as in other matters, Hughes was something of an anomaly; he was an "old-fashioned innovator." He was old-fashioned in the sense that he was drawn to the story-as-tale or the story-as-sketch and preferred a style less polished and less elliptical than that of most modernists. ⟨. . .⟩ But he was an innovator in the way he boldly handled issues of race and class in short fiction, made use of an oral tradition, and especially in the way he developed the very brief, dialogue-dependent Simple stories.

Examining a cross section of the narrative modes within Hughes's short fiction, at least three main forms emerge: the traditional dramatic story with a clear plot, conflict, and resolution; the sketch, with a journalistic or nonfiction texture and muted dramatic action; and the "oral" story, heavily dependent on monologue and dialogue and often featuring different kinds of wordplay. ⟨. . .⟩

Hughes's narrative counterrevolution in favor of plot did not spring from literary conservatism, however, nor from an antipathy to Joyce, Mansfield, or any of the writers who would later be termed modernists. Hughes's main link to the modernists, after all, is D. H. Lawrence, himself an odd-person-out with regard to narrative style and structure. In part because he was inspired by Lawrence's direct, socially alert stories, Hughes started writing short fiction with social critique uppermost in mind. A lyrical, elliptical, subtle mode would not have served the purpose of presenting "the ways of white folks" and the collisions in society that racism caused. In other words, Hughes was often if not always drawn to the relatively uncomplicated narrative vehicle exemplified by Lawrence's fiction because it enabled him to dramatize racial friction. Ironically, what is so original about his short fiction, its economic and social critique of the racial "landscape," is exactly the element that drew him in many instances to a tried-and-true, conservative narrative mode. By contrast, Joyce, Mansfield, Hemingway, and Stein all seemed nearly obsessed with the stylistic "surface" of their stories, even if these writers offer social critique of a different kind. ⟨. . .⟩

Because the Simple stories embody many of the critical tenets Hughes defined early in his career, it may be tempting to overlook how different they are from his other short fiction; but if only *The Ways of White Folks* and *Laughing to Keep from Crying* were examined, Hughes would not be judged a master of the dialogue-based short story. The Simple stories clearly allowed him to link the orality of his plays and poetry with the short-fiction genre, without abandoning other elements which had made his earlier stories successful: his political and social alertness; his eye for dramatic situations; his allegiance to everyday subjects; and his psychological acumen.

Certainly, Hughes's milieu, his preoccupations, were significantly different from those of Ernest Hemingway, but in the Simple stories, Hughes equaled the Hemingway of "Hills Like White Elephants" or "A Clean, Well-Lighted Place," in his capacity to base a narrative almost entirely on dialogue and make it succeed. The Simple stories bringing Hughes acclaim for their humor, accessibility, and topicality, also earn him a place among the best innovators of short fiction.

> Hans Ostrom, *Langston Hughes: A Study of the Short Fiction* (New York: Twayne, 1993), pp. 56–57, 59

⊞ *Bibliography*

The Weary Blues. 1926.

Fine Clothes to the Jew. 1927.

Not without Laughter. 1930.

The Negro Mother and Other Dramatic Recitations. 1931.

Dear Lovely Death. 1931.

The Dream Keeper and Other Poems. 1932.

Popo and Fifina, Children of Haiti (with Arna Bontemps). 1932.

Scottsboro Limited: Four Poems and a Play in Verse. 1932.

The Ways of White Folks. 1934.

A New Song. 1938.

The Big Sea: An Autobiography. 1940.

Shakespeare in Harlem. 1942.

Freedom's Plow. 1943.

Jim Crow's Last Stand. 1943.

Lament for Dark Peoples and Other Poems. Ed. H. Driessen. 1944.

This Is My Land (with Toy Harper and La Villa Tullos). c. 1945.

Fields of Wonder. 1947.

Street Scene (adapter; with Kurt Weill). 1948.

Cuba Libre: Poems by Nicolás Guillén (translator; with Ben Frederic Carruthers). 1948.

Troubled Island (adapter; with William Grant Still). 1949.

One-Way Ticket. 1949.

The Poetry of the Negro 1746–1949 (editor; with Arna Bontemps). 1949, 1970.

Simple Speaks His Mind. 1950.

Montage of a Dream Deferred. 1951.

The First Book of Negroes. 1952.

Laughing to Keep from Crying. 1952.

Simple Takes a Wife. 1953.

Famous American Negroes. 1954.

The First Book of Rhythms. 1954.

Famous Negro Music Makers. 1955.

The First Book of Jazz. 1955.

The Sweet Flypaper of Life (with Roy De Carava). 1955.

The First Book of the West Indies. 1956.

I Wonder as I Wander: An Autobiographical Journey. 1956.

A Pictorial History of the Negro in America (with Milton Meltzer). 1956, 1963, 1968.

Selected Poems of Gabriela Mistral (translator). 1957.

Simple Stakes a Claim. 1957.

The Book of Negro Folklore (editor; with Arna Bontemps). 1958.

Famous Negro Heroes of America. 1958.

The Langston Hughes Reader. 1958.

Tambourines to Glory. 1958.

Simply Heavenly: A Comedy with Music (with David Martin). 1959.

Selected Poems. 1959.

An African Treasury (editor). 1960.

The First Book of Africa. 1960, 1964.

Ask Your Mama: Twelve Moods for Jazz. 1961.

The Best of Simple. 1961.

Fight for Freedom: The Story of NAACP. 1962.

Five Plays. Ed. Webster Smalley. 1963.

Poems from Black Africa (editor). 1963.

Something in Common and Other Stories. 1963.

New Negro Poets U.S.A. (editor). 1964.

Simple's Uncle Sam. 1965.

The Book of Negro Humor (editor). 1965.

The Best Short Stories by Negro Writers: Anthology from 1899 to the Present (editor). 1967.

Black Magic: A Pictorial History of the Negro in American Entertainment (with Milton Meltzer). 1967.

The Panther and the Lash: Poems of Our Times. 1967.

Black Misery. 1969.

Don't You Turn Back: Poems. Ed. Lee Bennett Hopkins. 1969.

Good Morning, Revolution: Uncollected Social Protest Writings. Ed. Faith Berry. 1973.

Langston Hughes in the Hispanic World and Haiti. Ed. Edward J. Mullen. 1977.

Arna Bontemps–Langston Hughes Letters 1925–1967. Ed. Charles H. Nichols. 1980.

Mule Bone: A Comedy of Negro Life (with Zora Neale Hurston). Ed. George Houston Bass and Henry Louis Gates, Jr. 1991.

Zora Neale Hurston
c. 1891–1960

ZORA NEALE HURSTON was born probably on January 7, 1891, although she frequently gave her birth date as 1901 or 1903. She was born and raised in America's first all-black incorporated town, Eatonville, Florida. Her father, John Hurston, was a former sharecropper who became a carpenter, preacher, and three-term mayor in Eatonville. Her mother, Lucy Hurston, died in 1904; two weeks after her death, Hurston was sent to Jacksonville, Florida, to school, but wound up neglected by her remarried father and worked a variety of menial jobs. A five-year gap in her personal history at this time has led some biographers to conjecture that she was married; however, no evidence exists to support or disprove this speculation. In 1917 she began studies at Morgan Academy in Baltimore and in 1918 attended Howard University, where her first short story appeared in the college literary magazine. She later won a scholarship to Barnard College to study with the eminent anthropologist Franz Boas.

While living in New York Hurston worked as a secretary to the popular novelist Fannie Hurst. Though she only lived in New York for a short time, Hurston is considered a major force in the Harlem Renaissance of the 1920s and 1930s. She was an associate editor for the one-issue avant-garde journal *Fire!!* and she collaborated on several plays with various writers, including *Mule Bone: A Comedy of Negro Life*, written with Langston Hughes. Boas arranged a fellowship for Hurston that allowed her to travel throughout the South and collect folklore. The result of these travels was the publication of Hurston's first collection of black folk tales, *Mules and Men* (1935). Hurston is thought to be the first black American to have collected and published Afro-American folklore, and both of her collections have become much used sources for myths and legends of black culture. Her interest in anthropology took her to several Latin American countries, including Jamaica, Haiti, and Honduras. Her experiences in Jamaica and Haiti appear in her second collection of folk tales, *Tell My Horse* (1938).

Hurston's first novel, *Jonah's Gourd Vine* (1934), is loosely based on the lives of her parents in Eatonville. It was written shortly after *Mules and Men* (although it was published first) and has been criticized as being more of an anthropological study than a novel. Her best-known work, the novel *Their Eyes Were Watching God*, was published in 1937. Written after a failed love affair, *Their Eyes Were Watching God* focuses on a middle-aged woman's quest for fulfillment in an oppressive society. Hurston also wrote *Moses, Man of the Mountain* (1939), an attempt to fuse biblical narrative and folk myth. In addition to her life as a writer, Hurston worked temporarily as a teacher, a librarian at an Air Force base, a staff writer at Paramount Studios, and as a reporter for the *Fort Pierce* (Florida) *Chronicle*.

Her autobiography, *Dust Tracks on a Road*, won the 1943 Annisfield Award. Her final novel, *Seraph on the Suwanee*, appeared in 1948. An attempt to universalize the issues addressed in *Their Eyes Were Watching God*, *Seraph* is Hurston's only novel to feature white protagonists. Hurston's other honors include Guggenheim Fellowships in 1936 and 1938. She wrote for various magazines in the 1950s, but her increasingly conservative views concerning race relations effectively alienated her from black intellectual culture. She died on January 28, 1960, in Fort Pierce, Florida.

▨ *Critical Extracts*

H. I. BROCK   The writer has gone back to her native Florida village—a Negro settlement—with her native racial quality entirely unspoiled by her Northern college education. She has plunged into the social pleasures of the black community and made a record ⟨*Mules and Men*⟩ of what is said and done when Negroes are having a good gregarious time, dancing, singing, fishing, and above all, and incessantly, talking. ⟨. . .⟩

The book is packed with tall tales rich with flavor and alive with characteristic turns of speech. Those of us who have known the Southern Negro from our youth find him here speaking the language of his tribe as familiarly as if it came straight out of his own mouth and had not been translated into type and transmitted through the eye to the ear. Which is to say that a very tricky dialect has been rendered with rare simplicity and fidelity into

symbols so little adequate to convey its true values that the achievement
is remarkable.

H. I. Brock, "The Full, True Flavor of Life in a Negro Community," *New York Times
Book Review*, 18 November 1935, p. 4

STERLING A. BROWN   Janie's grandmother ⟨in *Their Eyes Were
Watching God*⟩, remembering how in slavery she was used "for a work-ox
and a brood sow," and remembering her daughter's shame, seeks Janie's
security above all else. But to Janie, her husband, for all his sixty acres,
looks like "some old skull-head in de graveyard," and she goes off down
the road with slack-talking Jody Sparks. In Eatonville, an all-colored town,
Jody becomes the "big voice," but Janie is first neglected and then brow-
beaten. When Jody dies, Tea-Cake, with his contagious high spirits, whirls
Janie into a marriage, idyllic until Tea-Cake's tragic end. Janie returns home,
grief-stricken but fulfilled. Better than her grandmother's security, she had
found out about living for herself.

Filling out Janie's story are sketches of Eatonville and farming down "on
the muck" in the Everglades. On the porch of the mayor's store "big old
lies" and comic-serious debates, with the tallest of metaphors, while away
the evenings. The dedication of the town's first lamp and the community
burial of an old mule are rich in humor but they are not cartoons. Many
incidents are unusual, and there are narrative gaps in need of building up.
Miss Hurston's forte is the recording and the creation of folk-speech. Her
devotion to these people has rewarded her; *Their Eyes Were Watching God*
is chock-full of earthy and touching poetry. ⟨. . .⟩

But this is not *the* story of Miss Hurston's own people, as the foreword
states, for *the* Negro novel is as unachievable as the Great American Novel.
Living in an all-colored town, these people escape the worst pressures of
class and caste. There is little harshness; there is enough money and work
to go around. The author does not dwell upon the "people ugly from
ignorance and broken from being poor" who swarm upon the "muck" for
short-time jobs. But there is bitterness, sometimes oblique, in the enforced
folk manner, and sometimes forthright. The slave, Nanny, for bearing too
light a child with gray eyes, is ordered a terrible beating by her mistress,
who in her jealousy is perfectly willing to "stand the loss" if the beating is
fatal. And after the hurricane there is a great to-do lest white and black

victims be buried together. To detect the race of the long-unburied corpses, the conscripted grave-diggers must examine the hair. The whites get pine coffins; the Negroes get quick-lime. "They's mighty particular how dese dead folks goes tuh judgment. Look lak they think God don't know nothin' 'bout de Jim Crow law."

Sterling A. Brown, " 'Luck Is a Fortune,' " *Nation*, 16 October 1937, pp. 409–10

RICHARD WRIGHT   *Their Eyes Were Watching God* is the story of Zora Neale Hurston's Janie who, at sixteen, married a grubbing farmer at the anxious instigation of her slave-born grandmother. The romantic Janie, in the highly charged language of Miss Hurston, longed to be a pear in blossom and have a "dust-bearing bee sink into the sanctum of a bloom; the thousand sister-calyxes arch to meet the love embrace." Restless, she fled from her farmer husband and married Jody, an up-and-coming Negro business man who, in the end, proved to be no better than her first husband. After twenty years of clerking for her self-made Jody, Janie found herself a frustrated widow of forty with a small fortune on her hands. Tea Cake, "from in and through Georgia," drifted along and, despite his youth, Janie took him. For more than two years they lived happily; but Tea Cake was bitten by a mad dog and was infected with rabies. One night in a canine rage Tea Cake tried to murder Janie, thereby forcing her to shoot the only man she had ever loved.

Miss Hurston can write; but her prose is cloaked in that facile sensuality that has dogged Negro expression since the days of Phillis Wheatley. Her dialogue manages to catch the psychological movements of the Negro folk-mind in their pure simplicity, but that's as far as it goes.

Miss Hurston *voluntarily* continues in her novel the tradition which was *forced* upon the Negro in the theater, that is, the minstrel technique that makes the "white folks" laugh. Her characters eat and laugh and cry and work and kill; they swing like a pendulum eternally in that safe and narrow orbit in which America likes to see the Negro live: between laughter and tears.

⟨. . .⟩ The sensory sweep of her novel carries no theme, no message, no thought. In the main, her novel is not addressed to the Negro, but to a white audience whose chauvinistic tastes she knows how to satisfy. She exploits the phase of Negro life which is "quaint," the phase which evokes a piteous smile on the lips of the "superior" race.

Richard Wright, "Between Laughter and Tears," *New Masses*, 5 October 1937, p. 25

ZORA NEALE HURSTON   ⟨. . .⟩ I see nothing but futility in looking back over my shoulder in rebuke at the grave of some white man who has been dead too long to talk about. That is just what I would be doing in trying to fix the blame for the dark days of slavery and the Reconstruction. From what I can learn, it was sad. Certainly. But my ancestors who lived and died in it are dead. The white men who profited by their labor and lives are dead also. I have no personal memory of those times, and no responsibility for them. Neither has the grandson of the man who held my folks. I see no need in Button-holing that grandson like the Ancient Mariner did the wedding guest and calling for the High Sheriff to put him under arrest.

I am not so stupid as to think that I would be bringing this descendant of a slave-owner any news. He has heard just as much about the thing as I have. I am not so humorless as to visualize the grandson falling out on the sidewalk before me, and throwing an acre of fits in remorse because his old folks held slaves. No, indeed! If it happened to be a fine day and he had had a nice breakfast, he might stop and answer me like this:

"In the first place, I was not able to get any better view of social conditions from my grandmother's womb than you could from your grandmother's. Let us say for the sake of argument that I detest the institution of slavery and all that it implied, just as much as you do. You must admit that I had no more power to do anything about it in my unborn state than you had in yours. Why fix your eyes on me? I respectfully refer you to my ancestors, and bid you a good day."

If I still lingered before him, he might answer me further by asking questions like this:

"Are you so simple as to assume that the Big Surrender (Southerners, both black and white speak of Lee's surrender to Grant as the Big Surrender) banished the concept of human slavery from the earth? What is the principle of slavery? Only the literal buying and selling of human flesh on the block? That was

only an outside symbol. Real slavery is couched in the desire to
and the efforts of any man or community to live and advance
their interests at the expense of the lives and interests of others.
All of the outward signs come out of that. Do you not realize that
the power, prestige and prosperity of the greatest nations on earth
rests on colonies and sources of raw materials? Why else are great
wars waged? If you have not thought, then why waste time with
your vapid accusations? If you have, then why single *me* out?"
And like Pilate, he will light a cigar, and stroll on off without
waiting for an answer.

Anticipating such an answer, I have no intention of wasting my time
beating on old graves with a club. I know that I cannot pry aloose the
clutching hand of Time, so I will turn all my thoughts and energies on the
present. I will settle for from now on.

And why not? For me to pretend that I am Old Black Joe and waste my
time on his problems, would be just as ridiculous as for the government of
Winston Churchill to bill the Duke of Normandy the first of every month,
or for the Jews to hang around the pyramids trying to picket Old Pharaoh.
While I have a handkerchief over my eyes crying over the landing of the
first slaves in 1619, I might miss something swell that is going on in 1942.
Furthermore, if somebody were to consider my grandmother's ungranted
wishes, and give *me* what *she* wanted, I would be too put out for words.

Zora Neale Hurston, *Dust Tracks on a Road: An Autobiography* (1942; rpt. New York: HarperPerennial, 1991), pp. 206–8

WORTH TUTTLE HEDDEN   Though *Seraph on the Suwanee* is
the love story of a daughter of Florida Crackers and of a scion of plantation
owners, it is no peasant-marries-the-prince tale. Arvay Henson, true Cracker
in breeding, is above her caste in temperament; James Kenneth Meserve is
plain Jim who speaks the dialect and who has turned his back on family,
with its static living in the past, to become foreman in a west Florida
turpentine camp. Neither is it a romance of the boy-meets-girl school.
Beginning conventionally enough with a seduction (a last minute one when
Arvay is in her wedding dress), it ends twenty-odd years later when the
protagonists are about to be grandparents. In this denouement the divergent
lines of Miss Hurston's astonishing, bewildering talent meet to give us a
reconciliation scene between a middle-aged man and a middle-aged woman

that is erotically exciting and a description of the technique of shrimping that is meticulously exact. Emotional, expository; meandering, unified; naive, sophisticated; sympathetic, caustic; comic, tragic; lewd, chaste—one could go on indefinitely reiterating this novel's contradictions and still end helplessly with the adjective unique. ⟨. . .⟩

Reading this astonishing novel, you wish that Miss Hurston had used the scissors and smoothed the seams. Having read it, you would like to be able to remember every extraneous incident and every picturesque metaphor.

Worth Tuttle Hedden, "Turpentine and Moonshine: Love Conquers Caste Between Florida Crackers and Aristocrats," *New York Herald Tribune Books*, 10 October 1948, p. 2

ROBERT BONE   The genesis of a work of art may be of no moment to literary criticism but it is sometimes crucial in literary history. It may, for example, account for the rare occasion when an author outclasses himself. *Their Eyes Were Watching God* (1937) is a case in point. The novel was written in Haiti in just seven weeks, under the emotional pressure of a recent love affair. "The plot was far from the circumstances," Miss Hurston writes in her autobiography, "but I tried to embalm all the tenderness of my passion for him in *Their Eyes Were Watching God*." Ordinarily the prognosis for such a novel would be dismal enough. One might expect immediacy and intensity, but not distance, or control, or universality. Yet oddly, or perhaps not so oddly, it is Miss Hurston's best novel, and possibly the best novel of the period, excepting *Native Son*.

The opening paragraph of *Their Eyes Were Watching God* encompasses the whole of the novel's meaning: "Ships at a distance have every man's wish on board. For some they come in with the tide. For others they sail forever on the horizon, never out of sight, never landing, until the Watcher turns his eyes away in resignation, his dreams mocked to death by Time. That is the life of man" (p. 9). For women, the author continues, the dream is the sole reality. "So the beginning of this was a woman, and she had come back from burying the dead."

Janie has been gone for almost two years as the action of the novel commences. The townspeople know only that she left home in the company of a lover much younger than herself, and that she departed in fine clothes but has returned in overalls. Heads nod; tongues wag; and the consensus is that she has played the fool. Toward the gossiping women who, from the safety of a small-town porch "pass notions through their mouths," Janie feels only contempt and irritation: "If God don't think no mo' 'bout 'em than Ah do, they's a lost ball in de high grass." To Phoeby, her kissing-friend, she tells the story of her love for Tea-Cake, which together with its antecedents comprises the main body of the novel.

Robert Bone, *The Negro Novel in America* (New Haven: Yale University Press, 1958), pp. 127–28

ROBERT HEMENWAY   What I should like to conclude with is the hypothesis that one reason Zora Neale Hurston was attracted to the scientific conceptualization of her racial experience during the late twenties and early thirties was its *prima facie* offering of a structure for black folklore. That is, it offered a pattern of meaning for material that white racism consistently distorted into "Negro" stereotypes. A folk singer was a cultural object of considerable scientific importance to the collecting anthropologist precisely because his folk experience affirms his humanity, a fact that Hurston could know subjectively as she proved it scientifically. The scientific attraction became so strong that she was led into seriously planning a career as a professional anthropologist, and it continued to affect her writing even after she had rejected such a possibility. When she used Eatonville as fiction in *Jonah's Gourd Vine* (1934), and folklore as personal narrative in her collection, *Mules and Men* (1935), she was in the process of rejecting the scientific conceptualization, but had not yet reached the aesthetic resolution in fiction that characterized her two masterpieces of the late thirties, *Their Eyes Were Watching God* (1937), and *Moses, Man of the Mountain* (1939). Hurston never denied the usefulness of the Barnard training, but she made it clear that something more was needed for the creation of art. As she once told a reporter: "I needed my Barnard education to help me see my people as they really are. But I found that it did not do to be too detached as I stepped aside to study them. I had to go back, dress as they did, talk as they did, live their life, so that I could get into my stories the world I knew as a child."

In sum, then, Zora Neale Hurston was shaped by the Harlem Renaissance, but by Boas as well as by Thurman and Hughes, by Barnard as well as by Harlem. This should not necessarily suggest that the Boas experience was of a superior quality; in many ways it seriously hindered her development as an artist. Nor should it suggest that the aesthetic excitement among the Harlem literati failed to influence her thought. It does mean that the attraction of scientific objectivity was something Hurston had to work through to arrive at the subjective triumphs of her later books. But the ferment of the Harlem Renaissance should also not be underestimated. Hughes, in particular, showed Hurston the poetic possibilities of the folk idiom and she was continually impressed when a reading from Hughes's poems would break the ice with dock loaders, turpentine workers, and jook singers. The mutual effort involved in the creation of *Fire,* the nights at Charles S. and James Weldon Johnson's, the *Opportunity* dinners, even the teas at Jessie Fauset's helped make Zora Hurston aware of the rich block of material which was hers by chance of birth, and they stimulated her thinking about the techniques of collecting and presenting it.

> Robert Hemenway, "Zora Neale Hurston and the Eatonville Anthropology," *The Harlem Renaissance Remembered,* ed. Arna Bontemps (New York: Dodd, Mead, 1972), pp. 212–13

S. JAY WALKER   It comes as something of a shock to discover that Zora Neale Hurston's neglected 1937 masterpiece, *Their Eyes Were Watching God,* deals far more extensively with sexism, the struggle of a woman to be regarded as a person in a male-dominated society, than racism, the struggle of blacks to be regarded as persons in a white-dominated society. It is a treatment virtually unique in the annals of black fiction, and in her handling of it, Ms. Hurston not only shows an aching awareness of the stifling effects of sexism, but also indicates why the feminist movement has failed, by and large, to grasp the imaginations of black womanhood.

Janie Killicks Starks Woods, the heroine of the novel, is followed through three marriages, the first of which brings her safety, the second wealth and prestige, and the third love. On the surface, it sounds indistinguishable from the woman's-magazine fiction which has been denounced as the most insidious form of sexism. Yet a great deal goes on beneath the surface of Hurston's novel, leading to a final interpretation of love that denies not sexuality but sex-role stereotypes. The love that completes the novel is one that the previous marriages had lacked because it is a relationship between acknowledged equals. Janie and "Tea Cake," her husband, share resources, work, decisions, dangers, and not merely the marriage bed.

It is something less than a primer of romanticized love. At one point, Tea Cake, jealous of a suspected rival, beats Janie; at another, Janie, having the same suspicion, beats Tea Cake. Each has weaknesses, fears; but in the final analysis each respects the other as a person, and it is that respect that allows them to challenge the world's conventions and to find each other, and themselves.

> S. Jay Walker, "Zora Neale Hurston's *Their Eyes Were Watching God:* Black Novel of Sexism," *Modern Fiction Studies* 20, No. 4 (Winter 1974–75): 520–21

ALICE WALKER   It has been pointed out that one of the reasons Zora Neale Hurston's work has suffered neglect is that her critics never considered her "sincere." Only after she died penniless, still laboring at her craft, still immersed in her work, still following *her* vision and *her* road, did it begin to seem to some that yes, perhaps this woman *was* a serious artist after all, since artists are known to live poor and die broke. But you're up against a hard game if you have to die to win it, and we must insist that dying in poverty is an unacceptable extreme.

We live in a society, as blacks, women, and artists, whose contests we do not design and with whose insistence on ranking us we are permanently at war. To know that second place, in such a society, has often required more work and innate genius than first, a longer, grimier struggle over greater odds than first—and to be able to fling your scarf about dramatically while you demonstrate that you know—is to trust your own self-evaluation in the face of the Great White Western Commercial of white and male supremacy, which is virtually everything we see, outside and often inside our own homes. That Hurston held her own, literally, against the flood of whiteness and maleness that diluted so much other black art of the period in which she worked is a testimony to her genius and her faith.

As black women and as artists, we are prepared, I think, to keep that faith. There are other choices, but they are despicable.

Zora Neale Hurston, who went forth into the world with one dress to her name, and who was permitted, at other times in her life, only a single pair of shoes, rescued and recreated a world which she labored to hand us whole, never underestimating the value of her gift, if at times doubting the good sense of its recipients. She appreciated us, in any case, *as we fashioned ourselves*. That is something. And of all the people in the world to be, she chose to be herself, *and more and more of herself*. That, too, is something.

Alice Walker, "On Refusing to Be Humbled by Second Place in a Contest You Did Not Design: A Tradition by Now," *I Love Myself When I Am Laughing . . . and Then Again When I Am Looking Mean and Impressive: A Zora Neale Hurston Reader*, ed. Alice Walker (New York: The Feminist Press, 1979), p. 4

HENRY LOUIS GATES, JR.   Hurston's achievement in *Dust Tracks* is twofold. First, she gives us a *writer's* life—rather than an account of "the Negro problem"—in a language as "dazzling" as Mr. Hemenway says it is. So many events in the book were shaped by the author's growing mastery of books and language, but she employs both the linguistic rituals of the dominant culture and those of the black vernacular tradition. These two speech communities are the sources of inspiration for Hurston's novels and autobiography. This double voice unreconciled—a verbal analogue of her double experiences as a woman in a male-dominated world and as a black person in a non-black world—strikes me as her second great achievement.

Many writers act as if no other author influenced them, but Hurston freely describes her encounter with books, from Xenophon in the Greek through Milton to Kipling. Chapter titles and the organization of the chapters themselves reflect this urge to testify to the marvelous process by which the writer's life has been shaped by words. "The Inside Search" and "Figure and Fancy" reveal the workings of the youthful Hurston's mind as she invented fictional worlds, struggled to find the words for her developing emotions and learned to love reading. "School Again," "Research" and "My People! My People!"—printed in the original form for the first time—unveils social and verbal race rituals and customs with candor that shocks even today. Hurston clearly saw herself as a black woman writer and thinker first and as a specimen of Negro progress last. What's more, she structured her autobiography to make such a reading inevitable.

Henry Louis Gates, Jr., " 'A Negro Way of Saying,' " *New York Times Book Review*, 21 April 1985, pp. 43, 45

JOHN LOWE   Humor is a basic, continuing component in Hurston; to her, laughter was a way to show one's love for life, and a way to bridge the distance between author and reader. But more than this, she was determined to create a new art form based on the Afro-American cultural tradition, something she helped recover and define, as an anthropologist. ⟨. . .⟩ It now seems clear that humor played a crucial role in her initial reception by, and later relations with, the other members of the Harlem Renaissance; in her sense of folklore and its functions; in the anthropological aspect of Hurston's humor, which grew out of her training as a professional folklorist; and in the ever changing and increasing role humor played in her fiction, including her masterworks, *Their Eyes Were Watching God* and *Moses, Man of the Mountain.* ⟨. . .⟩

   Dust Tracks never bores the reader, largely because the book, in celebrating Zora Neale Hurston, also salutes the culture that made her. The text is larded with humor, both as structure and adornment. Hurston uses comic expressions, jokes, and entire collections of humorous effects, to amplify, underline, and sharpen the points she makes. These deceptively delightful words often contain a serious meaning, just as the slave folktales did. Hurston skillfully trims and fits folk saying into integral parts of her narrative; on the first page, for instance, she describes her hometown by saying "Eatonville is what you might call hitting a straight lick with a crooked stick. The town . . . is a by-product of something else." This type of description becomes more pungent when she combines these materials with her own imaginative coinages, as in the following description of her father's family: "Regular hand-to-mouth folks. Didn't own pots to pee in, nor beds to push 'em under. . . . No more to 'em than the stuffings out of a zero." This utterance alone gives utterance to Hurston's assertion that the Negro's greatest contributions to the language were (1) the use of metaphor and simile ("hand-to-mouth folks"); (2) the use of the double descriptive ("pot . . . nor beds"); and (3) the use of verbal nouns ("stuffings"). It also reveals the way such tools can be used to revitalize language by working simultaneously in the comic mode.

      John Lowe, "Hurston, Humor, and the Harlem Renaissance," *The Harlem Renaissance Re-examined,* ed. Victor A. Kramer (New York: AMS Press, 1987), pp. 284–85, 289

KARLA F. C. HOLLOWAY   Hurston develops her character Janie to the point that she is an assertive, self-fulfilled woman. Weaving her maturity through the natural imagery of the pear tree, through a fertile

farmland with Logan Killicks where her spirit is spoiled, and into a town
grown out of wilderness tamed, Hurston's word destroys sexual and natural
fertility. Her word sweeps through with the force of a hurricane destroying
all the structures so carefully framed from the opening pages of the novel.
Hurston's text has warned the reader from the same early pages of its
potential for destruction, teasing itself with the "ships at a distance" puzzle
that sets the narrative tone. This often-quoted paragraph (perhaps so much
so because its ambiguity invites a variety of critical comment) is a linguistic
trope, a tease. It is language used to tell on, to signify upon, itself. It warns
the reader through such signification that here is a text that talks its own
structure into existence. I think it is less important to try to discover
what Hurston's opening paragraphs mean than it is to point out that these
paragraphs signal a text with an internal force that will gather strength
through its manipulations of language. ⟨Henry Louis⟩ Gates's observation
of the importance of this text's structure clarifies its importance:

> Hurston . . . has made *Their Eyes Were Watching God* into a
> paradigmatic signifying text, for this novel resolves that implicit
> tension between the literal and the figurative contained in
> standard English usages of the term "signifying." *Their Eyes*
> represents the black trope of signifying both as thematic matter
> and as a rhetorical strategy of the novel itself.

I would take Gates's point further and assert that *Eyes* represents a vocal
structure that is something more basic than "strategy." He observes that
Janie, the protagonist, "gains her voice, as it were, in her husband's store
not only by engaging with the assembled men in the ritual of signifying . . .
but also by openly signifying upon her husband's impotency." I support this
statement with an emendation important to my thesis of voice: Janie gains
her voice from the available voice of the text and subsequently learns to
share it with the narrator ⟨. . .⟩ This is a vital extension of Gates's discussion
of *Eyes*. I must credit the voice gained to the structure itself. Certainly the
traditions of signifying belong to a black community, but Hurston has made
them belong to a literary text in ways that empower them to take on their
own life forms. This is a tradition of voice let loose in *Jonah* and re-merged
to the literary text in *Eyes*. I think it is the same voice because Hurston
uses it as character—investing it with active power. Sometimes her "word"
is a teasing ambiguity; other times, it is an innocent bystander. But lest we
fail to take it seriously, it returns in a whirlwind to exact its due on the

very world it had created in the beginning. We know this is so because in
the final pages of the novel, which are really the opening pages because
the novel is a flashback (another show of power by the recursive word),
Janie talks to her friend Phoeby, telling her what she must tell those who
criticize what she has done with her life. "Then you must *tell* [emphasis
added] them," Janie says, and if we have attended to that power of the word
to speak itself into being, we know that Janie too has learned that through
telling her spirit will rest fulfilled. "Love is lak de sea," she tells Phoeby,
while the narrative voice finishes the image that opened the novel and
speaks of Janie pulling "in her horizon like a great fish-net" and calling her
soul "to come and see." The images of water and air collapse in these final
pages; the wind turns peaceable and waits for its next embodiment.

Karla F. C. Holloway, *The Character of the Word: The Texts of Zora Neale Hurston*
(Westport, CT: Greenwood Press, 1987), pp. 39–40

JENNIFER JORDAN   Despite her lack of veracity, critics like Alice
Walker, Robert Hemenway, and Mary Helen Washington have managed
to maintain both a certain objectivity about Hurston's weaknesses and a
respectful fondness for her daring and talent. This same openmindedness and
tolerance for ambivalence are not always reflected in the critical responses to
her greatest work, *Their Eyes Were Watching God*. Hurston's independence,
her refusal to allow her love interests and marriages to hamper her career,
and her adventuresomeness in confronting the dangers of anthropological
research in the violent turpentine camps of the South and in the voodoo
temples of Haiti make her a grand candidate for feminist sainthood. Difficulties arise, however, when critics transfer their narrow conception of
Hurston's personal attitudes and history to their readings of *Their Eyes Were
Watching God*, a novel that reflects Hurston's ambiguity about race, sex,
and class. The result is the unsupportable notion that the novel is an
appropriate fictional representation of the concerns and attitudes of modern
black feminism. ⟨. . .⟩

Their Eyes Were Watching God is a novel that examines with a great deal
of artistry the struggle of a middle-class woman to escape the fetters of
traditional marriage and the narrow social restrictions of her class and sex.
But Janie Killicks Starks Woods never perceives herself as an independent,
intrinsically fulfilled human being. Nor does she form the strong female and

racial bonds that black feminists have deemed necessary in their definition of an ideologically correct literature. The novel fails to meet several of the criteria defined by black feminist criticism. Perhaps the acceptance and glorification of this novel as the bible of black women's liberation speak to the unconscious conflicts about emotional and financial dependence, sexual stereotyping, intraracial hostilities, and class interests inherent within the black feminist movement. In its very ambivalences Hurston's *Their Eyes Were Watching God* may serve as a Rorschach test by which these conflicts are revealed and thus is an appropriate manifesto for black feminism.

But the novel's success or failure as an ideological document does not diminish its aesthetic worth. It remains one of the great novels of black literature—a novel that is laughing out-loud funny, that allows black people to speak in their own wonderful voices, and that portrays them in all their human nobility and pettiness.

> Jennifer Jordan, "Feminist Fantasies: Zora Neale Hurston's *Their Eyes Were Watching God*," *Tulsa Studies in Women's Literature* 7, No. 1 (Spring 1988): 106–7, 115

NELLIE McKAY   Unlike the solitary but representative hero of male autobiography, Janie Starks and Zora Neale Hurston join voices to produce a personal narrative that celebrates an individual and collective black female identity emerging out of the search for an autonomous self. Although the structure of this text is different, the tradition of black women celebrating themselves through other women like themselves began with their personal narratives of the nineteenth century. Female slave narratives, we know, generally had protagonists who shared their space with the women who instilled pride of self and love of freedom in them. The tradition continued into the twentieth century. For instance, much of the early portion of Hurston's autobiography, *Dust Tracks on a Road*, celebrates the relationship she had with her mother and the lessons she learned, directly and indirectly, from other women in the community. Thus, Hurston's structure for Janie's story expands that already existing tradition to concretize the symbolic rendering of voice to and out of the women's community by breaking away from the formalities of conventional autobiography to make Janie's text an autobiography about autobiographical storytelling, in the tradition of African and Afro-American storytelling. Hurston, struggling with the pains and ambivalences she felt toward the realities of a love she had to reject for the restraints it would have placed on her, found a safe place to embalm the tenderness and passion of her feelings in the autobiographical voice of Janie Crawford, whose life she made into a very fine crayon enlargement of life.

Nellie McKay, " 'Crayon Enlargements of Life': Zora Neale Hurston's *Their Eyes Were Watching God* as Autobiography," *New Essays on* Their Eyes Were Watching God, ed. Michael Awkward (New York: Cambridge University Press, 1990), pp. 68–69

MAYA ANGELOU   Zora Neale Hurston chose to write her own version of life in *Dust Tracks on a Road*. Through her imagery one soon learns that the author was born to roam, to listen and to tell a variety of stories. An active curiosity led her throughout the South, where she gathered up the feelings and the sayings of her people as a fastidious farmer might gather eggs. When she began to write, she used all the sights she had seen, all the people she encountered and the exploits she had survived. One reading of Hurston is enough to convince the reader that Hurston had dramatic adventures and was a quintessential survivor. According to her own account in *Dust Tracks on a Road*, a hog with a piglet and an interest in some food Hurston was eating taught the infant Hurston to walk. The sow came snorting toward her, and Zora, who had never taken a step, decided that the time had come to rectify her reluctance. She stood and not only walked but climbed into a chair beyond the sow's inquisitive reach.

That lively pragmatism which revealed itself so early was to remain with Hurston most of her life. It prompted her to write and rewrite history. Her books and folktales vibrate with tragedy, humor and the real music of Black American speech.

⟨. . .⟩ Is it possible that Hurston, who had been bold and bodacious all her life, was carrying on the tradition she had begun with the writing of *Spunk* in 1925? That is, did she mean to excoriate some of her own people, whom she felt had ignored or ridiculed her? The *New Yorker* critic declared the work a "warm, witty, imaginative, rich and winning book by one of our few genuine grade A folk writers."

There is, despite its success in certain quarters, a strange distance in this book. Certainly the language is true and the dialogue authentic, but the author stands between the content and the reader. It is difficult, if not impossible, to find and touch the real Zora Neale Hurston. The late Larry Neal in his introduction to the 1971 edition of *Dust Tracks on a Road* cited,

"At one moment she could sound highly nationalistic. Then at other times she might mouth statements which in terms of the ongoing struggle for Black liberation were ill conceived and were even reactionary."

There is a saying in the Black community that advises: "If a person asks you where you're going, you tell him where you've been. That way you neither lie nor reveal your secrets." Hurston called herself the "Queen of the Niggerati." She also said, "I like myself when I'm laughing." *Dust Tracks on a Road* is written with royal humor and an imperious creativity. But then all creativity is imperious, and Zora Neale Hurston was certainly creative.

Maya Angelou, "Foreword," *Dust Tracks on a Road* (New York: HarperPerennial, 1991), pp. viii–xii

⊞ *Bibliography*

Jonah's Gourd Vine. 1934.

Mules and Men. 1935.

Their Eyes Were Watching God. 1937.

Tell My Horse. 1938, 1939 (as *Voodoo Gods: An Inquiry into Native Myths and Magic in Jamaica and Haiti*).

Moses, Man of the Mountain. 1939.

Dust Tracks on a Road: An Autobiography. 1942.

Caribbean Melodies for Chorus of Mixed Voices and Soloists by William Grant Still (editor). 1947.

Seraph on the Suwanee. 1948.

I Love Myself When I Am Laughing . . . and Then Again When I Am Looking Mean and Impressive: A Zora Neale Hurston Reader. Ed. Alice Walker. 1979.

The Sanctified Church. 1981.

Spunk: Selected Stories. 1985.

Mule Bone: A Comedy of Negro Life (with Langston Hughes). Ed. George Houston Bass and Henry Louis Gates, Jr. 1991.

James Weldon Johnson
1871–1938

NEITHER OF JAMES WELDON JOHNSON'S parents had been slaves before the Civil War. His father, James, was born free in Virginia in 1830; his mother, Helen Duttel, was part Haitian, part French, and a member of the Bahamian black middle class. James William ("James Weldon" after 1913) was born on June 17, 1871, in Jacksonville, Florida, after his family escaped the economic depression in Nassau at that time.

In Florida, James, Sr., provided his family with a middle-class life accessible to only a small minority of blacks in the South of the late 1800s. As a teenager, Johnson visited New York and became fascinated with city life. At seventeen he worked as a secretary to a white physician and research scientist, Thomas Osmond Summers, whose character greatly influenced him. Summers saw Johnson as a social equal, encouraging the young man to read and write poetry.

At Atlanta University, modeled after Yale, Johnson received a classical education and wished to pursue public service; he was often an active participant in formal debates on the issue of race. Upon graduation, and after a stint as a principal, Johnson established the first high school for blacks, as well as creating America's first black daily newspaper, the Jacksonville *Daily American*. Upon its financial collapse, Johnson studied law and in 1896 was admitted to the Florida bar.

Johnson practiced law for part of the year but traveled to New York in the summer months to work with his brother, John Rosamond, and other black performers bound for Broadway and Europe. The Johnson brothers employed popular black imagery but avoided standard racist vocabulary. One of the earliest songs composed by the Johnsons, "Lift Every Voice and Sing," was composed for a celebration of Abraham Lincoln's birthday in 1900; this song was later adopted by the NAACP as their official song.

Johnson, in his early dialect poems and lyrics, drew upon a genre full of racial stereotypes, but he also accepted the reality of that dialect as an authentic language. He wished to reveal the deeper themes of history and

119

the emotions of black Americans; yet he, and his critics as well, found the use of dialect problematic at best. Even today it continues to be a topic for debate.

In 1906 Johnson entered foreign service as a U.S. consul in Venezuela and wrote his only work of fiction, *The Autobiography of an Ex-Colored Man* (published anonymously in 1912), a story modeled on an autobiographical narrative. After publishing his first book of poems, *Fifty Years and Other Poems* (1917), Johnson became Secretary of the NAACP and led a battle for a federal antilynching law, using his talents as a lawyer, public speaker, and lobbyist. Johnson was perhaps the leading proponent of black American culture in the 1920s. However, he became increasingly at odds with other black leaders and rejected communism, separatism, and violence as alterna- tives in the struggle for racial equality.

In 1930 Johnson published *Black Manhattan*, a still valuable study of black theatre in New York. His autobiography, *Along This Way*, followed in 1933. The last books to appear in his lifetime were the trenchant essay *Negro Americans, What Now?* (1934) and a selection of his poetry, *Saint Peter Relates an Incident* (1935).

Johnson died a sudden death when, on his sixty-seventh birthday (June 17, 1938), his automobile collided with a train while he was vacationing in Maine. He is buried in Greenwood Cemetery in Brooklyn, New York.

▨ *Critical Extracts*

SHERMAN, FRENCH & COMPANY   This vivid and startlingly new picture of conditions brought about by the race question in the United States makes no special plea for the Negro, but shows in a dispassionate, though sympathetic, manner conditions as they actually exist between the whites and blacks to-day. Special pleas have already been made for and against the Negro in hundreds of books, but in these books either his virtues or his vices have been exaggerated. This is because writers, in nearly every instance, have treated the colored American as a *whole*; each has taken some one group of the race to prove his case. Not before has a composite and proportionate presentation of the entire race, embracing all of its various groups and elements, showing their relations with each other and to the whites, been made.

It is very likely that the Negroes of the United States have a fairly correct idea of what the white people of the country think of them, for that opinion has for a long time been and is still being constantly stated; but they are themselves more or less a sphinx to the whites. It is curiously interesting and even vitally important to know what are the thoughts of ten millions of them concerning the people among whom they live. In these pages it is as though a veil had been drawn aside: the reader is given a view of the inner life of the Negro in America, is initiated into the "freemasonry," as it were, of the race.

These pages also reveal the unsuspected fact that prejudice against the Negro is exerting a pressure which, in New York and other large cities where the opportunity is open, is actually and constantly forcing an unascertainable number of fair-complexioned colored people over into the white race.

In this book the reader is given a glimpse behind the scenes of this race-drama which is being here enacted,—he is taken upon an elevation where he can catch a bird's-eye view of the conflict which is being waged.

Sherman, French & Company, "Preface," *The Autobiography of an Ex-Colored Man* by
James Weldon Johnson (1912; rpt. New York: Penguin Books, 1990), pp. xxxiii–xxxiv

BRANDER MATTHEWS   In the following pages Mr. James Weldon Johnson ⟨. . .⟩ gathers together a group of lyrics, delicate in workmanship, fragrant with sentiment, and phrased in pure and unexceptionable English. Then he has another group of dialect verses, racy of the soil, pungent in flavor, swinging in rhythm and adroit in rhyme. But where he shows himself as a pioneer is the half-dozen larger and bolder poems, of a loftier strain, in which he has been nobly successful in expressing the higher aspirations of his own people. It is in uttering this cry for recognition, for sympathy, for understanding, and above all, for justice, that Mr. Johnson is most original and most powerful. In the superb and soaring stanzas of "Fifty Years" (published exactly half-a-century after the signing of the Emancipation Proclamation) he has given us one of the noblest commemorative poems yet written by any American,—a poem sonorous in its diction, vigorous in its workmanship, elevated in its imagination and sincere in its emotion. In it speaks the voice of his race; and the race is fortunate in its spokesman.

In it a fine theme has been finely treated. In it we are made to see something of the soul of the people who are our fellow citizens now and forever,— even if we do not always so regard them. In it we are glad to acclaim a poem which any living poet might be proud to call his own.

Brander Matthews, "Preface," *Fifty Years and Other Poems* by James Weldon Johnson (Boston: Cornhill Co., 1917), pp. xiii–xiv

---

JAMES WELDON JOHNSON   In a general way, these poems were suggested by the rather vague memories of sermons I heard preached in my childhood; but the immediate stimulus for setting them down came quite definitely at a comparatively recent date. I was speaking on a Sunday in Kansas City, addressing meetings in various colored churches. When I had finished my fourth talk it was after nine o'clock at night, but the committee told me there was still another meeting to address. I demurred, making the quotation about the willingness of the spirit and the weakness of the flesh, for I was dead tired. I also protested the lateness of the hour, but I was informed that for the meeting at this church we were in good time. When we reached the church an "exhorter" was just concluding a dull sermon. After his there were two short sermons. These sermons proved to be preliminaries, mere curtain-raisers for a famed visiting preacher. At last he arose. He was a dark-brown man, handsome in his gigantic proportions. He appeared to be a bit self-conscious, perhaps impressed by the presence of the "distinguished visitor" on the platform, and started in to preach a formal sermon from a formal text. The congregation sat apathetic and dozing. He sensed that he was losing his audience and his opportunity. Suddenly he closed the Bible, stepped out from behind the pulpit and began to preach. He started intoning the old folk-sermon that begins with the creation of the world and ends with Judgement Day. He was at once a changed man, free, at ease and masterful. The change in the congregation was instantaneous. An electric current ran through the crowd. It was in a moment alive and quivering; and all the while the preacher held it in the palm of his hand. He was wonderful in the way he employed his conscious and unconscious art. He strode the pulpit up and down in what was actually a very rhythmic dance, and he brought into play the full gamut of his wonderful voice, a voice—what shall I say?—not of an organ or a trumpet, but rather of a trombone, the instrument possessing above all the others the power to express the wide and varied range of emotions encompassed by the human voice—and with greater amplitude. He intoned, he moaned, he pleaded— he blared, he crashed, he thundered. I sat fascinated; and more, I was, perhaps against my will, deeply moved; the emotional effect upon me was irresistible. Before he had finished I took a slip of paper and somewhat surreptitiously jotted down some ideas for the first poem, "The Creation."

James Weldon Johnson, "Preface," *God's Trombones* (New York: Viking Press, 1927), pp. 5–7

COUNTEE CULLEN   James Weldon Johnson has blown the true spirit of the pentecostal trumpeting of the dark Joshuas of the race in *God's Trombones*, composed of seven sermon-poems and a prayer. The seven sermons are like the seven blasts blown by Joshua at Jericho. "The Creation", "The Prodigal Son", "Go Down Death—A Funeral Sermon", "Noah Built the Ark", "The Crucifixion", "Let My People Go", and "The Judgement Day", they are all great evangelical texts. And the magnificent manner in which they are done increases our regret that Mr. Johnson was not intrigued into preaching "The Dry Bones in the Valley", the *pièce de résistance* in the repertoire of every revivalist to whom a good shout is a recommendation of salvation well received. ⟨. . .⟩

The poet here has admirably risen to his intentions and his needs; entombed in this bright mausoleum the Negro preacher of an older day can never pass entirely deathward. Dialect could never have been synthesized into the rich mortar necessary for these sturdy unrhymed exhortations. Mr. Johnson has captured the peculiar flavor of speech by which the black sons of Zebedee, lacking academic education, but grounded through their religious intensity in the purest marshalling of the English language (the King James' version of the Bible) must have astounded men more obviously letter-trained. This verse is simple and awful at once, the grand diapason of a musician playing on an organ with far more than two keys.

There is a universality of appeal and appreciation in these poems that raises them, despite the fact that they are labled "Seven Negro Sermons in Verse", and despite the persistent racial emphasis of Mr. Douglas' beautiful illustrations, far above a relegation to any particular group of people. Long ago the recital of the agonies and persecutions of the Hebrew children under Pharaoh ceased to chronicle the tribulations of one people alone. So in

"Let My People Go" there is a world-wide cry from the oppressed against the oppressor, from the frail and puny against the arrogant in strength who hold them against their will. From Beersheba to Dan the trusting wrench, rich in nothing but his hope and faith, holds this axiomatic solace:

> Listen!—Listen!
> All you sons of Pharaoh,
> Who do you think can hold God's people
> When the Lord himself has said,
> Let my people go?

Countee Cullen, "And the Walls Came Tumblin' Down," *Bookman* (New York) 66, No. 2 (October 1927): 221

DAVID LITTLEJOHN   J. W. Johnson's *The Autobiography of an Ex-Colored Man* (1912) is more a social phenomenon than a novel, and its notoriety—some of which has endured—is the combined product of its once-daring title, its anonymous publication (which led readers to presume it factual for fifteen years), and the novelty of its "outspoken" message to 1912 America. It reveals itself today as an utterly artless, unstructured, unselective sequence of Negro-life episodes, written in a style as flat and directionless as the floor of an enormous room. The climactic episodes, moreover—the hero's high life in Bohemian New York as a ragtime pianist, his European tour with a millionaire patron—betray only adolescent fantasies beneath the dull surface of prose. More interesting is what Johnson reveals, of America and himself, between the lines of plot. His essayette digressions, for example, offer a fair view of the antediluvian race relations in America during this period, albeit a view peculiarly fogged by his own prejudices: W. E. B. DuBois is a far more dependable authority. The prejudices themselves, though, the self-revelation, may have for some white readers still a strangely pathetic appeal. He—the "hero," if not Johnson—is a pure example of the self-styled "better class of Negroes," a member of DuBois' "Talented Tenth," who hoped in these distant, deluded years to effect a liaison with "the better class of whites," and to detach himself utterly from the despised lower Negro classes.

> The unkempt appearance, the shambling slouching gait and loud talk and laughter of these people aroused in me a feeling of almost repulsion.

... odd as it may sound, refined coloured people get no more pleasure out of riding with offensive Negroes than anybody else would get. . . .

Happily, this class represents the black people of the South far below their normal physical and moral condition, but in its increase lies the possibility of grave dangers. . . .

I can imagine no more dissatisfied being than an educated, cultured, and refined coloured man in the United States.

Along with this class consciousness goes a dilettantish championing of the popular Negro arts, reminiscent of the detached folklorist's interest one feels in *God's Trombones*. His hero lists, in fact, the Uncle Remus stories, the Jubilee songs, ragtime, and the cake-walk as the four great cultural contributions of the American Negro, and paragraphs of his prose are devoted to the latter two. *The Autobiography* is anything but a "good" book; but, for all the naïveté, the snobbery, the fantasy, and the flatness, it does afford a unique and perhaps useful portrait of a period and a type.

David Littlejohn, *Black on White: A Critical Survey of Writing by American Negroes* (New York: Grossman, 1966), pp. 26–27

RICHARD A. LONG   The verse output of James Weldon Johnson falls into four groups: lyrics in standard English, poems in the dialect tradition, folk-inspired free verse, and a long satirical poem. The first two groups are contemporary and were published in the volume *Fifty Years and Other Poems* (Boston, 1917). The prayer and seven Negro sermons of the third group constitute *God's Trombones* (New York, 1927). The last group is represented by the poem "St. Peter Relates an Incident of the Resurrection Day," privately printed in 1930, and republished with a selection of earlier poems in 1935.

The early poetry of Johnson belongs to the late nineteenth century tradition of sentimental poetry in so far as its techniques and verse forms are concerned, seldom rising above the mediocrity characteristic of American poetry in the period 1890–1910, during which it was written for the most part. In purpose, however, Johnson's early verse was a species of propaganda, designed sometimes overtly, sometimes obliquely, to advance to a reading public the merits and the grievances of blacks. In this sense the poetry of Johnson is an integral part of a coherent strain in the poetry of Afro-Americans beginning with Phillis Wheatley:

Remember, Christians, Negroes, black as Cain,
May be refined, and join th' angelic train.
      (Phillis Wheatley, "On Being Brought from Africa
      to America")

More particularly we may note the relationship of Johnson's early poetry to that of Paul Laurence Dunbar, his much admired friend and contemporary. Though they were about the same age, Dunbar was by far the more precocious, and his virtuosity had an obvious impact on Johnson, though little of Dunbar's verse bears any obvious burden of racial protest, in spite of the real personal suffering Dunbar underwent because of misunderstanding and neglect that he ascribed to his color.

Another factor of importance in the early verse of Johnson is his composition of verses to be set to music by his brother J. Rosamond Johnson; the search for euphony and piquancy and the use of devices such as internal rhyme betrays the hand of the librettist.

The division of Johnson's poetry into standard lyrics and dialect verse, as in the case of Dunbar's poetry, reflects a self-conscious distinction made by the author himself. Johnson's first collection of his poetry, which appeared eleven years after Dunbar's death, presents forty-eight standard poems, followed by a segregated group of sixteen "Jingles and Croons." The dialect poems reflect of course a literary tradition of their own since in point of fact the themes and forms of such a dialect of poetry as was written by Dunbar and Johnson and many others reflects no tradition of the folk who used "dialect." In point of fact, it is useful to remember that the dialect poets learned mainly from their predecessors and employ for the most part uniform grammatical and orthographic conventions which suggest that they did not consciously seek to represent any individual or regional dialect. Johnson himself gives a brief account of the dialect literary tradition in his introductions to Dunbar and other dialect poets in *The Book of American Negro Poetry* (New York, 1931).

    Richard A. Long, "A Weapon of My Song: The Poetry of James Weldon Johnson," *Phylon* 32, No. 4 (Winter 1971): 374–75

EUGENE LEVY   Like many creative writers, Johnson felt that art and social criticism were fundamentally different forms of expression, though each might be of use to the other. Art could not be produced for the purpose of propaganda. Art such as Forster's *A Passage to India* or the singing of Ethel Waters, however, in certain subtle ways could expand our understanding of a social problem like racism. Writers such as McKay and Hughes, Johnson believed, demonstrated to the American public that black men could create valid art by drawing for their material upon a significant social phenomenon—the life of the Afro-American. Johnson saw this as contributing to the breakdown of racial separation in American society, thus pushing society closer to his goal of integration.

For those who believed that goal to be both invalid and unrealizable, however, men like Hughes, McKay, and Johnson were simply deceiving blacks when they claimed that demonstrating one's ability would bring opportunity. Perhaps the most outspoken advocate in the 1920s of this viewpoint was Marcus Garvey, a man with few friends among intellectuals, either black or white. Garvey did nothing to conceal the profound distrust he felt toward whites, or toward blacks who tried to convince whites they ought to share the wealth and power of Euro-America with its black population. W. E. B. Du Bois, one of Garvey's most vitriolic critics, nevertheless shared with the Back to Africa leader a profound skepticism toward putting faith in whites. The white power structure, at least as it existed in the United States in the 1920s, seemed unlikely to be converted to brotherhood by the artistry of Ethel Waters or the insight of Gertrude Stein. Along with the sexual prudery of his views toward the Renaissance, Du Bois firmly believed that only the fist of hard-hitting propaganda, not the velvet glove of art, would stop the oppression of white over black.

On one matter Garvey, Du Bois, Johnson, and the writers of the Renaissance agreed: the necessity of pride in the race's past and present accomplishments. Booker T. Washington expressed it for them when he wrote: "It was with a race as it is with an individual: it must respect itself if it would win the respect of others." Johnson, along with most of the younger writers, however, was far more optimistic than Garvey or Du Bois as to the influence black writers might have on American society. He had his differences with the younger writers, largely stemming from his attachment to what was essentially a modified "melting pot" conception of America's future. Blacks should further develop their own culture so as to establish themselves in American society, but, once that had been accomplished, it would be wisest and safest, Johnson had maintained for many years, to meld into a fully unified national culture. Black writers such as Locke, Hughes, and Countee Cullen, on the other hand, put much more emphasis on maintaining a unique black culture. They adhered to a "nation of nations" conception: black Americans, like Euro-American ethnic groups, would develop their own hyphenated culture, but all Americans would cooperate in maintaining an equitable and productive society. Such differences in ends were theoretical in the social situation of the 1920s. Those of the Renaissance agreed on means, and especially on the role of art in race progress and reconciliation. After reading *The Autobiography of an Ex-Colored Man*, Aaron Douglas— the black artist who illustrated many of the books of the Renaissance, including *God's Trombones*—wrote Johnson: "The post-war Negro, blinded by the glare and almost sudden bursting of a new day, finds much difficulty in realizing the immense power and effort . . . the pre-war Negro . . . made to prepare the country for what we now feel to be the new awakening." The "new awakening," of course, awoke fewer than Douglas, in his enthusiasm, seemed to think—a fact many black writers were to learn in the 1930s. Nevertheless, the sense of change as well as of continuity with the past which he expressed in his letter reflected both a feeling and a reality which Johnson had done much to foster.

Eugene Levy, *James Weldon Johnson: Black Leader, Black Voice* (Chicago: University of Chicago Press, 1973), pp. 219–21

ARTHUR P. DAVIS   The second volume, *God's Trombones*, though appearing only ten years after the first, shows far more than ten years of poetic growth and understanding on the part of Johnson. An index to this maturing is found in the preface to *The Book of American Negro Poetry*, an anthology published in 1922. In this lengthy preface Johnson voiced his dissatisfaction with the limitations of dialect writing and his interest in a new vehicle for Negro expression:

> What the colored poet in the United States needs to do is
> something like what Synge did for the Irish; he needs to find a
> form that will express the racial spirit by symbols from within
> rather than by symbols from without, such as the mere mutilation
> of English spelling and pronunciation. He needs a form that is
> freer and larger than dialect, but which will still hold the racial
> flavor; a form of expressing imagery, the idioms, the peculiar turns
> of thought, and the distinctive humor and pathos, too, of the
> Negro, but which will also be capable of voicing the deepest and

highest emotions and aspirations, and allow the widest range of
subject and the widest scope of treatment.

In *God's Trombones*, using the old-time Negro folk sermon as his vehicle,
Johnson successfully puts his theories into practice. In these eight free-verse
poems, without the distortion and limitation of dialect, he captures the
rhythm, intonation (as far as one can write it down), sentence structure,
breaks, and repetitions of the illiterate black folk preacher. Johnson has
shown great skill in transforming folk material into sophisticated art. Note,
for example, how he renders the characteristic intoning of the folk sermon;
note the interrupted flow of the phrases, the dramatic breaks:

> Jesus, my sorrowing Jesus,
> The sweat like drops of blood upon his brow,
> Talking with his Father,
> While the three disciples slept,
> Saying: Father,
> Oh, Father,
> Not as I will
> Not as I will,
> But let thy will be done.

The spiritual as well as the sermon influence is found in these free-verse
poems. Johnson's success with these folk forms had considerable effect on
the later Renaissance writers. It gave impetus to the folk emphasis which
characterized much Renaissance verse. Johnson used the spiritual sermon
and, of course, certain forms common to dialectic poetry. Langston Hughes,
Sterling Brown, Waring Cuney, and others added ballad and blues forms
and otherwise widened the range of folk expression. Johnson, however, was
a pioneer influence. He saw the possibilities of folk influence as early as
1922. Because of its folk undergirding, *God's Trombones*, in all probability,
will outlast the rest of Johnson's poetry. ⟨. . .⟩

Johnson's full-length autobiography, *Along This Way* (1930), adopts the
pattern of Negro autobiography of the age: a combination of middle-class
success story, racial vindication, and social commentary, rather than "pure"
delineation of personality. The work, however, is valuable because Johnson
had such a varied and outstanding career and knew so many prominent
persons, white and black, of his age. The most fascinating parts are not the
ones connected with the Dyer Anti-Lynching Bill and other important
political matters, but rather those dealing with the vignettes that crop up:
Paul Laurence Dunbar's reaction to the poetry of Walt Whitman, midnight

parties with black celebrities at the old Marshall Hotel, contacts with Broadway characters such as Flo Ziegfeld and Anna Held, and, above all, Black Bohemia in the 53rd Street area. One enjoys reading *Along This Way*, yet leaves it with a feeling that this success story is too successful, too upward looking; it is all peaks with few or no pits of failure and ugliness. The reason, perhaps, is the best-foot-foremost philosophy that motivated Johnson's generation. Determined to prove to white America that they could make the grade, these writers became automatic salesmen, selling the Talented Tenth to the nation, although by 1935 they would not have used the phrase. What *Along This Way* really says is this: See what I have done in spite of the pressures you put on me. I am like you—the best of you, of course; so count me in.

Arthur P. Davis, *From the Dark Tower: Afro-American Writers 1900 to 1960* (Washington, DC: Howard University Press, 1974), pp. 28–29, 31

CHIDI IKONNÉ   In a way, *The Autobiography of an Ex-Colored Man* is a celebration of the Negro folk. This can also be said of James Weldon Johnson's more serious dialect poems—such as the lilting lullaby entitled "De Little Pickaninny's Gone to Sleep," and the folktale "Brer Rabbit, You's de Cutes' of 'em All" which dramatizes the mythical weakness of the overconfident and aggressively strong in the face of the bodily weak but mentally strong nature. It is, however, in "The Creation" (1918) that the exaltation reached its apogee in Johnson's work, at least before this Negro sermon was combined with other poems like it and published in the volumes of *God's Trombones* (1927).

Operating from the consciousness of a folk preacher, who speaks to a group of believers whose lives, like his, are rooted in warm human relations, in the soil, the water, and other elements of nature (from which they derive all their needs including "pictures," to use Zora Neale Hurston's terms, with which to "adorn" their "expression") the poem is simple and direct. It eschews metaphysical abstractions and reflects the conception of *Obatala*, God the creator, in the Negro folklore: a being more human than the Bible concedes. Thus he feels lonely and seeks company. He almost suffers from the blues. He smiles in happiness. Zora Neale Hurston, the folklorist, as distinct from the fictionist, documents this concept of a human God:

Negro folklore is not a thing of the past. . . . God and the Devil
are paired, and are treated no more reverently than Rockefeller
and Ford. . . . The angels and the apostles walk and talk like
section hands. And through it all walks Jack, the greatest culture
hero of the South; Jack beats them all—even the Devil, who is
often smarter than God.

The Devil is next after Jack as a culture hero. He can outsmart
everyone but Jack. God is absolutely no match for him. He is
good-natured and full of humour.

Chidi Ikonné, *From Du Bois to Van Vechten: The Early New Negro Literature 1903–1926*
(Westport, CT: Greenwood Press, 1981), pp. 70–71

LADELL PAYNE   Johnson's "I" ⟨in *The Autobiography of an Ex-
Colored Man*⟩ was born in Georgia shortly after the Civil War. Rather
than telling the reader that his narrator is black, Johnson has him recall
impressions of the house, the flowers, the glass-bottle hedge, the wash tubs,
the vegetable garden which surrounded him, the bread and molasses which
he ate. In short, he remembers details which tell us that he almost certainly
came from a southern rural Negro home. He also remembers the tall man
with the shiny boots, the gold chain, and the watch, who visited his mother
from time to time and who hung a ten dollar gold piece with a hole drilled
in it around his neck as a gift when the narrator and his mother moved
north to Connecticut. In Connecticut the narrator demonstrates some musical talent and is given piano lessons. He is also a good student. He is
splendidly happy until one day, when he is about ten years old, his teacher
identifies him as a Negro before the class. Like many other southern protagonists, black and white, he is shattered by a knowledge he cannot comprehend.
In Faulkner's *Absalom, Absalom!* (1936), Mr. Compson imagines Charles
Etienne de Saint Velery Bon, when he is told "that he was, must be, a
negro," looking at himself in "the shard of broken mirror" during "what
hours of amazed and tearless grief . . . examining himself . . . with quiet and
incredulous incomprehension." In Johnson's 1912 novel, the protagonist
rushes to his room and goes quickly to his looking glass.

For an instant I was afraid to look, but when I did, I looked long
and earnestly. . . . I was accustomed to hear remarks about my
beauty; but now, for the first time, I became conscious of it and

recognized it. I noticed the ivory whiteness of my skin, the beauty
of my mouth, the size and liquid darkness of my eyes. . . . I
noticed the softness and glossiness of my dark hair. . . . How long
I stood there gazing at my image I do not know. . . . I ran
downstairs and rushed to where my mother was sitting. . . . I
buried my head in her lap and blurted out: "Mother, mother, tell
me, am I a nigger?"

He is, in effect, asking his mother who he is. She answers that he is neither
a "nigger" nor white; her refusal even to name his father makes his identity
even more equivocal. Nameless, raceless, fatherless, like the Joe Christmas
of Faulkner's *Light in August,* he is a person without a definable self. And
also like Christmas, he assumes a racial identity based, as Cleanth Brooks
has pointed out, on a state of mind rather than on the possession of Negro
genes: "And so I have often lived through that hour, that day, that week,
in which was wrought the miracle of my transition from one world into
another; for I did indeed pass into another world. From that time I looked
out through other eyes, my thoughts were coloured, my words dictated, my
actions limited by one dominating, all-pervading idea which constantly
increased in force and weight until I finally realized in it a great, tangible
fact."

Ladell Payne, "Themes and Cadences: James Weldon Johnson, 1871–1938." *Black
Novelists and the Southern Literary Tradition* (Athens: University of Georgia Press,
1981), pp. 28–29

SUSAN J. KOPRINCE   A study of the women in Johnson's sermons
⟨. . .⟩ not only reveals the poet's attitude toward the female sex, but, in a
broader sense, helps to explain his enchantment with Harlem during the
1920s—the same Harlem which Johnson evokes so vividly in his cultural
treatise *Black Manhattan* (1930).

Several poetic sermons in *God's Trombones* make clear Johnson's view
of women as powerful temptresses. The poem "Noah Built the Ark" intro-
duces the figure of Eve, the archetypal temptress "With nothing to do the
whole day long / But play all around in the garden" with her consort, Adam.
Although Eve disobeys God out of vanity ("You're surely goodlooking,"
Satan tells her, offering her a mirror), Adam does so out of uxoriousness
and a fatal desire for this beautiful, sensuous woman. "Back there, six

thousand years ago," Johnson says, "Man first fell by woman— / Lord, and he's doing the same today." 〈. . .〉

But Johnson also presents a different image of women in *God's Trombones:* that of the saintly mother, the sympathetic and loving comforter. In his sermon "The Crucifixion," for instance, Johnson pictures the Virgin Mary at the scene of her son's death, weeping as she watches "her sweet, baby Jesus on the cruel cross." 〈. . .〉

So important for Johnson is this dichotomy between the sensual and the spiritual, between the whorish and the maternal, that he employs it not only to describe the women of *God's Trombones*, but to depict Harlem of the twenties in his cultural study *Black Manhattan*. Just as Johnson tends to divide women into two extreme types—the sexual temptress and the saintly mother—so does he picture Harlem as a city containing the extremes of sensuality and spirituality. For Johnson, Harlem is at once a voluptuous temptress and a spiritual mother—a force which inspires both amorous passion and creative genius—a city which is seductive and vibrant.

Susan J. Koprince, "Femininity and the Harlem Experience: A Note on James Weldon Johnson," *CLA Journal* 29, No. 1 (September 1985): 52–54

HOWARD FAULKNER   What I want to argue is that *The Autobiography* is the first black novel to be totally of a piece: a small masterpiece of control. What critics have faulted is not truly digression or artlessness. Rather, the insipid style and the apparent lack of purposeful selectivity are a direct expression of the narrator's character and of his inability to feel deeply what is happening to him and to put those events in perspective; similarly, the discussion and analysis of black life and people are not adventitious nor are they intrusions of Johnson's own beliefs, but further revelations of character. Our reaction is more problematic than it would be were the irony less subtle, for the narrator is an educated, articulate, and sensitive hero, or anti-hero, and we are thus likely to begin by giving his ideas credence. But we must never mistake the persona for Johnson or think that Johnson lets the ironic tone drop: He does not, in his life story of a man who finally realizes that he has had no life to report.

It is a novel to set beside such other small works of "the unlived life" as Henry James' "The Beast in the Jungle," F. Scott Fitzgerald's "The Rich Boy," and Saul Bellow's *Seize the Day*. In each of these novellas, as in *The*

Autobiography, a protagonist of sufficient intelligence, means, and sophistication has a chance to make of his life something significant. Each work is structured around a series of events which involves a protagonist who fails to act or whose action may more accurately be defined as a withdrawal. Each story thus risks boredom; the "fallacy of imitative form" seems for each author a real peril: how to portray boredom without becoming wearisome. The protagonists have chance after chance to act, to learn, to be, but fail over and over again, and the story must present this slow, willful, and consistent failure in order for us to understand the texture of their lives. Because the focus is consistently on one character and because that character's lack of perception is the tonal key, the narrative style must have about it a certain flatness. Finally, each story ends with the protagonist's epiphany, his understanding that though he remains literally alive, his chance to live meaningfully is behind him; ironically, though, the habits of their lifetimes make the protagonists unable even to feel completely the horror of that understanding. In each of the works, that epiphany follows immediately the death of another character: James' protagonist learns after the death of Mary Bartram, the woman who has loved him; Fitzgerald's learns after the death of his first love, Paula Legendre. For Bellow's protagonist the funeral he stumbles into is of a man he has not known, and yet his sorrow rises like waves, engulfing him; and in *The Autobiography*, the protagonist has just realized what he calls the second great sorrow of his life, the death of his wife. ⟨. . .⟩

The Autobiography of an Ex-Coloured Man is the first fully realized black American novel, a beautiful story of the fear of never living, of being only a detached observer of life. Johnson gives it the peculiar twist that the birthright sold, the beast in the jungle that never springs, the day that is never seized—all depend on the acceptance of blackness, of manhood, of life with all its dangers and impurities. The ex-coloured man is the first protagonist in black fiction to be destroyed from within. In his striving to free himself from limitation, he is perfectly successful in effacing himself, in reducing himself and his life to invisibility.

Howard Faulkner, "James Weldon Johnson's Portrait of the Artist as Invisible Man," *Black American Literature Forum* 19, No. 4 (Winter 1985): 148, 151

▨ *Bibliography*

The Autobiography of an Ex-Colored Man. 1912.

Fifty Years and Other Poems. 1917.

The Changing Status of Negro Labor. 1918.

Africa in the World Democracy (with others). 1919.

Self-Determining Haiti. 1920.

The Book of American Negro Poetry (editor). 1922, 1931.

The Race Problem and Peace. c. 1924.

The Book of Negro Spirituals (editor; with J. Rosamond Johnson). 1925.

The Second Book of American Negro Spirituals (editor; with J. Rosamond John-
        son). 1926.

God's Trombones: Seven Negro Sermons in Verse. 1927.

Native African Races and Culture. 1927.

Saint Peter Relates an Incident of the Resurrection Day. 1930.

Black Manhattan. 1930.

The Shining Life: An Appreciation of Julius Rosenwald. 1932.

Along This Way: The Autobiography of James Weldon Johnson. 1933.

Negro Americans, What Now? 1934.

Saint Peter Relates an Incident: Selected Poems. 1935.

Claude McKay
1890–1948

CLAUDE MCKAY was born in Sunny Ville, Jamaica, on September 15, 1890. After being apprenticed to a wheelwright in Kingston, he emigrated to the U.S. in 1912 and studied agriculture at the Tuskegee Institute and at Kansas State University. He abandoned his studies in 1914 and moved to Harlem, where he became a leading radical poet. Before coming to America, McKay had published a collection of poetry entitled *Songs of Jamaica* (1912). While in Harlem he frequently wrote under the pseudonym Eli Edwards, a name derived from that of his wife, Eulalie Imelda Edwards. This marriage ended in 1914 after only six months; McKay's wife gave birth to a daughter whom he never saw.

"If We Must Die," perhaps McKay's best-known poem, was published in Max Eastman's magazine, the *Liberator*, in 1919. This stirring call to arms was written after the race riots that followed the end of World War I. McKay lived in London from 1919 to 1921; during this time he first read Karl Marx and worked for the Marxist periodical *Worker's Dreadnought*. In 1922—the year he published his celebrated poetry collection *Harlem Shadows*—he made a "magic pilgrimage" to the USSR where he was warmly welcomed by the Communist leaders and addressed the Third Communist International. He wrote two works that were translated into Russian by P. Okhrimenko in 1923: *Sudom Lincha*, a collection of three stories, and the treatise *Negry v Amerike*. These works were translated into English by Robert Winter, the first (as *Trial by Lynching: Stories about Negro Life in America*) in 1977, the second (as *The Negroes in America*) in 1979. McKay's interest in Marx seems to have been based on his perception of its calls for a return to agrarian values and for racial equality. However, McKay never joined the Communist party and by the 1930s he had completely renounced all association with communism.

From 1923 to 1934 McKay lived overseas, having left the United States as a result of his alienation from the black American intelligentsia and from the leaders of the Harlem Renaissance. In Paris he came to feel that racial barriers separated him from "the lost generation"; he subsequently moved to Marseilles and later to Morocco. In Marseilles he wrote his first two novels, *Home to Harlem* (1928) and *Banjo* (1929). On its publication, *Home to Harlem* became the most popular novel ever written by a black author. In 1932 McKay published a collection of short stories, *Gingertown*, followed by a third novel, *Banana Bottom* (1933).

Returning to the U.S. in 1934, McKay worked briefly as a laborer in a welfare camp. In 1938 he wrote *A Long Way from Home*, an account of his life since first coming to America. In 1944 he was baptized into the Roman Catholic church and wrote essays on Christian faith. He died in Chicago on May 22, 1948.

◈ *Critical Extracts*

JAMES WELDON JOHNSON   McKay in 1911, when he was twenty, published a volume of verse, *Songs of Jamaica*. Most of the poems in this collection were written in the Jamaican dialect. It is important to note that these dialect poems of McKay are quite distinct in sentiment and treatment from the conventional Negro dialect poetry written by the poets in the United States; they are free from both the minstrel and plantation traditions, free from exaggerated sweetness and wholesomeness; they are veritable impressions of Negro life in Jamaica. Indeed, some of these dialect poems are decidedly militant in tone. It is, of course, clear to see that McKay had the advantage of not having to deal with stereotypes. He found his medium fresh and plastic. ⟨. . .⟩

McKay belongs to the post-war group and was its most powerful voice. He was preëminently the poet of the rebellion. More effectively than any other poet of that period he voiced the feelings and reactions the Negro in America was then experiencing. Incongruous as it seems, he chose as the form of these poems of protest, challenge, and defiance the English sonnet; and no poetry in American literature sounds a more portentous note than these sonnet-tragedies. Read "The Lynching" and note the final couplet:

> And little lads, lynchers that were to be,
> Danced around the dreadful thing in fiendish glee.

The terrifying summer of 1919, when race riots occurred in quick succession in a dozen cities in different sections of the country, brought from him the most widely known of these sonnets, a cry of defiant desperation, beginning with the lines:

> If we must die—let it not be like hogs
> Hunted and penned in an inglorious spot,

and closing with:

> Like men we'll face the murderous, cowardly pack,
> Pressed to the wall, dying, but fighting back!

This is masculine poetry, strong and direct, the sort of poetry that stirs the pulse, that quickens to action. Reading McKay's poetry of protest and rebellion, it is difficult to imagine him dreaming of his native Jamaica and singing as he does in "Flame Heart" or creating poetic beauty in the absolute as he does in "The Harlem Dancer," "Spring in New Hampshire," and many another of his poems. Of the major Negro poets he, above all, is the poet of passion. That passion found in his poems of rebellion, transmuted, is felt in his love lyrics.

James Weldon Johnson, *The Book of American Negro Poetry* (New York: Harcourt, Brace & World, 1922), pp. 165–67

W. E. B. DU BOIS   Claude McKay's *Home to Harlem* ⟨. . .⟩ for the most part nauseates me, and after the dirtier parts of its filth I feel distinctly like taking a bath. This does not mean that the book is wholly bad. McKay is too great a poet to make any complete failure in writing. There are bits of *Home to Harlem*, beautiful and fascinating: the continued changes upon the theme of the beauty of colored skins; the portrayal of the fascination of their new yearnings for each other which Negroes are developing. The chief character, Jake, has something appealing, and the glimpses of the Haitian, Ray, have all the materials of a great piece of fiction.

But it looks as though, despite this, McKay has set out to cater for that prurient demand on the part of white folk for a portrayal in Negroes of that utter licentiousness which conventional civilization holds white folk back from enjoying—if enjoyment it can be called. That which a certain decadent section of the white American world, centered particularly in New York, longs for with fierce and unrestrained passions, it wants to see written out in black and white, and saddled on black Harlem. This demand, as voiced by a number of New York publishers, McKay has certainly satisfied, and added much for good measure. He has used every art and emphasis to paint drunkenness, fighting, lascivious sexual promiscuity and utter absence of restraint in as bold and as bright colors as he can.

If this had been done in the course of a well-conceived plot or with any artistic unity, it might have been understood if not excused. But *Home to Harlem* is padded. Whole chapters here and there are inserted with no connection to the main plot, except that they are on the same dirty subject. As a picture of Harlem life or of Negro life anywhere, it is, of course, nonsense. Untrue, not so much as on account of its facts, but on account of its emphasis and glaring colors. I am sorry that the author of *Harlem Shadows* stooped to this. I sincerely hope that he will some day rise above it and give us in fiction the strong, well-knit as well as beautiful theme, that it seems to me he might do.

W. E. B. Du Bois, "Two Novels," *Crisis* 35, No. 6 (June 1928): 202

RUDOLPH FISHER   The first six stories ⟨of *Gingertown*⟩ are laid in Negro Harlem, which has apparently fascinated Mr. McKay, himself a British West Indian, precisely as it might fascinate any other outside observer. These scenes, however, are not definitely Harlem as they are definitely Negro; that is, while these things could not have happened to anybody but Negroes, they could have happened in any Negro community—any black belt. Merely to capitalize the "b" and call Harlem the "Belt" is not a sufficient distinction. But the themes have one commendably distinctive feature. Most stories about Negroes could just as well have been told about Jews, Swedes or Chinamen. The complexion or other racial characteristic, physical or mental, is not ordinarily the essence of the theme but merely an attribute. Such a story is "Truant," the sixth in this collection, describing a restless spirit which happened to be a Negro's but might just as well have been anybody's. Such also are the sketches following "Truant." But the five tales preceding it present difficulties which arise specifically out of the most obvious Negro characteristic—skin-color. And simple as this device is, it undeniably gives the first five narratives a flavor which the others lack. Accordingly, though the setting is not made unmistakable, and though the more general aspects of the themes are familiar, there is still a specifically complexional essence which sets these five apart as definitely Negro. These too, despite their distracting inaccuracies of dialect—strange West-Indianisms issue from the mouths of American blacks on occasion—are by far the most dramatic scenes of the collection. In all twelve, however, there is a robust vigor characteristic of all Mr. McKay's work.

Rudolph Fisher, "White, High Yellow, Black," *New York Herald Tribune Books*, 27 March 1932, p. 3

CLAUDE McKAY   A negro writer feeling the urge to write faithfully about the people he knows from real experience and impartial observation is caught in a dilemma (unless he possesses a very strong sense of esthetic values) between the opinion of this group and his own artistic consciousness. I have read pages upon pages of denunciation of young Negro poets and story-tellers who were trying to grasp and render the significance of the background, the fundamental rhythm of Aframerican life. But not a line of critical encouragement for the artistic exploitation of the homely things— of Maudy's wash tub, Aunt Jemima's white folks, Miss Ann's old clothes for work-and-wages, George's Yessah-boss, dining car and Pullman services, barber and shoe shine shop, chittling and corn-pone joints—all the lowly things that go to the formation of the Aframerican soil in which the best, the most pretentious of Aframerican society still has its roots.

My own experience has been amazing. Before I published *Home to Harlem* I was known to the Negro public as the writer of the hortatory poem "If We Must Die." This poem was written during the time of the Chicago race riots. I was then a train waiter in the service of the Pennsylvania Railroad. Our dining car was running between New York, Philadelphia and Pittsburgh, Harrisburg and Washington and I remember we waiters and cooks carried revolvers in secret and always kept together going from our quarters to the railroad yards, as a precaution against sudden attack.

The poem was an outgrowth of the intense emotional experience I was living through (no doubt with thousands of other Negroes) in those days. It appeared in the radical magazine the *Liberator*, and was widely reprinted in the Negro press. Later it was included in my book of poetry *Harlem Shadows*. At the time I was writing a great deal of lyric poetry and none of my colleagues on the *Liberator* considered me a propaganda poet who could reel off revolutionary poetry like an automatic machine cutting fixed patterns. If we were a rebel group because we had faith that human life might be richer, by the same token we believed in the highest standards of creative work.

"If We Must Die" immediately won popularity among Aframericans, but the tone of the Negro critics was apologetic. To them a poem that voiced the deep-rooted instinct of self-preservation seemed merely a daring piece of impertinence. The dean of Negro critics ⟨William Stanley Braithwaite⟩ denounced me as a "violent and angry propagandist, using his natural poetic gifts to clothe arrogant and defiant thoughts." A young disciple characterized me as "rebellious and vituperative."

Thus it seems that respectable Negro opinion and criticism are not ready for artistic or other iconoclasm in Negroes. Between them they would emasculate the colored literary aspirant. Because Aframerican group life is possible only on a neutral and negative level our critics are apparently under the delusion that an Aframerican literature and art may be created out of evasion and insincerity.

Claude McKay, "A Negro Writer to His Critics" (1932), *The Passion of Claude McKay: Selected Poetry and Prose 1912–1948*, ed. Wayne F. Cooper (New York: Schocken Books, 1973), pp. 133–34

ROBERT A. SMITH   One must admit that the author's most powerful dudgeon lay in this protest poetry. Whether he wrote an epigram, a sonnet, or a longer poem, his thought is sustained. He expressed the deepest resentment, but even when doing so his feelings were lucid. He did not stumble as he attempted to express himself. This dynamic force within his poetry caused him to be constantly read and re-read by his admirers and critics. They realized that here was a man of deepest emotions, as well as one who was a skilled craftsman.

In the sonnet, McKay had found a verse form peculiarly adaptable to his taste and ability. His talent was diversified, but this form with its rise and fall seemed quite the thing for the thought which he wished to convey to his readers. Sonnets that bear out this idea are "America," "If We Must Die," and "The Lynching." "America" does not show McKay's bitterness. It gives advice to Negro Americans to face squarely the tests and the challenges that come to them as a persecuted minority. "If We Must Die" reflects the author's acrimony toward the lynchers of Negroes. Written during the epidemic of race riots which swept the country in 1919, its theme is: "fight back; do not take a beating lying down".

Other poems which in content are racial protest are: "In Bondage," "Outcast," "The White City," and the "Barrier." The rebellious philosophy in McKay may be traced back through his turbulent youth, and his affiliation with radical organizations and people.

Occasionally, however, one sees another side of McKay. When he puts down his rancor, his lyricism is entirely clear. He paints pictures that are beautiful; especially is this true when he describes scenes of his native islands. One sees in the poet a sort of nostalgia for home, for relatives, and for the scenes of childhood days, long past. It is in this idyllic mood that McKay appears in an entirely different light. Possibly one of the best poems of this sort is "Flame-Heart." It contains beautiful lines of description such as "The poinsettia's red, blood red in warm December," and "Sweet with the golden threads of the rose apple." "To One Coming North" and "The Tropics in New York" are in the same vein. Although not concerned with the West Indies, they do picture scenes of nature and peacefulness. Their mood is one of quietness also. Others in this group show McKay's range and facility. There is sheer delight in reading them, and the collection would be richer with more of the same tone. ⟨. . .⟩

McKay took upon himself a tremendous task when he chose to be the leading spokesman of an oppressed race. The question always arises as to whether a poet loses any or all of his effectiveness when he takes upon his shoulders the problem of fighting. Does one's lyrical ability become clouded by his propaganda or bombast? is another question. This, it seems, may or may not be true. In the case of McKay, what he has had to say, for the most part has been important. Literary history is full of humanitarians who attacked conditions that were unsavory. Some were successful in their attacks; others were not. Although he was frequently concerned with the race problem, his style is basically lucid. One feels disinclined to believe that the medium which he chose was too small, or too large for his message. He has been heard.

Robert A. Smith, "Claude McKay: An Essay in Criticism," *Phylon* 9, No. 3 (September 1948): 272–73

ARTHUR D. DRAYTON   Outside Jamaican and Negro literary circles in the United States, the late Jamaican poet, Claude McKay, is known best and often only for his race-conscious verse, sometimes only by his much-quoted sonnet which Sir Winston Churchill helped to popularize during World War II. For many people, in the same way that 'The Negro Speaks of Rivers' is Langston Hughes, so this particular sonnet is McKay.

> If we must die, let it not be like hogs
> Hunted and penned in an inglorious spot,
> While round us bark the mad and hungry dogs,
> Making their mock at our accursed lot.
> If we must die, O let us nobly die,
> So that our precious blood may not be shed
> In vain; then even the monsters we defy
> Shall be constrained to honor us though dead!
> O kinsmen! we must meet the common foe!
> Though far outnumbered let us show us brave,
> And for their thousand blows deal one deathblow!
> What though before us lies the open grave?
> Like men we'll face the murderous, cowardly pack,
> Pressed to the wall, dying, but fighting back!

G. R. Coulthard has described his protest verse as 'bitter and violent', and has observed that 'his best poems are characterised by a racial hatred, or even a challenge, of the most violent kind'. Bitter and violent; a challenge: yes. But the charge of racial hatred is difficult to support; and unless we are to argue a complete change in McKay between this later protest verse and his earlier dialect poems, it is a strange assertion. For, quite apart from the evidence of the protest verse itself, it assumes a new dimension if one is familiar with McKay's two publications of dialect poems before he left Jamaica to take up residence in the United States.

But it is not surprising that McKay should have won recognition through his verse written around the theme of Negro suffering in the States. For this has the virility one might expect of a Caribbean poet shocked by what he discovers in America. Coming from quite a different kind of experience of Negro degradation in Jamaica, McKay was fired by what he saw in the States and helped to give to American Negro poetry a distinctly different voice.

⟨. . .⟩ McKay's early years in America coincided with crucial years for the Negro cause, and the virility of his verse was in keeping with the prevailing atmosphere. But, looked at closely, this virility reveals itself as based on something more than mere bitterness; it includes and depends on a certain resilience—perhaps stubborn humanity would be better—on the part of the poet. And this in turn is to be traced to McKay's capacity to react to Negro suffering, not just as a Negro, but as a human being; to react to human suffering as such. For there is a certain danger which is inherent in the Negro situation, one which can lead to great human tragedy, and has no doubt done so times without number in individual cases. It is that the Negro, because of the injustices which he has suffered and continues to suffer, reacts quite rightly as a Negro to the degradation of the Negro; but he is called upon to react in this way so continually, and at times so violently, that he is in danger of losing his capacity to react to suffering in a way which rises above this and includes it, to react simply and primarily as a human being. White bigotry has become so insistent that it is difficult to ask this of the Negro, and he is left in danger of not being touched by human suffering outside the Negro context, or outside a situation which closely resembles his own. And yet, if he is not to abdicate his humanity, he must retain his capacity for this larger and more basic reaction, since to be without it has frightful implications for his emotional growth and his stature as a human being.

For the poet, especially one handling 'racial' material, to lack it would be anathema. If he does not have it, he may as well go off and write about daffodils and lakes. But if by identifying himself with his own community or race he can proceed to that greater and more meaningful identification based on his humanity, he is qualified to handle 'racial' material. McKay always had this qualification, and it imparted to his verse a certain universal significance. Thus the sonnet 'If We Must Die' was written after and relates to the Washington race riot of 1919. Sir Winston Churchill, however, could use it to whip up defiant courage during World War II because it is essentially a cry of defiance from the human heart in the face of a threat to man's dignity and civilisation, a threat which was and is true of Nazism and the hatred of the Negro alike.

Arthur D. Drayton, "McKay's Human Pity: A Note on His Poetry," *Black Orpheus* No. 17 (June 1965): 39–40

ST. CLAIR DRAKE   Claude McKay came to this country from Jamaica in 1912, four years before Marcus Garvey, the organizer of the Universal Negro Improvement Association. He, like Garvey, had left the West Indies in search of wider opportunities for self-expression. Garvey's destiny led him toward a mass-leadership role, then to imprisonment and deportation to Jamaica. Claude McKay eventually won international acclaim as a writer; then came poverty, chronic illness, and finally his death—almost unnoticed.

His autobiography had contemporary relevance for a number of reasons. Black intellectuals are still involved in the quest for an identity and an ideology, and under circumstances similar to those of the period through which McKay lived. Present-day pilgrimages of black Americans, West Indians, and Africans to China and Cuba are reminiscent of the Moscow journeys of an earlier period. The dilemmas and contradictions that accompany attempts to reconcile Marxism and black nationalism are as perplexing to the intellectuals of the 1960s as they were to those of the 1920s and 1930s. Stokely Carmichael, Eldridge Cleaver, and James Forman find themselves confronted with the same type of problems that faced Paul Robeson, Richard Wright, and Langston Hughes. McKay came to grips with them earlier than any of the others, and his autobiography documents the processes of discovery, growth, inner conflict, and disillusionment that all sensitive black intellectuals experience in a world where racism is a pervasive reality.

A Long Way from Home, like the autobiography of other black writers since World War I, falls into a literary tradition that begins with the narratives of runaway slaves, including The Life and Times of Frederick Douglass, and continues in Booker T. Washington's Up from Slavery and W. E. B. Du Bois' Dusk of Dawn. The genre is one in which more intimate aspects of the autobiographer's personal experiences are subordinated to social commentary and reflections upon what it means to be a Negro in a world dominated by white men. There have been no black Marcel Prousts and André Gides. The traumatic effects of the black experience seem to have made confessional writing an intellectual luxury black writers cannot afford.

McKay's narrative is unique in one aspect. Other accounts by prominent black men of their encounter with America have been written by those who were born and bred in the United States. Claude McKay was one of the more talented individuals in the stream of immigrants from the British West Indies who have been seeking their fortune in the United States since the turn of the century. They were refugees from a poverty exacerbated by overpopulation, and from a social system in which British settlers and their mixed-blood descendants had kept most blacks in a subordinate position. During the twenties and thirties West Indians played an active role in the hectic politics of Harlem, a phenomenon that has been analyzed with insight and perception (and also some bias) by Harold Cruse in *The Crisis of the Negro Intellectual*.

McKay's life was a single episode in the 500-year-old drama of the black diaspora, that massive dispersal of millions of men and women out of the great African homeland to the Caribbean islands and onto the American continents. He symbolizes their wanderings backward and forward between Africa and the New World, and from both of these areas to Britain and Europe. They have become detribalized in the process and have developed a pan-African consciousness. McKay does not emphasize his West Indianness but rather his blackness, his solidarity with Afro-Americans and Africans. He was keenly conscious of being a child of the diaspora, revealing sentiments similar to those in the Negro spiritual: "Sometimes I feel like a motherless child, a long way from home." ⟨. . .⟩

McKay was a complex man who himself had enjoyed the hospitality of many a "fine white house." Compassionate and valuing his relations with specific white friends, he realized the danger of racial solidarity sliding over into hate, but he thought it was a risk that had to be taken. The last chapter of the autobiography is a plea for black unity, and it led him to the position that Dr. Du Bois had espoused in 1934 at the cost of his position on the board of the NAACP, and that the youth in the civil-rights movement came to thirty years later. We have no way of knowing how he would have reacted to the Deacons for Defense, Malcolm X's Afro-American Unity Organization, the Black Panthers, or the Republic of New Africa. But what he has to say about the general forms of organization that black communities should adopt have a startlingly contemporary ring.

> St. Clair Drake, "Introduction," *A Long Way from Home* (New York: Harcourt, Brace & World, 1970), pp. ix–xi, xvii

---

GEORGE E. KENT   The story of McKay's poetry is also the story of such novels as *Home to Harlem*, *Banjo*, and *Banana Bottom*, both with respect to the soul's embattlement and the quality of the fiction. In *Home to Harlem*, the soulful way is expressed through Jake, a former longshoreman who has returned to Harlem after deserting an American army intent upon exploiting him as a laborer instead of a fighter against Germans, and Ray, an educated Black whose alienation from both Blacks and Whites blocks him from the uncomplicated celebration of joy that Jake easily achieves. Ray's main function in the novel is to represent a contrast to Jake and to articulate a criticism of Western culture, Jake's to assert an incorruptible innocence while celebrating the joys of the flesh, comradeship, and love. His natural innocence is his salvation, no matter what situation he confronts: the army's attempt to reduce him, living with an English woman who unsuccessfully attempts to keep him tethered, living with a black woman who requires brutality as an ingredient of love, dealing with a labor situation that offers either scabbing or an insincere labor union.

The greatest threat to his sense of innocence derives from the thin plot of the novel. Returning to Harlem, he discovers in Felice, a woman who returns the money he has paid for sexual favors, a natural soulmate. After discovering their natural affinity, Jake loses her for most of the duration of the novel, a fact which allows McKay to explore Harlem joy life. When Jake finds her, she has become the common-law partner of Jake's comrade Zeddy—but has not taken him into the inner citadel of her heart. Zeddy, angered at the threatened loss of Felice, draws a razor, and Jake confronts him with a pistol. Thus the snake has entered the edenic garden of comradeship—but not for long. Both men suffer quick remorse over the threatened corruption of their souls. Zeddy apologizes, and his apology is quickly accepted by Jake. Jake's realization of the threat to his innocence is expressed as follows:

> His love nature was generous and warm without any vestige of the diabolical or sadistic.
> Yet here he was caught in the thing that he despised so thoroughly . . . Brest, London, and his America. Their vivid brutality tortured his imagination. Oh, he was infinitely disgusted with himself to think that he had just been moved by the same savage emotions as those vile, vicious, villainous white men who, like hyenas and rattlers, had fought, murdered, and clawed the entrails out of black men over the common commercial flesh of women.

The form of soul in *Home to Harlem* is really romantic bohemianism. The reader can admire the superiority of Jake and Felice's natural normality, but cannot forget that the real test comes when Jake has given hostages to fortune in the form of a wife and children, a situation in which the vibrations of the black man's condition in Western culture are not so easily brushed aside.

George E. Kent, "The Soulful Way of Claude McKay," *Blackness and the Adventure of Western Culture* (Chicago: Third World Press, 1972), pp. 46–48

WAYNE F. COOPER   Despite his genuine achievements in *Songs of Jamaica* and *Constab Ballads*, these volumes too often betrayed McKay's literary inexperience, emotional confusion, and intellectual immaturity. In "Bennie's Departure," a long description of his affection for and emotional dependence on a fellow recruit in the early days of their enlistment—a description, not incidentally, that bordered upon a passionate declaration of homosexual love—McKay observed that Bennie "was always quick and steady, / Not of wav'rin' min' like me." McKay's "wav'rin' min' " can in part be attributed to his youthful inexperience and in part to the deep-seated psychological insecurity with which he viewed his future. But his uncertainty was made even more acute by his ambivalent suspension at this stage of his life between the peasant culture and the literate colonial society. All these factors contributed to the stylistic problems and contradictory emotional and intellectual stances in his dialect poetry.

Despite his emotional loyalty to the Jamaican peasantry, his commitment to the dialect was not total because he could not adequately express through his dialect persona all those aspects of his own intellectual and literary experiences that he had assimilated as an educated colonial. His education claimed a part of his being as surely as did his peasant heritage and could not be denied expression, as its awkward manifestation in the dialect attested. Although tied emotionally and racially to the uneducated peasantry, he no longer fully shared their necessarily restricted world view. On the other hand, while sharing the literate consciousness of the race from whom he had acquired his education, he could not identify with it at the deepest levels of his emotions.

Given this dual estrangement, the wonder is not that so much of McKay's dialect poetry was bad but that he achieved in it as much as he did. In his later poetry and novels, he would handle the problems of alienation and identity with greater self-consciousness and with more sophistication.

Wayne F. Cooper, *Claude McKay: Rebel Sojourner in the Harlem Renaissance* (Baton Rouge: Louisiana State University Press, 1987), pp. 46–47

MELVIN DIXON   ⟨. . .⟩ in *Banjo* Ray rejects civilization as vehemently as he feels rejected by it. The extremity of this position leads to a self-righteous tone in Ray's proclamation, which is compromised by Ray's lack of productivity. McKay backs himself into such a corner that he all but extinguishes any hope that intellect and instinct, education and passion, can coexist for black writers as they have for Russian novelists like Tolstoy, whose art, Ray believes, grew from the soil. The quest McKay began with Ray meeting Jake on a moving train—an overground railroad—and continued until Ray's ultimate break with civilization and embrace of vagabonding finds a more balanced conclusion in *Banana Bottom*. In the earlier novels McKay attempted to survey the wilderness of black alienation and displacement. In his last novel, McKay finds peace with himself through his female protagonist Bita Plant who, uprooted from Jamaica and grafted with a European education, manages to transplant herself back in the native soil.

McKay's choice of a female protagonist to complete his quest shows his desire for regeneration. Bita fulfills the potential of McKay's bachelor wanderers. Her procreative union with her peasant husband Jubban, in which both are "nourished by the same soil," resolves McKay's dilemma of unification with land, culture, and self. McKay previously depicted divided sensibilities through oppositional friendships between men, which limit creativity to the realm of art. This is not to say that Jake and Banjo fail as mates for Ray, but that the union goes only so far. Through the "offspring" of literature Ray represents his racial ambivalence or displacement. And Ray does locate Harlem and the Ditch as places for the performance of his identity. Bita Plant, however, embodies regeneration.

By returning in *Banana Bottom* to the time and place of his West Indian upbringing, McKay frees himself from the overwhelming cultural tradition of Europe and from American myths of racial uplift through face-saving art (a dominant ideology during the Harlem Renaissance). McKay is also free to explore the range of characters, situations, and life opportunities a predominantly black environment provides. Readers encounter a similar ease in Zora Neale Hurston's fiction, which takes place in the all-black town of Eatonville, Florida. McKay and Hurston luxuriate in lavish descriptions of quotidian events, customs, and the various features of the land. Yet McKay worried about the possibility of exaggeration and imprecision in his writing. He once commented disparagingly in a letter to his longtime friend Max Eastman, "Whether poetry or prose, my writing is always most striking and true when it is a little reminiscent and nostalgic. The vividness of *Home* to *Harlem* was due to my being removed just the right distance from the scene. Doing *Banjo* I was too close to it. *Banana Bottom* was a lazy dream, the images becoming blurred from overdoing long-distance photography." The imagery, no matter how imprecise, clearly helped McKay resolve some long-standing, as well as long-distance, conflicts, for the novel celebrates Bita's successful reintegration into her home society.

Melvin Dixon, "To Wake the Nations Underground: Jean Toomer and Claude McKay," *Ride Out the Wilderness: Geography and Identity in Afro-American Literature* (Urbana: University of Illinois Press, 1987), pp. 52–53

TYRONE TILLERY   The reason ⟨McKay⟩ had chosen Marseilles as his setting ⟨for *Banjo*⟩ and had created such an episodic plot was rooted in the very criticism he challenged. His assertion that he knew more about African-American life than most American-born blacks was an exaggeration. In fact, McKay had little more experience among American blacks than some bohemian and radical whites. His relationship with the ordinary blacks celebrated in his poems and prose always remained perfunctory. He had worked alongside blacks in America only from 1916 to 1920, when he had left the United States to travel to his "spiritual homeland," England. From 1922 until 1934, he spent all of his time abroad. But even during the years when he had worked among lower-class American blacks, McKay managed to remain aloof from his environment.

His association with the black masses had never been voluntary; it had occurred as a result of his own failure to succeed at middle-class pursuits. By McKay's own admission, he had gleaned all he could from his Harlem experiences. Writing to Eastman after the publication of *Home to Harlem*, he had lamented that "all [his] hankering for the United States had disappeared," and, more important, "all of it [Harlem] had gone out in the first novel." Of the future projects he outlined for Eastman, none mentioned Harlem as a background.

The hostile reaction of Du Bois, White, and other blacks to McKay's books stemmed in part from their disappointment with the black settings and characters he chose to depict (low-life instead of middle-class life), in part from hostility to McKay as a West Indian who presumed to be an authority on American blacks, and in part from anger at his assault on middle-class blacks. By 1929, the year of *Banjo*'s publication, middle-class blacks had grown even more sensitive to the depiction of black Americans in fiction; the black audience who borrowed books from the library or who bought books for their homes wanted to see positive portraits of blacks. Thus, it is not surprising that the *New York Amsterdam News*, one of the few black newspapers to praise *Home to Harlem*, was outraged at *Banjo*, complaining that it was full of things that would please white readers, "Coon stuff."

Black writers and critics had logical reasons to be sensitive about literature that seemed to perpetuate old stereotypes concerning blacks. McKay tried to argue that the black middle class was offended by his subject matter because it identified more with whites and had no sympathy for the black lower class. But it is not true that the small black middle class turned its back on poorer blacks. Middle-class blacks during the twenties did not lead a life separated from lower-class black life. All blacks, whatever their economic circumstances, lived in the same neighborhoods, attended the same churches, shopped in the same stores, and so on. Even the Harvard-educated Du Bois, who occupied the heights of black society, had what today would seem a surprising amount of contact with lower-class African-Americans. According to George Kent, author of *Blackness and the Adventure of Western Culture*, many of the Renaissance writers and critics brought to their "task" a cosmopolitan range of experiences that protected them from a simple, myopic middle-class perspective. ⟨. . .⟩

In *Banjo*, McKay poured out much of what he was struggling to achieve in his own life: an understanding of his own identity. Too much of the person Claude McKay peered through the pages of *Banjo* for it to succeed as a dramatization of the conflict between the unspoiled folk and Western civilization. The catharsis so evident in *Banjo* represents McKay's personal journey to answer the question "Who am I?" At best, he was only able to respond in the manner of his black characters in *Banjo* who, when foreign officials asked for their papers, were distinguished by the official phrase: "Nationality Doubtful."

Tyrone Tillery, *Claude McKay: A Black Poet's Struggle for Identity* (Amherst: University of Massachusetts Press, 1992), pp. 112–13, 125

◙ Bibliography

Songs of Jamaica. 1912.

Constab Ballads. 1912.

Spring in New Hampshire and Other Poems. 1920.

Harlem Shadows. 1922.

Sudom Lincha. Tr. P. Okhrimenko. 1923.

Negry v Amerike. Tr. P. Okhrimenko. 1923.

Home to Harlem. 1928.

Banjo: A Story without a Plot. 1929.

Gingertown. 1932.

Banana Bottom. 1933.

A Long Way from Home. 1937.

Harlem: Negro Metropolis. 1940.

Selected Poems. 1953.

The Dialect Poetry. 1972.

The Passion of Claude McKay: Selected Prose and Poetry 1912–1948. Ed. Wayne
        F. Cooper. 1973.

My Green Hills of Jamaica and Five Jamaican Short Stories. 1979.

Jean Toomer
1894–1967

JEAN TOOMER was born Nathan Pinchback Toomer in Washington, D.C., on December 26, 1894, the son of Nathan and Nina Pinchback Toomer. At his grandfather's insistence he was called Eugene Toomer, and later he adopted the first name Jean because he thought it had a more literary connotation. Nathan Toomer abandoned the family soon after Jean was born, and Nina Toomer, after living with her parents for some years, moved in 1906 to New Rochelle, New York, where she lived with her white husband. She died in 1909, and Jean returned to Washington to live with his grandparents. At this time his grandfather, P. B. S. Pinchback, informed Toomer—who looked white and believed himself to be white—that he was of racially mixed ancestry.

Toomer attended several universities between 1914 and 1919, including the University of Wisconsin and the City College of New York, but finally abandoned academic life to pursue literature, writing poetry and fiction for such magazines as the *Little Review, Secession,* and *Broom.* Toomer disliked the use of race labels, insisting he was neither white nor black but "simply an American." He held the belief that race was not a fundamental constituent in one's self-definition, and was accordingly criticized for the lack of a black focus in his later works.

Toomer is best remembered for his first book, *Cane* (1923), a miscellany of stories, verse, and a drama concerned with the lives of black Americans in the United States. Much of the source material for this work was derived from a trip to Georgia he took in the fall of 1921. *Cane* is now regarded as one of the most remarkable novels of its time because of its prose-poetic language, its amalgamation of literary genres, and its rich evocation of the lives of both northern and southern black Americans.

Toomer's other works are the plays *Balo, Natalie Mann,* and *The Sacred Factory;* the novella "York Beach" (1929); *Essentials* (1931), a collection of aphorisms; the 800-line poem "The Blue Meridian" (1936), a radical expansion of an earlier poem entitled "The First American"; and other stories, essays, and poems. Many of these works, as well as a selection from his autobiographical writings, have been gathered in *The Wayward and the Seeking: A Collection of Writings by Jean Toomer* (1980), edited by Darwin Turner. Several novels, plays, and stories remain unpublished.

In the mid-1920s Toomer became interested in the work of the mystic Georges Ivanovitch Gurdjieff. Gurdjieff's philosophy stressed the union of physical, mental, and psychological functions to achieve inner harmony, and Toomer taught the Gurdjieff method between 1925 and 1933. In 1931 he resided in a communal arrangement with eight unmarried male and female friends in Portage, Wisconsin; later he married one of the participants, Margery Latimer, who died while giving birth to their only child. Alternative spiritual disciplines obsessed Toomer, who devoted himself successively to Quakerism and to L. Ron Hubbard's Scientology. It is frequently asserted that Toomer's devotion to Gurdjieff, Scientology, and other pseudoscientific religions ruined him as a writer, as it made his later work dogmatic and excessively didactic.

In 1934 Toomer married again, this time to Marjorie Content, whose father gave the couple a farm in Bucks County, Pennsylvania. Aside from a trip to India in 1939, Toomer lived in seclusion on the farm, writing little and suffering increasing health problems. He died on March 30, 1967.

Critical Extracts

WALDO FRANK   Reading his book ⟨*Cane*⟩, I had the vision of a land, heretofore sunk in the mists of muteness, suddenly rising up into the eminence of song. Innumerable books have been written about the South; some good books have been written about the South. This book *is* the South. I do not mean that *Cane* covers the South or is the South's full voice. Merely this: a poet has arisen among our American youth who has known how to turn the essences and materials of his Southland into the essences and materials of literature. A poet has arisen in that land who writes, not as a Southerner, not as a rebel against Southerners, not as a Negro, not as apologist or priest or critic: who writes as a *poet*. The fashioning of beauty is ever foremost in his inspiration: not forcedly but simply, and because these ultimate aspects of his world are to him more real than all its specific problems. He has made songs and lovely stories of his land . . . not of its yesterday, but of its immediate life. And that has been enough. ⟨. . .⟩

How typical is *Cane* of the South's still virgin soil and of its pressing seeds! and the book's chaos of verse, tale, drama, its rhythmic rolling shift from lyricism to narrative, from mystery to intimate pathos! But read the book through and you will see a complex and significant form take substance from its chaos. Part One is the primitive and evanescent black world of Georgia. Part Two is the threshing and suffering brown world of Washington, lifted by opportunity and contact into the anguish of self-conscious struggle. Part Three is Georgia again . . . the invasion into this black womb of the ferment seed: the neurotic, educated, spiritually stirring Negro. As a broad form this is superb, and the very looseness and unexpected waves of the book's parts make *Cane* still more *South*, still more of an esthetic equivalent of the land.

Waldo Frank, "Foreword [to the 1923 edition of *Cane*]," *Cane* by Jean Toomer(New York: W. W. Norton, 1988), pp. 138–40

GORHAM B. MUNSON   There can be no question of Jean Toomer's skill as a literary craftsman. A writer who can combine vowels and liquids to form a cadence like "she was as innocently lovely as a November cotton flower" has a subtle command of word-music. And a writer who can break the boundaries of the sentences, interrupt the placement of a fact with a lyrical cry, and yet hold both his fact and his exclamation to a single welded meaning as in the expression: "A single room held down to earth . . . O fly away to Jesus . . . by a leaning chimney . . .", is assuredly at home in the language and therefore is assuredly free to experiment and invent. Toomer has found his own speech, now swift and clipped for violent narrative action, now languorous and dragging for specific characterizing purposes, and now lean and sinuous for the exposition of ideas, but always cadenced to accord with an unusually sensitive ear.

It is interesting to know that Toomer, before he began to write, thought of becoming a composer. One might have guessed it from the fact that the early sketches in *Cane* (1923) depend fully as much upon a musical unity as upon a literary unity. "Karintha," for example, opens with a song, presents a theme, breaks into song, develops the theme, sings again, drops back into prose, and dies away in a song. But in it certain narrative functions—one might mention that lying back of the bald statement, "This interest of the male, who wishes to ripen a growing thing too soon, could mean no good to her"—are left undeveloped. Were it not for the songs, the piece could scarcely exist.

But electing to write, Toomer was too canny to try to carry literature further into music than this. *Cane* is, from one point of view, the record of his search for suitable literary forms. We can see him seeking guidance and in several of the stories, notably "Fern" and "Avey," it is the hand of Sherwood Anderson that he takes hold. But Anderson leads toward formlessness and Toomer shakes him off for Waldo Frank in such pieces as "Theatre" where the design becomes clear and the parts are held in a vital esthetic union. Finally, he breaks through in a free dramatic form of his own, the play *Kabnis* which still awaits production by an American theatre that cries for good native drama and yet lacks the wit to perceive the talent of Toomer. ⟨. . .⟩

He is a dynamic symbol of what all artists of our time should be doing, if they are to command our trust. He has mastered his craft. Now he seeks a purpose that will convince him that his craft is nobly employed. Obviously, to his search there is no end, but in his search there is bound to occur a fusion of his experience, and it is this fused experience that will give profundity to his later work. His way is not the way of the minor art master, but the way of the major master of art. And that is why his potential literary significance outweighs the actualized literary significance of so many of his contemporaries.

Gorham B. Munson, "The Significance of Jean Toomer," *Opportunity* 3, No. 3 (September 1925): 262–63

JEAN TOOMER   In my writing I was working, at various times, on all the main forms. Essays, articles, poems, short stories, reviews, and a long piece somewhere between a novel and a play. Before I had even so much as glimpsed the possibility of writing *Cane*, I had written a trunk full of manuscripts. The phrase "trunk full" is often used loosely. I mean it literally and exactly. But what difficulties I had! I had in me so much experience so twisted up that not a thing would come out until by sheer force I had dragged it forth. Only now and again did I experience spontaneous writing.

Most of it was will and sweat. And nothing satisfied me. Not a thing had I done which I thought merited publication—or even sending to a magazine. I wrote and wrote and put each thing aside, regarding it as simply one of the exercises of my apprenticeship. Often I would be depressed and almost despair over the written thing. But, on the other hand, I became more and more convinced that I had the real stuff in me. And slowly but surely I began getting the "feeling" of my medium, a sense of form, of words, of sentences, rhythms, cadences, and rhythmic patterns. And then, after several years work, suddenly, it was as if a door opened and I knew without doubt that I was *inside. I knew literature!* And what was my joy!

But many things happened before that time came! ⟨. . .⟩

I came in contact with an entirely new body of ideas. Buddhist philosophy, the Eastern teachings, occultism, theosophy. Much of the writing itself seemed to me to be poorly done; and I was certain that the majority of the authors of these books had only third or fourth-rate minds, or less. But I extracted the ideas from their settings, and they seemed to me among the most extraordinary I had ever heard. It is natural to me to put my whole heart into anything that really interests me—as long as I am interested. For the time being, only that thing exists in the world. These ideas challenged and stimulated me. Despite my literary purpose, I was compelled to know something more about them. So, for a time, I turned my back on literature and plunged into this kind of reading. I read far and wide, for more than eight months. Then, I became dissatisfied with just reading. I wanted to do some of the things they suggested. I wanted to see some of the things with my own eyes. I myself wanted a personal all-around experience of the world these books seemed to open. I tried several of the exercises; but then, abruptly stopped them. I concluded they were not for me. In general, I concluded that all of that was not for me. I was in this physical, tangible, earthly world, and I knew little enough of it. It was the part of wisdom to learn more and to be able to do more in this, before I began exploring and adventuring into other worlds. So I came back to earth and to literature. But I had profited in many ways by my excursion. The Eastern World, the ancient scriptures had been brought to my notice. Also, our own Christian Bible. I had read it as if it were a new book. Just simply as a work of literature I was convinced that we had nothing to equal it. Not even Shakespeare— my old God—wrote language of such grand perfection. And my religious nature, given a cruel blow by Clarence Darrow and naturalism and atheism, but not, as I found, destroyed by them—my religious nature which had been sleeping was vigorously aroused. ⟨. . .⟩

Once during this period I read many books on the matter of race and the race problem in America. Rarely had I encountered the nonsense contained in most of these books. It was evident to me, who had seen both the white and the colored worlds, and both from the inside, that the authors of these writings had little or no experience of the matters they were dealing with. Their pages showed very little more than strings of words expressive of personal prejudices and preferences. I felt that I should write on this matter. I did write several fragments of essays. And I did a lot of thinking. Among other things, I again worked over my own position, and formulated it with more fullness and exactitude. I wrote a poem called, "The First American," the idea of which is, that here in America we are in the process of forming a new race, that I was one of the first conscious members of this race.

> Jean Toomer, "The *Cane* Years" (c. 1932), *The Wayward and the Seeking: A Collection of Writings by Jean Toomer*, ed. Darwin T. Turner (Washington, DC: Howard University Press, 1980), pp. 117–21

ROBERT BONE   In spite of his wide and perhaps primary association with white intellectuals, as an artist Toomer never underestimated the importance of his Negro identity. He attained a universal vision not by ignoring race as a local truth, but by coming face to face with his particular tradition. His pilgrimage to Georgia was a conscious attempt to make contact with his hereditary roots in the Southland. Of Georgia, Toomer wrote: "There one finds soil in the sense that the Russians know it—the soil every art and literature that is to live must be embedded in." This scene of soil is central to *Cane* and to Toomer's artistic vision. "When one is on the soil of one's ancestors," his narrator remarks, "most anything can come to one."

What comes to Toomer, in the first section of *Cane*, is a vision of the parting soul of slavery:

> . . . for though the sun is setting on
> A song-lit race of slaves, it has not set;
> Though late, O soil, it is not too late yet
> To catch thy plaintive soul, leaving, soon gone.

The soul of slavery persists in the "supper-getting-ready songs" of the black women who live on the Dixie Pike—a road which "has grown from a goat path in Africa." It persists in "the soft, listless cadence of Georgia's South," in the hovering spirit of a comforting Jesus, and in the sudden violence of the Georgia moon. It persists above all in the people, white and black, who have become Andersonian "grotesques" by virtue of their slave inheritance. Part I of *Cane* is in fact a kind of Southern *Winesburg, Ohio*. It consists of the portraits of six women—all primitives—in which an Andersonian narrator mediates between the reader and the author's vision of life on the Dixie Pike.

> Robert Bone, *The Negro Novel in America* (New Haven: Yale University Press, 1958), pp. 81–82

DARWIN T. TURNER   The actual beginning of Jean Toomer, writer, probably can be dated from ⟨. . .⟩ the spring of 1920. While chasing many gleams, he had read extensively in atheism, naturalism, socialism, sociology, psychology, and the dramas of Shaw. To these scientific, philosophical, and social writings, he had added *Wilhelm Meister* of Goethe, the romances of Victor Hugo, and the verse of Walt Whitman. After his abortive crusade in the shipyard, he had reaccepted capitalism as a necessary evil. Dismayed because his atheism had shocked a Quaker girl, he had reaffirmed his faith in God and in religion, even though he refused to believe in orthodox creeds and churches. Introduced now to a literary world of such people as Lola Ridge, Edwin Arlington Robinson, and Waldo Frank, he was dazzled with the prospect of retiring from arid philosophies into a cultural aristocracy.

Looking back from a diary written in 1930, he saw the Toomer of the early twenties as a vanity-burdened poseur who adopted the manners of a poet, a poet's appearance, and a French-sounding name—Jean. A more objective observer sees a seriously confused young man of twenty-five, who was not content to be average, but who had discovered nothing at which to be great; who wanted to guide, to instruct, to lead, to dominate, but who would withdraw completely if he could not; and who habitually discontinued studies with startling abruptness, not because he had mastered them, but because he had lost interest or, as with music, had decided that he could not become a master. This, however, was the tortured soul hidden by the

ever present mask of intellect, confidence, and charm which caused Waldo
Frank to write, "You are one of those men one must see but once to know
the timbre and the truth of."

Darwin T. Turner, "Jean Toomer: Exile," *In a Minor Chord: Three Afro-American Writers and Their Search for Identity* (Carbondale: Southern Illinois University Press, 1971), pp. 10–11

CHARLES W. SCRUGGS   ⟨A⟩ fuller understanding of *Cane* comes
from Toomer's letter to Waldo Frank upon completion of the novel. Critics
may be skeptical about finding any structure in the work, and certainly
Cane may be appreciated without one, but Toomer himself apparently had
a plan. "My brother!" he says to Frank on December 12, 1922:

> Cane is on its way to you! For two weeks I have worked steadily
> at it. The book is done. From three angles, Cane's design is a
> circle. Aesthetically, from simple forms to complex ones, and back
> to simple forms. Regionally, from the South up into the North,
> and back into the South again. Or from the North down into the
> South and then a return North. From the point of view of the
> spiritual entity behind the work, the curve really starts with Bona
> and Paul (awakening), plunges into Kabnis, emerges in Karintha
> etc. swings upward into Theatre and Box Seat, and ends (pauses)
> in Harvest Song. . . . Between each of the three sections, a curve.
> These, to vaguely indicate the design.

Toomer's outline both puzzles and informs. It puzzles because, although the
novel moves from South to North to South, it does not parallel the spiritual
pattern he employs. The published work begins with the Karintha section
and ends with "Kabnis." The curves drawn on separate pages between the
sections hint at a circular design, but the reader tends to associate them
only with the South-North-South structural scheme.

The key, I think, lies in the word "pauses" (". . . and ends (pauses) in
Harvest Song"). Toomer is describing *Cane* in organic terms, and therefore
it never really ends. It is simply a matter of beginning all over again with
"Bona and Paul," the story that follows "Harvest Song."

Organic form interests Toomer as he reacts to the industrialization of his
age. In a letter to Gorham Munson (March 19, 1923) he compares his
aesthetic form to a tree, with the sap as the sustenance and the arrangement

of leaves as the meaning. "A machine," he says, "is all form, it has no leaves. Its very abstraction is . . . the death of it." Even earlier, in a letter to Waldo Frank (July 19, 1922), he mentions plans for a collection entitled *Cane* with the sections "Cane stalks and choruses" ("Kabnis" and "K.C.A."—probably "Karintha," "Carma," and "Avey"); "leaves and syrup songs" (the poems), and "Leaf Traceries in Washington" (the vignettes).

Charles W. Scruggs, "The Mark of Cain and the Redemption of Art: A Study of Theme and Structure of Jean Toomer's *Cane*," *American Literature* 44, No. 2 (May 1972): 279–80

JEAN WAGNER   "Blue Meridian" is beyond a doubt the concluding step in a long process of meditation, for its central idea is already contained in embryo in an essay published seven years earlier and entitled "Race Problems and Modern Society."

In this essay, Toomer begins by noting "the changes of forms and of modes" that had occurred at a constantly accelerated pace during his own lifetime: "The principles of cohesion and crystallization are being rapidly withdrawn from the materials of old forms, with a consequent break up of these forms, a setting free of these materials, with the possibility that the principles of cohesion and crystallization will recombine the stuff of life and make new forms." These cataclysms affect not only the material features of man's life but also the actual forms of relationships between men.

Alongside this development there is, contrariwise, a strengthening of some other forms of modern society which, remaining exempt from the dissolution noted above, even tend to expand and establish themselves more firmly. In particular these are, according to Toomer, the Western world's economic, political, legal, and military concepts, which dig themselves in and work against the evolutionary forces.

He proceeds by placing, within the context of these related yet hostile movements, the racial problems, especially those of the United States, which cannot be considered apart from the other principal forms of the social order. Here the effect of the evolutionary factors is to bring about an ever closer resemblance between such Negro social types as the businessman, politician, educator, student, writer, etc., and the corresponding white types. Yet, on the other hand, whites and blacks shut themselves up ever more tightly in their separatism with the consequence, for example, that interracial marriage becomes no less heinous in the eyes of blacks than of whites.

Given this crystallization of the race question, Toomer is led to advocate, as a way out of the impasse, "a selective fusion of the racial and cultural factors of America, in order that the best possible stock and culture may be produced."

Though the line of argument in this essay is buttressed by scientific considerations, Toomer's thinking is essentially that of a poet and humanist. We are, in any case, under no obligation to pass judgment on the feasibility of the plan, which concerns us only insofar as it may serve to throw light on the genesis of "Blue Meridian."

Race, in this poem, acquires a totally different dimension from what we encountered in *Cane*. As in the essay discussed above, it takes place in the much vaster setting of the "Myth of America," to adopt Hart Crane's expression. For is not America indeed, as Walt Whitman declared it, "the race of races" and also "the greatest poem"? "Blue Meridian" quite certainly owes something to *The Bridge*, but both alike are indebted to Whitman and, through him, to the American tradition born with the Pilgrim Fathers, according to which the New World must necessarily be new, in the most literal sense of the word.

The fundamental thesis of "Blue Meridian" is the need for a regenerated America, to be achieved through the regeneration of each individual and each community composing it, of an America once more united around the spiritual dream of its founders.

> It is a new America,
> To be spiritualized by each new American.

What must be found once more is the whole man in his primordial unity, whether this is brought about by the collective effort of millions of men or attained by an elite of apostles ("twelve men") among whom, as Toomer saw things, one would have to place poets:

> Lift, lift thou walking forces!
> Let us feel the energy of animals,
> The energy of rumps and bull-bent heads
> Crashing the barrier to man.
> It must spiral on!
> A million men, or twelve men,
> Must crash the barrier to the next higher form.

Jean Wagner, *Black Poets of the United States: From Paul Lawrence Dunbar to Langston Hughes*, tr. Kenneth Douglas (Urbana: University of Illinois Press, 1973), pp. 272–74

SUSAN L. BLAKE   Between Jean Toomer and ⟨Cane's⟩ characters is a creative persona—represented sometimes by a narrator, sometimes simply by the narrative voice—who shares his characters' goals and whose story unifies the book. Like Kabnis, like any artist, he wants to give form to experience, and Cane is the record of his attempt. Gorham B. Munson has called this persona the "spectatorial artist," a term which suggests the artistic process outlined in the book: the persona progresses from a spectator in the first stories to an artist in "Kabnis." His progress is measured by his distance from his characters. Both the spectator and the artist are detached from their material, but the understanding that distinguishes the detached creator of the final story from the detached observer of the first comes from a transitional stage of involvement.

The central conflict in Cane is the struggle of the spectatorial artist to involve himself in his material. The characters in the individual stories are engaged in the same conflict. Their "material" is life; involvement for them means acceptance of its chaos. The protagonists in the first stories are unaware of the conflict; the men who try to buy Karintha do not know what they are missing, "do not know that the soul of her was a growing thing ripened too soon." Kabnis knows; and the sight of "hills and valleys, heaving with folk-songs, so close to me that I cannot reach them" drives him mad. For the spectatorial artist, involvement in his material means identification with his characters and recognition that the dilemma he is portraying in them is also his dilemma. Their characters become more complex as they become more aware of their experience; they become more aware as their creator, becoming more involved with them, put his own awareness into them. Thus characters and creative voice develop in parallel in Cane, and the book resembles neither a novel nor a collection of short stories as much as it does a sketchbook—a record of artistic development.

Susan L. Blake, "The Spectatorial Artist and the Structure of Cane," CLA Journal 17, No. 4 (June 1974): 516–17

RICHARD ELDRIDGE   While the poetic quality of Toomer's prose is in many respects bolder and more successful than much of his poetry, the poems nevertheless are an essential part of his "song." As in his prose, many of his poems are dusk songs, reflecting not only the mood of the land but also the sense of the people. "Nullo" is a poem which shows the deep

connection between earth and sky at a time of day when limits are hard
to define and therefore blend with the limitless:

> A spray of pine-needles,
> Dipped in western horizon gold,
> Fell onto a path.
> Dry moulds of cow-hoofs.
> In the forest.
> Rabbits knew not of their falling,
> Nor did the forest catch aflame.

The poem places before the reader the merest glimpse of a moment when
a spectacle occurs without notice but for the poet: the sun setting fire to
the edges of a spray of pine-needles as it falls to the ground. The visual
impression is precise; not only are we shown the path, but the shapes in
the path, "Dry moulds of cow-hoofs." The silence of such an eventful non-
event protects it from all but the poet's eye: "Rabbits knew not of their
falling, / Nor did the forest catch aflame." The pine spray catches the fire
yet does not spread it beyond the spray's own beauty. The cows have parted
until the next day, and the rabbits are unconscious of the passing. Such
is the attraction of sunset, when the poet's eye can make the seemingly
insignificant moment into a significant statement.

As in the sadness of Karintha's waste, Toomer's dusk poems often are
commentaries on the sadness of a dying culture. "Song of the Son" has
correctly been singled out as embodying the central idea of Toomer's Southern experience. In the poem, dusk is connected most clearly with Toomer's
thesis of the "swan-song" of the black folk heritage. The poem's message
is that the narrator, ostensibly Toomer, has returned to his Southern roots
in time to record the rural life in art which will outlast the black man. A
letter to Waldo Frank clarifies the point of view with which Toomer wrote
the poem:

> There is one thing about the Negro in America which most
> thoughtful persons seem to ignore: the Negro is in solution, in the
> process of solution. As an entity, the race is loosing [sic] its body,
> and its soul is approaching a common soul. If one holds his eye to
> individuals and sections, race is starkly evident, and racial
> continuity seems assured. One is even led to believe that the
> thing we call Negro beauty will always be attributable to a clearly
> defined physical source. But the fact is, that if anything comes up
> now, pure Negro, it will be a swan-song. The negro [sic] of the
> folk-song has all but passed away: the Negro of the emotional

church is fading. A hundred years from now these Negroes, if they exist at all will live in art. . . . The supreme fact of mechanical civilization is that you become part of it, or get sloughed off (under). Negroes have no culture to resist it with (and if they had, their position would be identical to that of the Indians), hence industrialism the more readily transforms them. A few generations from now, the Negro will still be dark, and a portion of his psychology will spring from this fact, but in all else he will be a conformist to the general outlines of American civilization, or of American chaos. In my own stuff, in those pieces that come closest to the old Negro, to the spirit saturated with folk-song: Karintha and Fern, the dominant emotion is sadness derived from a sense of fading, from a knowledge of my futility to check solution. There is nothing about these pieces of the bouyant [sic] expression of new race. The folk-songs themselves are of the same order. The deepest of them: "I ain't got long to stay here."

If the expression of folk-roots is to be recorded in art, what better way to record it than by creating a pattern of song to drift from story to story, poem to poem, usually at dusk when toil and need are reflected upon with a soul-response? If the culture is dying, what better moment to frame that death than the moment of day which heightens life by the very imminence of darkness and, symbolically, death?

Richard Eldridge, "The Unifying Images in Part One of Jean Toomer's *Cane*," CLA *Journal* 12, No. 3 (March 1979): 194–96

NELLIE Y. McKAY   *Balo* and *Natalie Mann* are products of the brief time during which Toomer had the desire to add the unique richness of the Afro-American experience to American literature. ⟨. . .⟩

Balo and *Natalie Mann* are two very different plays, and in them Toomer explores two distinctly separate forms of dramatic techniques. The first is a one-act folk play, the second, a full-length experiment in expressionist theater. In *Balo*, the southern setting, the single-day action, and the poor, rural, close-to-the-earth and very religious characters contrast sharply with the living rooms of the Washington, D.C., middle class, the cabarets of the counterculture, the year-long action, and the affluent, urbane, and upwardly mobile characters who make "refined" culture their religion, who engage in endless conversations about the definition of art and whom we meet in *Natalie Mann*. In these plays, the differences in basic values between these two groups of people—a result of the development of class differences among black people between the end of the Civil War and 1920—becomes clear as Toomer describes folk culture and regionalism in one and the black need for erudition and cosmopolitanism in the other. ⟨. . .⟩

The differences between *Balo* and *Natalie Mann* make it clear that although Toomer was critical of some of the realities of black folk life, its good qualities made a positive impression on his imagination, whereas there was little he could recommend in the culture of middle-class America, the negative aspects of which he wanted to expose. From an emotional and philosophical standpoint, Toomer looked back to the African/American folk culture, identified himself with what he found spiritually uplifting in it, and made it a source of artistic inspiration.

Nellie Y. McKay, *Jean Toomer, Artist: A Study of His Literary Life and Work 1894–1936* (Chapel Hill: University of North Carolina Press, 1984), pp. 60–61, 79

CYNTHIA EARL KERMAN and RICHARD ELDRIDGE

⟨Toomer⟩ was not seeking a shift in a category attached to his own name, such as from black to white; he wished to be neither white nor black. The vision of the universal man was the benchmark of his identity, and perhaps he accurately perceived himself as the embodiment of the greater American soul, a concept that Waldo Frank and others continued to encourage. Toomer's appearance, he noted, caused people on separate occasions to think that he was of eleven different nationalities. As for biological forebears, he could not be sure but was probably somewhere between one-eighth and one-sixteenth black. And he had lived among blacks, among whites, among Jews, and in groups organized without racial labels around a shared interest such as literature or psychology, moving freely from any one of these groups to any other. One mark of membership in the "colored" group, he said, was acceptance of the "color line" with its attendant expectations; neither his family nor he had ever been so bound. To be in the white group would also imply the exclusion of the other.

> What then am I?
> I am at once no one of the races and I am all of them.
> I belong to no one of them and I belong to all.
> I am, in a strict racial sense, a member of a new race.

This new race of mixed people, now forming all over the world but especially in America, "may be the turning point for the return of mankind, now divided into hostile races, to one unified race, namely, to the human race." It was a new race, but also the oldest. The different racial and national groups could still contribute their distinctive richness: "I say to the colored group that, as a human being, I am one of them. . . . I say to the white group that, as a human being, I am one of them. As a white man, I am not one of them. . . . I am an American. As such, I invite them [both], not as [colored or] white people, but *as Americans*, to participate in whatever creative work I may be able to do."

Thus Toomer propounded the rather unpopular view that the racial issue in America would be resolved only when white America could accept the fact that its racial "purity" was a myth, that indeed its racial isolation produced blandness and lack of character. On the other hand, racial purity among blacks was just as much a myth and only encourages defensiveness and unconscious imitation, like that of an adolescent who defines his revolt against his parents by the very values he is trying to renounce. Race, he said, was a fictional construct, of no use for understanding people: "Human blood is human blood. Human beings are human beings. . . . No racial or social factors can adequately account for the uniqueness of each—or for the individual differences which people display concurrently with basic commonality."

Cynthia Earl Kerman and Richard Eldridge, *The Lives of Jean Toomer: A Hunger for Legibility* (Baton Rouge: Louisiana State University Press, 1987), pp. 341–42

CHARLES R. LARSON   Toomer was raised as a white person. Sociologically and culturally that is what he considered himself to be until the 1909 conversation with his grandfather, when P. B. S. informed him that Eliza Stewart may have been of mixed heritage. Until that moment, he had apparently never seriously considered the possibility, though the effect of this knowledge so traumatized him that he altered it and called himself an American. There were the years following Nina Toomer Coombs's death, when Jean and his grandparents lived in a racially mixed neighborhood and he attended a predominantly black school. But as soon as he graduated from high school, he made a hasty withdrawal from this first foray into black life and skittered off to Wisconsin. His autobiographical writings make the significance of that location absolutely clear: if he continued to live in a racially mixed community, people might begin to regard him as a Negro. ⟨. . .⟩

Toomer's connection to and with Harlem Renaissance might best be called an accident of time and place. If he had not told Waldo Frank and others that he was P. B. S. Pinchback's grandson, he might never have been connected with the Renaissance. If he had not used Waldo Frank's friendship and influence among New York publishers—blatantly, to his own advantage, it should be said—he might have remained unpublished. More likely, he would have found a publisher who would not have tried to promote him as a black writer, and today he would simply be regarded as another American author (like Waldo Frank, Sherwood Anderson, or even William Faulkner) who chose to write about black life in the United States. Clearly, by the time *Cane* saw print, Toomer deeply regretted being classified as a Negro author.

To his surprise and horror, the classification stuck. Why wouldn't it? *Cane* is one of the masterpieces of twentieth-century American fiction. Though its mixed form is often initially confusing, the statement it makes about ethnic pride through the nourishment of one's roots is absolutely indisputable. On a personal level, *Cane* is not simply about Jean Toomer's inability to accept his blackness but about America's failure to accept its Africanness. Still, people of differing ethnic origins have been proud to claim the novel, as if proprietary rights are a guarantee of artistic greatness. Fortunately, the work can stand on its own creative merit, with or without the ethnic claimants. Like *Huckleberry Finn* and *Light in August* and *Invisible Man*, Toomer's novel addresses one of the major issues of American life— racism in the United States. It is very much a social document about that specific American malady, yet its affirmation of blackness is never weighted down by the romantic sentiment of some of Toomer's contemporaries' work.

Instead, one might say that *Cane* catalogues the frustrations and psychoses of black life in a kleptomaniacal world, where one culture steals from another while simultaneously beating it down. In the jealousy that binds the two cultures together, Toomer discovers not only life and heritage but also poetry. *Cane* was Toomer's ultimate homage to black life, his praise song of a way of life he himself was unable to embrace.

Charles R. Larson, *Invisible Darkness: Jean Toomer and Nella Larsen* (Iowa City: University of Iowa Press, 1993), pp. 201–2

▨ *Bibliography*

Cane. 1923.

Essentials. 1931.

The Flavor of Man. 1949.

The Wayward and the Seeking: A Collection of Writings. Ed. Darwin T. Turner. 1980.

Collected Poems. Ed. Robert B. Jones and Margery Toomer Latimer. 1988.

◈ ◈ ◈

Richard Wright
1908–1960

RICHARD NATHANIEL WRIGHT was born on September 4, 1908, near Natchez, Mississippi, to a schoolteacher mother and an illiterate sharecropper father. His father abandoned the family when Wright was very young, and he was raised by his maternal grandmother. After ninth grade, he dropped out of school and moved to Memphis, then to Chicago and New York. He educated himself, and was particularly interested in literature, sociology, and psychology. In 1932 he joined the Communist party, and his literary career was encouraged by the Communist-affiliated John Reed Club. Much of his early writing appeared in leftist publications. He worked for the Federal Negro Theatre Project and the Federal Writers' Project; while associated with these organizations he published *12 Million Black Voices* (1941), a Marxist analysis of the American class struggle. He was Harlem editor for the *Daily Worker* in New York. In 1938 he married Rose Dhima Meadman; they were later divorced, and Wright married Ellen Poplar, with whom he had two children. From 1947 until his death he lived in Paris.

Wright first came to the attention of the American reading public with the publication of *Uncle Tom's Children: Four Novellas* in 1938; the stories concern the struggles to maturity of oppressed black women and men. An augmented edition including the novelette "Bright and Morning Star" appeared in 1940. Wright's second book, *Native Son* (1940), was his major critical and popular breakthrough, and remains one of the most influential American novels of the twentieth century. It concerns the life and destruction of Bigger Thomas, a poor black youth from the slums of Chicago. Wright's evocative portrayal of a life of fear and enslavement struck a powerful chord with his readership, despite some critics' complaints that the latter third of the book is expository and slow-moving.

Though none of Wright's subsequent books had the immediate impact of *Native Son*, he was admired as a solid stylist and spokesman for the poor and oppressed. His later novels are *The Outsider* (1953), *Savage Holiday* (1954), *The Long Dream* (1958), and *Lawd Today* (1963). *Eight Men*, a collection of stories, was published posthumously in 1961. His autobiography, *Black Boy: A Record of Childhood and Youth* (1945), and his sociological studies, including *Black Power: A Record of Reactions in a Land of Pathos* (1954), *The Color Curtain: A Report on the Bandung Conference* (1956; originally published in French in 1955), *Pagan Spain* (1956), and *White Man, Listen!* (1957), were also widely read and admired. Wright died on November 28, 1960. Another autobiography, *American Hunger*, was published in 1977; *Richard Wright Reader*, edited by Ellen Wright and Michel Fabre, was published in 1978.

▨ *Critical Extracts*

ZORA NEALE HURSTON   This ⟨*Uncle Tom's Children*⟩ is a book about hatreds. Mr. Wright serves notice by his title that he speaks of people in revolt, and his stories are so grim that the Dismal Swamp of race hatred must be where they live. Not one act of understanding and sympathy comes to pass in the entire work.

But some bright new lines to remember come flashing from the author's pen. Some of his sentences have the shocking-power of a forty-four. That means that he knows his way around among words. With his facility, one wonders what he would have done had he dealt with plots that touched the broader and more fundamental phases of Negro life instead of confining himself to the spectacular. For, though he has handled himself well, numerous Negro writers, published and unpublished, have written of this same kind of incident. It is the favorite Negro theme just as how the stenographer or some other poor girl won the boss or the boss's son is the favorite white theme. What is new in the four novelettes included in Mr. Wright's book is the wish-fulfillment theme. In each story the hero suffers but he gets his man. ⟨. . .⟩

Since the author himself is a Negro his dialect is a puzzling thing. One wonders how he arrived at it. Certainly he does not write by ear unless he is tone-deaf. But aside from the broken speech of his characters, the book contains some beautiful writing. One hopes that Mr. Wright will find in Negro life a vehicle for his talents.

Zora Neale Hurston, "Stories of Conflict," *Saturday Review*, 2 April 1938, p. 32

RICHARD WRIGHT   It was not until I went to live in Chicago that I first thought seriously of writing of Bigger Thomas. Two items of my experience combined to make me aware of Bigger as a meaningful and prophetic symbol. First, being free of the daily pressure of the Dixie environment, I was able to come into possession of my own feelings. Second, my contact with the labor movement and its ideology made me see Bigger clearly and feel what he meant.

I made the discovery that Bigger Thomas was not black all the time; he was white, too, and there were literally millions of him, everywhere. The extension of my sense of the personality of Bigger was the pivot of my life; it altered the complexion of my existence. I became conscious, at first dimly, and then later on with increasing clarity and conviction, of the vast, muddied pool of human life in America. It was as though I had put on a pair of spectacles whose power was that of an x-ray enabling me to see deeper into the lives of men. Whenever I picked up a newspaper, I'd no longer feel that I was reading of the doings of whites alone (Negroes are rarely mentioned in the press unless they've committed some crime!), but of a complex struggle for life going on in my country, a struggle in which I was involved. I sensed, too, that the Southern scheme of oppression was but an appendage of a far vaster and in many respects more ruthless and impersonal commodity-profit machine. ⟨. . .⟩

The more I thought of it the more I became convinced that if I did not write of Bigger as I saw and felt him, if I did not try to make him a living personality and at the same time a symbol of all the larger things I felt and saw in him, I'd be reacting as Bigger himself reacted: that is, I'd be acting out of *fear* if I let what I thought whites would say constrict and paralyze me.

As I contemplated Bigger and what he meant, I said to myself: "I must write this novel, not only for others to read, but to free *myself* of this sense of shame and fear." In fact, the novel, as time passed, grew upon me to the extent that it became a necessity to write it; the writing of it turned into a way of living for me.

Richard Wright, "How 'Bigger' Was Born" (1940), *Native Son* (1940; rpt. New York: Harper & Row, 1989), pp. xiv–xv, xxi–xxii

---

MARGARET MARSHALL   Mr. Wright's style often reminds one of a stream "riled" by a heavy storm. Its element of Biblical rhetoric is not out of place since it is part of the colloquial heritage of the Negro in America, but there is in addition a bookish quality, often encountered in the self-educated writer, which should be weeded out. Mr. Wright's boldness in choosing to develop his theme through the story of a "bad nigger" is all to the good, but his flair for the melodramatic could bear curbing.

These defects cannot be described as minor, but they are extenuated by the wealth of evidence in *Native Son* that they can be overcome by a writer whose talent and seriousness are apparent on every page, who displays a maturity of thought and feeling beside which the eloquence of *The Grapes of Wrath* grows pale. And Mr. Wright's youth demonstrates once more that maturity is not necessarily a matter of years.

Margaret Marshall, "Black Native Son," *Nation*, 16 March 1940, pp. 367–68

RICHARD WRIGHT   I ran across many words whose meanings I did not know, and I either looked them up in a dictionary or, before I had a chance to do that, encountered the word in a context that made its meaning clear. But what strange world was this? I concluded the book with the conviction that I had somehow overlooked something terribly important in life. I had once tried to write, had once reveled in the feeling, had let my crude imagination roam, but the impulse to dream had been slowly beaten out of me by experience. Now it surged up again and I hungered for books, new ways of looking and seeing. It was not a matter of believing or disbelieving what I read, but of feeling something new, of being affected by something that made the look of the world different.

As dawn broke I ate my pork and beans, feeling dopey, sleepy. I went to work, but the mood of the book would not die; it lingered, coloring everything I saw, heard, did. I now felt that I knew what the white men were feeling. Merely because I had read a book that had spoken of how they lived and thought, I identified myself with that book. I felt vaguely guilty. Would I, filled with bookish notions, act in a manner that would make the whites dislike me? ⟨. . .⟩

I knew of no Negroes who read the books I liked and I wondered if any Negroes ever thought of them. I knew that there were Negro doctors, lawyers, newspapermen, but I never saw any of them. When I read a Negro newspaper I never caught the faintest echo of my preoccupation in its pages. I felt trapped and occasionally, for a few days, I would stop reading. But a vague hunger would come over me for books, books that opened up new avenues of feeling and seeing, and again I would forge another note to the white librarian. Again I would read and wonder, feeling that I carried a secret, criminal burden about with me each day.

> Richard Wright, *Black Boy* (1945), *Richard Wright Reader*, ed. Ellen Wright and Michel Fabre (New York: Harper & Row, 1978), pp. 18, 21

RALPH ELLISON   As a writer, Richard Wright has outlined for himself a dual role: to discover and depict the meaning of the Negro experience; and to reveal to both Negroes and whites those problems of a psychological and emotional nature which arise between them when they strive for mutual understanding.

Now, in *Black Boy*, he has used his own life to probe what qualities of will, imagination and intellect are required of a Southern Negro in order to possess the meaning of his life in the United States. Wright is an important writer, perhaps the most articulate Negro American, and what he has to say is highly perceptive. Imagine Bigger Thomas projecting his own life in lucid prose, guided, say, by the insights of Marx and Freud, and you have an idea of this autobiography.

Published at a time when any sharply critical approach to Negro life has been dropped as a wartime expendable, it should do much to redefine the problem of the Negro and American Democracy. Its power can be observed in the shrill manner with which some professional "friends of the Negro people" have attempted to strangle the work in a noose of newsprint.

What in the tradition of literary autobiography is it like, this work described as a "great American autobiography"? As a non-white intellectual's statement of his relationship to Western culture, *Black Boy* recalls the conflicting pattern of identification and rejection found in Nehru's *Toward Freedom*. In its use of fictional techniques, its concern with criminality (sin) and the artistic sensibility, and in its author's judgement and rejection of the narrow world of his origin, it recalls Joyce's rejection of Dublin in *A Portrait of the Artist*. And as a psychological document of life under oppressive conditions, it recalls *The House of the Dead*, Dostoievsky's profound study of the humanity of Russian criminals.

Such works were perhaps Wright's literary guides, aiding him to endow his life's incidents with communicable significance; providing him with ways of seeing, feeling and describing his environment. These influences, however, were encountered only after these first years of Wright's life were past and were not part of the immediate folk culture into which he was born. In that culture the specific folk-art form which helped shape the writer's attitude toward his life and which embodied the impulse that contributes much to the quality and tone of his autobiography was the Negro blues. This would bear a word of explanation:

The blues is an impulse to keep the painful details and episodes of a brutal experience alive in one's aching consciousness, to finger its jagged grain, and to transcend it, not by the consolation of philosophy but by squeezing from it a near-tragic, near-comic lyricism. As a form, the blues is an autobiographical chronicle of personal catastrophe expressed lyrically. And certainly Wright's early childhood was crammed with catastrophic incidents. In a few short years his father deserted his mother, he knew intense hunger, he became a drunkard begging for drinks from black stevedores in Memphis saloons; he had to flee Arkansas, where an uncle was lynched; he was forced to live with a fanatically religious grandmother in an atmosphere of constant bickering; he was lodged in an orphan asylum; he observed the suffering of his mother, who became a permanent invalid, while fighting off the blows of the poverty-stricken relatives with whom he had to live; he was cheated, beaten and kicked off jobs by white employees who disliked his eagerness to learn a trade; and to these objective circumstances must be added the subjective fact that Wright, with his sensitivity, extreme shyness and intelligence, was a problem child who rejected his family and was by them rejected.

Thus along with the themes, equivalent descriptions of milieu and the perspectives to be found in Joyce, Nehru, Dostoievsky, George Moore and Rousseau, *Black Boy* is filled with blues-tempered echoes of railroad trains, the names of Southern towns and cities, estrangements, fights and flights, deaths and disappointments, charged with physical and spiritual hungers and pain. And like a blues sung by such an artist as Bessie Smith, its lyrical prose evokes the paradoxical, almost surreal image of a black boy singing lustily as he probes his own grievous wound.

Ralph Ellison, "Richard Wright's Blues" (1945), *Shadow and Act* (New York: Random House, 1964), pp. 77–79

JAMES BALDWIN   Now the most powerful and celebrated statement we have yet had of what it means to be a Negro in America is unquestionably Richard Wright's *Native Son*. The feeling which prevailed at the time of its publication was that such a novel, bitter, uncompromising, shocking, gave proof, by its very existence, of what strides might be taken in a free democracy; and its indisputable success, proof that Americans were now able to look full in the face without flinching the dreadful facts. Americans, unhappily, have the most remarkable ability to alchemize all bitter truths into an innocuous but piquant confection and to transform their moral contradictions, or public discussions of such contradictions, into a proud decoration, such as are given for heroism on the field of battle. Such a book, we felt with pride, could never have been written before— which was true. Nor could it be written today. It bears already the aspect of a landmark; for Bigger and his brothers have undergone yet another metamorphosis; they have been accepted in baseball leagues and by colleges hitherto exclusive; and they have made a most favorable appearance on the national screen. We have yet to encounter, nevertheless, a report so indisputably authentic, or one that can begin to challenge this most signifi-cant novel. ⟨. . .⟩

Negroes are Americans and their destiny is the country's destiny. They have no other experience besides their experience on this continent and it is an experience which cannot be rejected, which yet remains to be embraced. If, as I believe, no American Negro exists who does not have his private Bigger Thomas living in the skull, then what most significantly fails to be illuminated here is the paradoxical adjustment which is perpetually made, the Negro being compelled to accept the fact that this dark and dangerous and unloved stranger is part of himself forever. Only this recogni-tion sets him in any wise free and it is this, the necessary ability to contain and even, in the most honorable sense of the word, to *exploit* the "nigger," which lends to Negro life its high element of the ironic and which causes the most well-meaning of their American critics to make such exhilarating errors when attempting to understand them. To present Bigger as a warning is simply to reinforce the American guilt and fear concerning him, it is most forcefully to limit him to that previously mentioned social arena in which he has no human validity, it is simply to condemn him to death. For he has always been a warning, he represents the evil, the sin and suffering which we are compelled to reject. It is useless to say to the courtroom in which this heathen sits on trial that he is their responsibility, their creation, and his crimes are theirs; and that they ought, therefore, to allow him to live, to make articulate to himself behind the walls of prison the meaning of his existence. The meaning of his existence has already been most adequately expressed, nor does he wish, particularly not in the name of democracy, to think of it any more; as for the possibility of articulation, it is this possibility which above all others we most dread. Moreover, the courtroom, judge, jury, witnesses and spectators, recognize immediately that Bigger is their creation and they recognize this not only with hatred and fear and guilt and the resulting fury of self-righteousness but also with that morbid fullness of pride mixed with horror with which one regards the extent and power of one's wickedness. They know that death is his portion, that he runs to death; coming from darkness and dwelling in darkness, he must be, as often as he rises, banished, lest the entire planet be engulfed. And they know, finally, that they do not wish to forgive him and that he does not wish to be forgiven; that he dies, hating them, scorning that appeal which they cannot make to that irrecoverable humanity of his which cannot hear it; and that he *wants* to die because he glories in his hatred and prefers, like Lucifer, rather to rule in hell than serve in heaven.

James Baldwin, "Many Thousands Gone" (1951), *Notes of a Native Son* (Boston: Beacon Press, 1955), pp. 23–24, 33–35

DAN McCALL   Wright asserted that in the act of killing, his black boy had begun to *be*. Throughout the narrative ⟨of *Native Son*⟩ the author insisted,

> It was a kind of eagerness he felt, a confidence, a fullness, a freedom; his whole life was caught up in a supreme and meaningful act.

> He had murdered and created a new life for himself.

> His crime was an anchor weighing him safely in time; it added to him a certain confidence. . . .

And Bigger Thomas was no Raskolnikov, no Dostoevskyan hero who at least had some massive (albeit depraved) intellectual force behind his act of killing. Bigger had no *Ubermensch* leading him on; no Idea had twisted his humanity. He killed because everything in his life had wrung humanity out of him and he only wanted to become a one-man lynch mob. ⟨. . .⟩

Now it is surely true that, and E. R. Embree has said, "Richard Wright wanted to write not a book but a bomb." And it is also true that Wright, like his fictional creation, had an obsession with violence. Toward the end of *Black Boy* Wright says that "it was perhaps an accident that I had never killed." And in "How Bigger Was Born" he confesses of the Bigger 1, "Maybe I longed secretly to be like him." Nelson Algren said in his review that "Thomas forced recognition by an act of murder, Wright by an act of art," the implication being that it was very lucky Wright was able to educate himself, to have a "socially approved" outlet for his violence so that he could murder on paper instead of in the flesh. And when Samuel Sillen ran a series on "*Native Son*: Pros and Cons" in the *New Masses*, other black men of letters came to the defense of Wright's portrait of racial hate; Chester Himes said that Bigger "had to hate them to keep himself a human being, knowing that when he gave in to being afraid of them without hating them he would lose everything which impelled his desire to fly a plane or build a bridge." Yet Wright himself was disturbed that in the controversy too many readers and critics had been extremely careless in their understanding of what Bigger's hate meant and how he, the author, had portrayed it. Wright was moved to passionate italics in the *Atlantic* (June 1940): "No *advocacy* of hate is in that book. *None!*"

Bigger is "the beast in the skull." The difficulty in thinking clearly and talking clearly about "the beast in the skull" is that one can become so intensely, obsessively conscious of it that one lets it out, lets it out not to expose it but to let it do its damage. If one lives too long and too carelessly with the beast, one can love it. After fighting it for so long, after hating it so deeply, one feels something break inside; the hate turns to love, the fierce denial turns to passionate embrace. It is an enormously complicated problem for the black writer, trying to make sense of himself and his world. Wrestling in such agony with the beast he may begin to pump it. Becoming an intellectual Bigger Thomas, he deals in fantasies without ever seeing them for what they are. How Wright faced the problem in *Native Son* involves the question of what kind of book it is, and when one looks carefully at it one can see several indications that Wright is trying to understand the fantasy for what it is and provide some imaginative controls to direct its power.

Dan McCall, "The Bad Nigger," *The Example of Richard Wright* (New York: Harcourt, Brace & World, 1969), pp. 64, 66–67

EDWARD MARGOLIES   When Richard Wright planned *The Long Dream* he evidently foresaw it as the first in a series of books dwelling on the life and career of Fishbelly Tucker, a Mississippi Negro boy who goes to live in France. The autobiographical resemblances between the author and his protagonist are not however confined to mere geography. In many respects the psychic lives of the two appear to be very close—not to mention the fact that they both seem to have shared almost identical traumatic experiences. A reading of *Black Boy* alongside *The Long Dream* is instructive in this regard. Both Wright and Fishbelly, for example, at the age of six discover that their fathers are having illicit relations with women. Both boys have dreadful fears of being abandoned by their mothers; indeed Fishbelly has a dream not unlike the nightmares the four-year-old Wright suffered in the opening pages of *Black Boy*. Both boys do not come into any real contact with the brutality of the white world until their adolescent years, a fact which may account for their singular independence of spirit and defiance of caste ordinances. As a result both Fishbelly and Wright come to the conclusion that they are unable to accept the traditions and values of either white world or black, and must therefore seek the meaning of their lives in a different environment. In *The Long Dream* and *Black Boy* critical moments are described relating to the lynching and mutilation of a Negro bellhop who had been having an affair with a white prostitute. For both Fishbelly and Wright the death of the bellhop provides central insights into the connection between sex and caste. The Negro, they discover, who submits to white oppression is as much castrated psychologically as the bellhop is physically. Thus, for them the lynchings become symbolic of the roles they are expected to play in life. Finally, one is almost tempted to say that both Wright and Fishbelly share certain bourgeois backgrounds. Although Fishbelly is relatively affluent and Wright frequently destitute, both are reared in a middle-class milieu. (Wright's mother, aunts, and uncles, it will be remembered, were school teachers—and his grandparents owned property in Jackson.) Whatever else may be said of *The Long Dream* it would be difficult to deny that Wright was once again reliving deeply embedded memories as a primary source for his new novel.

Edward Margolies, *The Art of Richard Wright* (Carbondale: Southern Illinois University Press, 1969), pp. 129–30

RUSSELL CARL BRIGNANO   In *The Outsider*, Cross Damon, a Negro, is isolated and alienated from other men *because* he is a man. The novel is one of the few examples in American fiction of an author's conscious attempt to shape existential themes. The work also offers an unflattering commentary on the Communist Party. In many respects, and especially in its treatment of the Party, *The Outsider* may be compared to Ralph Ellison's *Invisible Man* (1952), published only a few months before Wright's novel. One striking parallel between Ellison's unnamed central narrator and Cross Damon is their search for identity beyond the context of racial conflict. In both works it is the Party that feels it can provide a basis for identity, and in both works it is the Party that exploits the fact of the main figure's color, for political and propagandistic gain. In terms of the Marxist content in *The Outsider* ⟨. . .⟩, the Party's treatment of Cross Damon clearly echoes words set down by Wright in a 1945 publication, only months before his formal break with the Party, but years before he wrote *The Outsider*: "Both the political Left and the political Right try to change the Negro problem into something that they can control, thereby denying the humanity of the Negro, excluding his unique and historic position in American life." This attitude is essentially the basis for Wright's attack on the Party in *The Outsider*. It reflects the position that he had taken earlier in his essay in *The God That Failed*.

Russell Carl Brignano, *Richard Wright: An Introduction to the Man and His Works* (Pittsburgh: University of Pittsburgh Press, 1970), pp. 82–83

JEAN-FRANÇOIS GOUNARD   Obviously, the controversial reaction to *Black Boy* was typical of the attitudes of American society to black achievements—while Wright gained recognition for his work as a writer, he continued to encounter many bitter and demeaning personal experiences all caused by the color of his skin. In New York where he and his white Jewish wife lived, the painfulness of these experiences was undoubtedly intensified by the fact that he had received acceptance as a writer.

Recognition of Wright's literary achievements even came from abroad, and the French government extended an official invitation for the black author and his family to come to France. Given the frustrating circumstances he encountered in the United States, it is not surprising that Wright readily accepted this considerable honor, and from May to December 1946, he and his family lived in Paris. Here they were treated as privileged guests by many French admirers, and Wright could not help but be impressed by the respect for human dignity and relative lack of racial prejudice in France. After retasting the bitter realities of life in New York for only six months, Wright and his family returned to France to live permanently in July 1947. ⟨. . .⟩

Why did Wright choose to address his audience from the viewpoint of an exile? Oddly enough, some critics state quite adamantly that the reason why Richard Wright chose exile was that he hated black people and, consequently, loathed himself. Talking about this much-debated point, Robert Bone tells us: "Wright suffers, no doubt, from rootlessness, but the source of that rootlessness is self-hatred." Such a statement is rather serious and most damaging to make. Obviously, Robert Bone does not seem to consider, or remember, that many projects and ideas Richard Wright had in mind when he once wrote a childhood friend: "There is a great novel yet to be written about the Negro in the South; just a simple, straight, easy, great novel, telling how they feel each day; what they do in the winter, spring, summer and fall. Just a novel telling of the quiet ritual of their lives. Such a book is really needed."

Richard Wright did hate conditions in the Southern United States, but it seems totally unfair to maintain that he disliked black people on the grounds that they had absolutely nothing to offer. He was painfully aware that any fault in the matter lay with the white man, not the black. In "Big Boy Leaves Home" and "Long Black Song," for instance, Big Boy and Sarah lead a happy and carefree life in the Garden of Eden we know to be Richard Wright's South. Unfortunately, the beautiful dream is brutally destroyed by the fatal intrusion of the white man; Big Boy has to escape hurriedly to the North, and Sarah helplessly witnesses her husband's violent but courageous death.

There was a certain type of Negro that Richard Wright did hate—the apathetic and humble black man who accepted his tragic and inhuman plight in complete surrender. For Richard Wright, such a Negro was as guilty as his white torturers because he was an accomplice in his own humiliation and sufferings. Tom, in "The Man Who Saw The Flood," represents quite well that type of dull Negro who is totally submitted to the powerful will of the white world. Richard Wright was very fond of his own people and was also deeply attached to his native South. In other words, when Wright left the United States, he was simply fleeing the inhuman atmosphere created by the whites. His activities abroad indicate that his own heart always kept a secret, special and affectionate place for his colored brothers.

Jean-François Gounard, "Richard Wright as a Black American Writer in Exile," *CLA Journal* 17, No. 3 (March 1974): 308, 312–13

MICHEL FABRE   The depiction of the black struggle under adverse social and racial conditions often explicitly constitutes the subject of Wright's writing, but because of his sometimes conflicting attitudes towards black life in the United States the coherence of his purpose is not always apparent. It does not appear, either, that his major purpose was to demonstrate the universality of the black struggle as a reflection and example of the condition of modern man (although certainly much can be made, as will be seen, of Wright's contention that "the Negro is America's metaphor"). Wright's enduring concern was in fact, more personal and more basic: it amounted to nothing less than the interchange and conflict between the individual and society.

Rooted as it is in an existential sense of freedom, Wright's blossoming into print should be constructed as an act of defiance, an assertion of the equation between literature and rebellion, an avatar of the myth of Prometheus who stole fire and knowledge from the Gods for the benefit of all men. In Wright's case, the gap between life and literature is so narrow that the awakening and development of his avocation closely follow the expanding circles of his self-awareness and his intellectual growth.

Michel Fabre, "Introduction," *Richard Wright Reader*, ed. Ellen Wright and Michel Fabre (New York: Harper & Row, 1978), p. ix

---

PAUL NEWLIN   Although Wright set out to compose a novel so hard that it would deny tears over the fate of the victims, he claims consciously to have then worked in a guilt theme after completing the first draft. By implication, he acknowledges that guilt was hinted at in the first draft, and it seems impossible to me that it was not there from the establishment of Bigger's character-destiny in the scene with the rat. Wright doesn't elaborate on *who* is guilty for *what* in "How 'Bigger' Was Born," but guilt is part of "the heritage of us all" and need not be spelled out except when it plays a dramatic purpose, as it does with Jan's and Mary's pathetic attempts at expiation in their uneasy gestures at brotherhood. Guilt is everywhere— from Mrs. Thomas' cruel questioning of why she brought Bigger into this world, Mrs. Dalton's collective guilt as a symbolic representation of a blind, self-praising, affluent white society, and Bigger's own irascible bullying of his street pals in an effort to assuage his fears, to Max's appalled recognition of what Wright called the moral of the novel: "the horror of Negro life in the United States." ⟨. . .⟩

The horror of which Richard Wright wrote in 1940 still infuses *Native Son* today. In telling us how Bigger was born, Wright has also told us why Bigger lives on. One can make a strong case that "the horror of Negro life in the United States" has diminished since Bigger was born in 1940. Yet black youngsters still wake up to battle rats or worse in ever-enlarging black urban ghettoes, and though Bigger and Gus currently could sit undisturbed in the orchestra of Chicago's movie houses, one need look no further than the June 1986 *FBI Law Enforcement Bulletin* to know how Bigger's presence in Mary Dalton's bedroom would be interpreted in Chicago today. Bigger Thomas' position in the literary canon of twentieth-century American litera-ture is secure precisely because rape remains "the representative symbol of the Negro's uncertain position in America." Passage of time modifies heritage but slowly, and the fear, the guilt, the horror of Wright's *Native Son* infuses each generation of readers with its moral: "the horror of Negro life in the United States." Is there any wonder my students are affected by *Native Son* as by no other book I teach?

Paul Newlin, "Why 'Bigger' Lives On: Student Reaction to *Native Son*," *Richard Wright: Myths and Realities*, ed. C. James Trotman (New York: Garland, 1988), pp. 143–45

MARGARET WALKER   Although these eight stories ⟨in *Eight Men*⟩ are uneven in quality, they uphold Wright's literary reputation as being at his best in the short story form. Tautness of plot, organization, excellent characterization, lively dialogue, heightened suspense, Freudian psychology, and general thematic structure, as well as melodramatic tone, are evident in these pieces. Perhaps the critics are biased when they generally agree that the four earlier stories, written before Wright's exile, are better in that they are less contrived, more artfully formed, and show greater skill in craftsmanship. There may be, however, some natural differences of opinion here. Neither "Slit" nor the newly named "The Man Who Saw the Flood" is as fine a piece as "Down by the Riverside." Why? For a number of reasons: the frenetic or even daemonic quality of "Down by the Riverside" reveals not only the freshness of Wright's imagery and the southern welter of black folklore and feeling out of which it comes, but like all the stories in Uncle Tom's Children, it also shows Wright's early obsession with revision, writing, and rewriting until he could be satisfied with a sharpened effect. The tensions in the work are poignant, the suspense heightened, the emotional effects of the words have stunning impact. Wright's genius is never more daemonic or frenetic than in those four novellas which comprise Uncle Tom's Children.

Dialogue is another well-crafted element in the first stories of Eight Men which is not nearly as effective as in the last four. The latter stories are perhaps most innovative in subject matter and theme, for there is almost as much variety as there are tales. I have already explored the mythic nature of "The Man Who Lived Underground," its surrealism and existentialism. "The Man Who Killed a Shadow" is also surreal, but instead of existentialism there is an element of Freudianism. Both "Big Black Good Man" and "Man, God Ain't Like That" deal with a folk belief or primitive religious concern, including ethical constructs in African and Afro-American religious and superstitious beliefs. "Man of All Works" deals cynically with economic determinism and satirizes Communists or the lumpenproletariat as victims. Two pieces are patently autobiographical, "The Man Who Was Almost a Man" and "The Man Who Went to Chicago." There is no doubt in my mind, however, that all of the stories have autobiographical elements in them because as demonstrated again and again, Wright was writing and rewriting one story, the story of himself. Eight Men or ten men, they were all one man. The subject was universal man, the specific man was everyman.

Margaret Walker, Richard Wright, Daemonic Genius (New York: Warner, 1988), pp. 330–31

JOHN M. REILLY   ⟨. . .⟩ it is Wright's decision to use a narrative point of view closely identified with Bigger's, though not identical to it, that accounts for readers' taking his side. Closely associated with Bigger's thought and expository of his feelings, the presiding narrative voice blurs the color lines and gives readers—white and black—the sensations and perspective of an underclass character. The subtle narrative reports Bigger's thought and preconscious feeling in the language of third-person story-telling; but while maintaining the third-person reference, the narrative also suggests a simulation of the character's own mental discourse. That technique, known as "free indirect discourse," is not in itself unusual. When employed in the service of a character like Bigger, however, it becomes a remarkable innovation in American realistic fiction, rarely matched before 1940 except by Mark Twain's giving the frontier ruffian Huck Finn the right to tell his own story, or by Theodore Dreiser's investment of subjectivity in working women like Carrie Meeber. In the line of realism, from the frontier sketches through the fiction of William Dean Howells and Stephen Crane, when outsiders or bottom dogs such as frontier settlers, immigrants, and ethnic characters appear, they are presented in a frame story or through the mediation of narrative voice firmly middle-class in its language, taste, and orientation. Thus the frontier humor of the Old Southwest is often reported by a narrator who comes from a metropolitan center, introducing an exotic country person who is allowed to tell a story in dialect before the reporter reestablishes his presence in standard English. Even the city of New York can appear to be full of aliens in such a novel as Howell's A Hazard of New Fortunes, which presents the industrial working class as beyond the ken of the editor Basil March, who is the focal point of the narrative, or Crane's Maggie, in which the narrative voice reductively presents its Irish-American subjects with hardly any indication that they even possess consciousness. Each of these representative texts in the tradition of American realism illustrates the habit of enforcing the perception shared by a dominant class. By distancing the narrative from socially subordinate groups distinguished by strong differences in dialect or appearance, by withholding explanation of their behavior, and above all by establishing a narrative viewpoint readily identifiable as old stock, formally educated, and more learned than frontier settlers, workers, and ethnics, these normative texts create an identification between readers and authors that expresses the monopoly of discourse by a ruling caste or class. That monopoly is exactly what Richard Wright aims to subvert in Native Son by use of a narrative point of view that draws readers beneath the externals of surface realism, so that as they are led into empathy with Bigger, they will be denied the conventional attitudes of American racial discourse.

John M. Reilly, "Giving Bigger a Voice: The Politics of Narrative in Native Son," New Essays on Native Son, ed. Keneth Kinnamon (New York: Cambridge University Press, 1990), pp. 45–46

ALFRED KAZIN   At a time when white supremacy was especially cruel and hysterical among poor whites in the rural South, and the young boy could be knocked down for forgetting to say "sir" immediately to any cretin who seemed to live for violence to blacks, Richard Wright was stripped naked by his mother and beaten with a barrel stave until he became feverish because he had fought back against white boys. His grandmother, a fanatical Seventh-day Adventist, slapped him around for listening to a story—"Devil stuff in my house"—and after he had finally retaliated with an obscene remark, beat him so horribly that he was sure she would kill him if he did not get out of her reach.

"I used to mull over the strange absence of real kindness in Negroes," Wright wrote in *Black Boy*, that extraordinary personal history of almost unrelieved opression in and out of the black community that becomes a great literary accomplishment through Wright's superb sense of momentum—of how to build up a narrative so that the reader duplicates his own intensity. As he was not afraid to admit, he had more than a touch of cruelty himself. When his terrible father ordered his sons to get rid of a kitten, Richard and his brother hanged it from a tree as a way of triumphing over their father.

Killing is as routine in Wright's work as in Dostoyevsky's great crime novels. Dostoyevsky used the act of murder to highlight everything hidden in the human soul. The race question in Wright is certainly not hidden. As for all black writers, it is the atmosphere they breathe, it is America itself. What makes Wright so remarkable an artist of this extreme situation is that the rage at the center of his work becomes a wholly individual drama without ceasing to be an accusation of our society in general. You can quarrel with the belief that the "Negro," as Wright still put it, was a tabula rasa given his character entirely by slavery. Whether he believed this or not in his erratic political career as a sometime Marxist (and he often contradicted himself in his search for a position), Wright was always more convincing describing characters in terms of action, pulse, deed on deed, than in ascribing reasons for their actions.

Alfred Kazin, "Too Honest for His Own Time," *New York Times Book Review*, 29 December 1991, p. 3

◈ *Bibliography*

Uncle Tom's Children: Four Novellas. 1938, 1940 (as *Uncle Tom's Children: Five Long Stories*).

Bright and Morning Star. 1938.

Native Son. 1940.

How "Bigger" Was Born: The Story of Native Son, *One of the Most Significant Novels of Our Time, and How It Came to Be Written.* 1940.

Native Son (The Biography of a Young American) (drama; with Paul Green). 1941.

The Negro and Parkway Community House. 1941.

12 Million Black Voices: A Folk History of the Negro in the United States. 1941.

Black Boy: A Record of Childhood and Youth. 1945.

A Hitherto Unpublished Manuscript by Richard Wright: Being a Continuation of Black Boy. c. 1946.

The F B Eye Blues. 1949.

The Outsider. 1953.

Savage Holiday. 1954.

Black Power: A Record of Reactions in a Land of Pathos. 1954.

The Color Curtain: A Report on the Bandung Conference. 1956.

Pagan Spain. 1956.

White Man, Listen! 1957.

The Long Dream. 1958.

Eight Men. 1961.

Lawd Today. 1963.

Letters to Joe C. Brown. Ed. Thomas Knipp. 1968.

The Man Who Lived Underground. Ed. Michael Fabre, tr. Claude Emonde Magny. 1971.

American Hunger. 1977.

Richard Wright Reader. Ed. Ellen Wright and Michel Fabre. 1978.

⟨*Works.*⟩ 1991. 2 vols.